BRIGADIER GENERAL ROBERT L. MCCOOK
and
COLONEL DANIEL MCCOOK, JR.

ALSO BY WAYNE FANEBUST

*Major General Alexander M. McCook, USA:
A Civil War Biography* (McFarland, 2013)

Brigadier General Robert L. McCook *and* Colonel Daniel McCook, Jr.

A Union Army Dual Biography

Wayne Fanebust

McFarland & Company, Inc., Publishers
Jefferson, North Carolina

All photographs are from the Library of Congress unless otherwise noted.

LIBRARY OF CONGRESS CATALOGUING-IN-PUBLICATION DATA

Names: Fanebust, Wayne, author.
Title: Brigadier General Robert L. McCook and Colonel Daniel McCook, Jr. : a Union Army dual biography / Wayne Fanebust.
Description: Jefferson, North Carolina : McFarland & Company, Inc., Publishers, 2017. | Includes bibliographical references and index.
Identifiers: LCCN 2017020709 | ISBN 9781476669861 (softcover : acid free paper) ∞
Subjects: LCSH: McCook, Robert Latimer, 1827–1862. | McCook, Daniel, Jr., 1834–1864. | Generals—United States—Biography. | United States—History—Civil War, 1861–1865—Biography. | Ohio—History—Civil War, 1861–1865—Biography. | United States—History—Civil War, 1861–1865—Campaigns. | Carrollton (Ohio)—Biography. | McCook family.
Classification: LCC E467 .F36 2017 | DDC 973.7/4710922 [B] —dc23
LC record available at https://lccn.loc.gov/2017020709

BRITISH LIBRARY CATALOGUING DATA ARE AVAILABLE

ISBN (print) 978-1-4766-6986-1
ISBN (ebook) 978-1-4766-2907-0

© 2017 Wayne Fanebust. All rights reserved

No part of this book may be reproduced or transmitted in any form or by any means, electronic or mechanical, including photocopying or recording, or by any information storage and retrieval system, without permission in writing from the publisher.

Front cover: (left to right) Brigadier General Robert L. McCook and Colonel Daniel McCook, Jr. (Library of Congress)

Printed in the United States of America

McFarland & Company, Inc., Publishers
 Box 611, Jefferson, North Carolina 28640
 www.mcfarlandpub.com

Table of Contents

Preface	1
Introduction: The Fighting Irish and the McCook Family	5

ROBERT L. MCCOOK

1. Commander of the 9th Ohio Infantry Regiment	18
2. The Union Takes West Virginia	31
3. The Battle of Mill Springs	43
4. Trouble on the Road to Corinth	54
5. The Killing of Robert L. McCook	72
6. Frank B. Gurley: Soldier or Murderer?	85

DANIEL MCCOOK, JR.

7. Fighting Lawyer in Kansas	102
8. On the Warpath: Shiloh, Perryville and Stones River	119
9. Morgan's Raid and the Death of Daniel McCook, Sr.	138
10. The Chattanooga Campaign and the Battle of Chickamauga	152
11. A Dead Stop at Kennesaw Mountain	168
12. A Soldier's Death	180

Tribute: Remembering Bob and Dan	197
Chapter Notes	209
Bibliography	225
Index	231

Preface

Unfurled in 1787, the Constitution of the United States was truly a remarkable document because it signaled to the rest of the world that a nation of immigrants digging in on a new continent were embarking on an experiment in government and culture. Whereas for centuries the people of planet Earth had toiled and suffered under oppressive rulers, the former colonists declared to the world that the foot of the tyrant would never walk on American soil. Instead, the proud, free people had created a "more perfect Union," rooted in a Declaration of Independence that declared "all men are created equal." It was a system of government unlike any that had existed before, so new and so radical that it must have seemed to some like the product of utopian dreamers rather than realists. Freedom, individual freedom, was unleashed in the New World.

It was an uneasy freedom from the beginning because of a word that is nowhere found in the Constitution: *slavery*. Since the founders failed to mention that word, some might presume that they were embarrassed by slavery. Looking back now, all reasonable people would agree that the founders, those intelligent and idealistic men, were, at the very least, uneasy about the existence of slave labor in America. There was, after all, a certain built-in hypocrisy looming over the new nation, "conceived in liberty," when in fact an entire race of people were considered unworthy of freedom. America was shackled by an ugly truth: for in a society with freedom as its guiding star, the right of one man to own another can never be morally or legally justified.

And yet serious men went to great pains to justify slavery during the span of years historians call the "antebellum" period of American history, the time leading up to the Civil War. It was during this time that the energy fueling the economy of the country was slave labor, wealth piling upon wealth, from Southern plantations to New York City banks. The slave trade was "officially" ended by law in 1808, but that didn't stop the "peculiar institution" from spreading and thriving.

The voices of opposition tried to keep pace with those working to permanently weave slavery into the fabric of democracy. The noise from the arguments and counter-arguments was not confined to America, but was heard around the world. Europeans were tuned in to the spectacle, wondering if the great experiment in representative democracy would fail. No doubt there were many men gloating and just waiting to say: "I told you so."

The abolitionists argued on moral grounds that slavery was evil and pointed out that most countries had abolished it. They wanted the federal government to take action to free the slaves. The slaveholders shouted back that the federal government had no right to take such action for they believed that national authority was subservient to states rights. In other words, the powers of at the federal level were, under the Constitution, merely delegated to Congress and to the president and therefore the states could simply take those powers away. If the federal government overstepped its authority, any state had the right to engage in remedial measures, including secession. Slaves, like horses, were simply property, and the right to deal with property was solely in the hands of the states. This was gospel throughout the South.

Slaves in the slave states were, in fact, the greatest asset on the books and it was believed that should the abolitionists win the argument, the South would be cast into ruin and chaos. Facing such dire prospects, the South stiffened, refusing to change, for any change, no matter how slight, was a threat to its existence. Furthermore, Southerners felt superior to Northerners, and cloaked in feelings of invincibility, they resolved to take up arms rather than retreat. The threatened extinction of slavery loomed large following the election of 1860 when Abraham Lincoln, known for his strong opposition to slavery, became the president. Thus America experienced secession and the Civil War.

This book is about two soldiers among the hundreds of thousands who fought on both sides of that war. Robert L. and Daniel McCook were brothers from a Scots-Irish, well-connected and politically-prominent Ohio family, known as the "Fighting McCooks." Both Bob and Dan were brigadier generals when they died from battle wounds. Dan was a colonel throughout most of the war, promoted to brigadier genearl as he lay dying of wounds he received at the battle of Kennesaw Mountain. During the four years of fighting, men died at an alarming rate and did so anonymously, but the manner of the deaths of the McCooks, combined with the fame of their family, created national sensations. Public outrage and anger over the killing of the McCook brothers launched them up and into the realm of heroes.

Robert L. McCook had gained fame for leading a bayonet charge in a Kentucky battle in 1862. Later that same year he was killed by Rebel cavalry while sick and riding in an ambulance. Since he and his small escort were attacked by superior numbers, by men not wearing uniforms, and because he was in poor condition, his death was deemed a murder. The Northern press and the public screamed for revenge, and when the soldier who admittedly killed General McCook was captured, he was not treated as a prisoner of war. He was jailed and tried and convicted of murder and sentenced to be hanged.

Daniel McCook, Jr., by existing standards, died a more glorious and certainly a more spectacular death than did his older brother. He was a brigade commander in General W. T. Sherman's mammoth army during the famous march to Atlanta in the summer of 1864. Sherman and McCook were friends. Prior to the war they practiced law together in a ramshackle office in Leavenworth, Kansas.

McCook's brigade was selected to participate in an ill-advised and dangerous assault up Georgia's Kennesaw Mountain, against well-fortified Rebels. The Union force was beaten back amid great slaughter. Among those mortally wounded was Daniel McCook, Jr., who, sword in hand, was leading the charge. The death of McCook haunted his friend Sherman who, later in life, admitted in print that he was responsible for it.

Bob and Dan McCook were heroes in the minds of people of the North, for they died heroes' deaths. They had served with honor and distinction and gave their lives for the cause of the Union in a war to defeat slavery and secession. Although during the years following the Civil War their star power has diminished, it is altogether fitting and proper that Americans grant them the respect they have earned and never allow them to be forgotten.

The research for this book has taken me to faraway places, but finding the Newspaper Archives on the Library of Congress website while sitting in front of my computer was one of the strongest and most rewarding discoveries. The easy-to-use website revealed a large number of newspaper articles that were very useful to my writing and, had the website not been available, much valuable detail would have been missed entirely.

An actual visit to the Library of Congress in Washington, D.C., was truly unforgettable and the McCook Manuscript Collection located there was invaluable, as were the McCook letters at the archives of the Connecticut Landmarks at Hartford and the vast assortment of research materials at the Ohio State Historical Society in Columbus.

I am grateful to other libraries and their Civil War collections, with special thanks to the library at Augustana University in Sioux Falls, South Dakota. It was at "Augie" that I was able to access, in book form, *The War of the Rebellion, Official Records*. Other libraries I want to thank include the public libraries in Sioux Falls, Pierre and Yankton, South Dakota, along with the public libraries in San Diego, California, Columbus, Ohio, and Hartford, Connecticut.

I have received support from many friends and colleagues, all of whom have an interest in the Civil War. I gladly extend special thanks to Richard Nordstrom, David Swan, David Davis, Steve Bointe, Bruce Blake, Tom Maldari, Paula Habbena, Ron Robinson and Civil War writer Mark Dunkelman. I want to acknowledge and salute all my friends and colleagues of the San Diego Independent Scholars, the Center for Western Studies at Augustana University, and the Minnehaha County Historical Society, Sioux Falls, South Dakota, for their support of my writing.

And best of all, to my dear family, my brothers, sisters, in-laws and cousins, all of whom have crowned my life with their love and affection, I send my heartfelt thanks. To my daughter Danae, son-in-law Steven, granddaughter Angelina, and to the newest member of the family, grandson Hunter Steven Perreira, I love you all very much and I hope you never get tired of hearing about "the next book."

Introduction:
The Fighting Irish
and the McCook Family

"In common with all the northern states, Ohio has much to be proud of in the war. But her family of "fighting McCooks" was unmatched by any in the Union army."—*Omaha Daily Bee*, February 17, 1885

Among the ethnic groups represented in the Civil War, the Irish emerge as the most conspicuous and most publicized. With volunteer regiments on both sides of the war, the Irish more than proved their mettle as fighters and leaders, displaying a fierce and courageous form of patriotism to their chosen side. Their aggressive, fighting spirit was a trait that they brought with them to America from the old country. When a Utah newspaper said, "The Irishman is by natural instinct a first-rate fighting man," it was expressing popular belief.[1] By reputation, the Irish were a proud, hot-blooded, determined people, a characteristic that Civil War leaders from both the North and South sought to exploit. After the shooting started, Northern Irish were killing Southern Irish, and vice versa. Among their many character traits was the strange willingness of the "Sons of Erin" to kill their kith and kin.

The Irish presence in America was well-established by the pre-revolutionary era. Immigration increased after independence was won, due to tension and hardship under British rule, and because of the great potato famine in Ireland that inflicted additional suffering on a proud people. Between the years 1815 and 1845, a million-plus Irish people gave up on Ireland, one of the poorest of European countries.[2] Too many people and too many problems.

Coming to America and gathering in cities, the Roman Catholic Irish struggled to assimilate while bucking the tide of discrimination and exploitation. They lived under the worst conditions, crowded in filthy tenement houses, referred to by a reporter as "tombs for the poor."[3] The desperate men took any work available, including dangerous jobs in mines, factories and on the railroads.

Their religion and ethnicity aroused the bigoted passions of anti–Irish Catholic Americans who saw in that class of immigrants a vaguely defined papal plot with headquarters in Rome. Bizarre conspiracy theories grew out of the belief that the pope was plotting to take over America. But paranoia went even further, and following a cholera outbreak in 1832 in Eastern cities, the Irish and other immigrants were blamed for causing and spreading that deadly disease.[4]

There was no papal plot, but the fear-struck leaders of a powerful, nativist movement convinced enough people to believe that there was, and the fictitious fear scared the hell out of non–Catholics. Believing America was a Protestant nation, and taking action to meet the "Roman threat," the faithful looked for convenient targets. They found them in Irish families. Tension turned into bloody riots in urban areas; it was xenophobia run amuck. It was as if a religious war had broken out in the land where religious freedom was enshrined in the Constitution. News of the violence reached other parts of America, adding to the anti–Irish sentiment.[5]

Through no fault of their own, the struggling Irish acquired a bad reputation. Denied even second class citizenship, Irish Catholic neighborhoods were associated with prostitution, pestilence, gambling, drinking and violent behavior. While this attitude was false or overblown, it isolated the Irish, creating stereotypes that would prove to have a long life. Although their lives were reduced to an angry struggle to survive, they still managed to send millions of dollars every year back home to relatives in Ireland.[6]

The paranoia and ethnic hate ultimately coalesced into politics. The nativist movement gave rise to the American Republican Party, also known as Nativist Party, in Philadelphia on May 3, 1844.[7] Better known as the "Know-Nothings," the odd political party was evasive but not invisible and owed its existence largely to its anti–Irish, anti–Catholic attitude, although other immigrants, such as the Germans, were also deemed undesirable. This attitude fueled the urgent belief that unless something was done to overcome the threatening influence of immigrants, "real" Americans would lose their identity, heritage and power. Nationality had to be protected.

The wave of anti-immigrant furor reached its peak in the 1850s. The Nativist Party with secrets and veiled activities thrived, feeding on the venomous hatred of immigrants in general and Irish in particular. Always elusive, when a member of the party was asked questions about political activities, he would invariably say, "I know nothing."[8]

Fighting against grinding poverty and rampant discrimination, the Irish people, over time, nevertheless made great strides toward a leadership role in American politics. Thomas Jefferson's party, the democratic republicans, being hostile toward monarchies, generally welcomed the new Irish. The party became known as the Democratic Party, and the Irish were attracted to it. The other major political party, the Whig Party, did not appeal to them.

The Irish tended to be anti-aristocratic but they were not abolitionists. It wasn't because they approved of slavery, but rather it was believed that free black people would compete with them for the low-paying jobs many Irish were struggling to keep. To a poor Irishman, struggling to feed his family, life as a wage slave was little, if at all, better than being an actual slave or indentured servant. But they recognized the economic advantage of being in America for there was no rush to get back to Ireland.

Much like the Irish-Catholics, another group of Irish, called the Scots-Irish, Protestants with deep roots in Scotland, found America to be a place far more desirable than Ireland. Also referred to as "Scotch-Irish," these tough-minded, hard-working and devoutly religious people began the long journey across the Atlantic in the early 1700s. After having lived in Ulster in Northern Ireland for about 100 years, an estimated 250,000 of Scots-Irish people came to America in the 18th and 19th centuries.[9]

Prior to becoming Americans, the Scots-Irish had been urged by the English to leave Scotland and move to and settle in Ulster. Once there, many of them maintained their Protestantism, but some joined the Catholic Church out of resentment of the English. The two religious groups shared a rebellious attitude toward the English monarchy, a defiance that they took with them to America. But unlike the Irish Catholics, most of the Scots-Irish settled in the South. In Virginia, Georgia and the Carolinas, they became leaders in the development of the distinctly Southern culture that over time formed the basis of the Confederacy.

From the time of the first Irish immigration to America until about 1830, all people coming from Ireland were simply referred to as "Irish." This designation stayed in place until the time that Irish Catholics out-numbered their Protestant brethren. After that turning point, the term "Irish" was applied to Irish Catholics. Hostility between two groups resulted in the Irish Protestants disassociating themselves from simply being called "Irish," the term having acquired negative connotations, such as "superstitious papists and illiterate ditch diggers." The Scots-Irish wanted nothing to do with the desperately poor Irish Catholics that fled Ireland during the famine years of the 1840s and 1850s.[10]

By 1860, America was home to a large urban population of Irish people of both religions. Philadelphia became the home of thousands. In New York alone, Irish-born immigrants were a full one-quarter of that city's total population. It became the largest Irish enclave in America. Ohio cities also received a large number of Irish, including Cincinnati where 12 percent of the population listed their birthplace as Ireland. Like all immigrant groups, the Irish were fruitful and multiplied and America found that it had acquired a hardy, loyal and patriotic people with a strong military tradition.

An uneasy peace existed between the two sets of Irish while America became mired in the sectional conflicts leading up to the Civil War. The Scots-Irish found the going a little easier because they were Protestant in a time of strong, anti–Catholic backlash. Nevertheless, all Irish people were being absorbed into the complex tapestry of American life that offered rewards for those whose talents and ambitions were exceptional.

Among the roster of American luminaries of Scots-Irish descent are Mark Twain, William Faulkner, Davy Crockett, Andrew Jackson, Sam Houston and General George Patton. Not a bad lineup of writers, political leaders and fighters. To this group we can add the McCook family of Ohio. This family was of Scots-Irish descent, and like most of their kindred, they were Presbyterians and proud of it. The McCook family was also damn proud of being American and it was their patriotism that forced them into action when their country was threatened, thus turning stout middle-class people into good soldiers. Long after the war ended the press sang the praises of the McCook family, crediting their "Scotch-Irish blood" for their determination, bravery and success as soldiers.[11]

The U.S. born McCook clan had common ancestors in George and Catherine McCook, who came from Ireland to America in 1790, the year that saw approximately 60,000 Irish leave Ireland. Of this number about 60 percent were Presbyterians.[12] Settling in western Pennsylvania, George McCook was one of those fiery, rebellious Scots-Irishmen who gave the English fits. In trouble for his outspoken and radical political beliefs, and fearing punishment, he and his wife immigrated to America where the proliferation of McCook boys and girls began.

The newly minted American, George McCook, found himself mired in controversy and trouble in western Pennsylvania during a dust-up called the "Whiskey Rebellion" of 1794. He was a member of a group that violently protested a federal tax on whiskey. In a contest with the young, national government over the right impose a federal law on a state, the protestors lost. McCook was arrested along with others but he did not face punishment.[13] From this point on, the McCook family prospered and worked its way into middle-class America, their "Irishness" tempered by an industrious attitude and a desire to live a comfortable, middle-class life.

George and Catherine McCook were the parents of four children: a girl, Fanny, the oldest, and three boys, Daniel, George and John. The family eventually left Pennsylvania and settled in Ohio, the state that became their home and headquarters. All three boys were educated and successful in their professional and personal lives; all three were motivated by strong parents who conferred upon them the importance of goal-directed hard work. Daniel, who is featured in this book, attended Jefferson College in Pennsylvania, but did not graduate; he was too restless and eager to get on with life, so he read law in the office of a Canonsburg attorney and was admitted to the bar.

The impatient young man was not slow in taking a wife. He married Martha Latimer, a fifteen-year-old girl, on August 28, 1817. The groom was only nineteen. The teenage couple got right down to the business of procreation, and in 1824, Daniel, Martha and their four little children moved to New Lisbon, Ohio.[14] Eventually the "New" was dropped and the small, pastoral town of wooded green hills was called "Lisbon."

Daniel McCook was one of the founders of the Presbyterian church in New Lisbon. This son of an immigrant was a tough-minded man who would not be intimidated or deterred by the pounding drums of nativism. He was also a devoutly religious man who saw the influence of God in all things. It was said that he raised his family "in fear of the lord." Translation: corporal punishment was regularly inflicted to instill proper respect and obedience.

Martha Latimer was born at Washington, Pennsylvania, on March 8, 1802.[15] She would prove to be a rock-solid, kind, strong and patient wife, traits she would need in order to keep pace with her headstrong husband and sons. Martha could look to her own family history for pride and strength. It was reported that she had deep roots in British history and was a descendant of Hugh Latimer, one of the great religious leaders of England in the 16th century. He was a Catholic bishop who switched sides and became a leader of the Protestant movement, and during the reign of Queen Mary Tudor, also known as "Bloody Mary," Latimer was arrested, charged with heresy and burned at the stake in 1555.[16] Like her illustrious ancestor, and the man she married, religious faith was at the very center of Martha's life.

By 1832 the McCook family was living in Carrollton, Ohio, a new city in a new county that Daniel and his business partner, Isaac Atkinson, were instrumental in creating. In Carrollton, McCook and Atkinson put their entrepreneurial skills to the test and both men became wealthy. McCook built a large, stylish home on the public square for his wife and children.[17] Always a stickler for good morals, Daniel McCook became a founding member of the Carrollton Total Abstinence Society, created in December of 1841.[18] The following year their son John, third oldest child, serving in the navy, died at sea while on a training mission to South America. He was buried in Rio De Janeiro.[19]

But trouble seemed to stalk the aggressive, crafty McCook as he increased the reach of his business connections. In 1846 when he was the business partner of Moses G. Beach, a New York banker and the publisher of the *New York*

Sun, McCook ran afoul of the law. Beach's bank, styled a "wild cat" bank, had been under scrutiny by the Pennsylvania legislature and it was facing a demand that its charter be pulled. Beach convinced Daniel McCook to lobby against any action adverse to the bank. While trying to spread some money around, McCook found he was in over his head and he was arrested for attempting to bribe a legislator.[20]

Of course someone used the incident to make political hay. A correspondent of the *New York Daily Tribune*, a Whig newspaper, feigning indignation and seeing a chance to take a shot at the Democratic Party, cried out: "Bribery, bold, high handed bribery has been attempted upon a member of the House of Representatives…." The reporter made sure everyone knew that all those involved were "incorruptible" Democrats.[21] McCook made some noise about being the victim of a scheme, "to bring him into the difficulties which now surround him."[22] Represented by a young Thaddeus Stevens, McCook was tried, found guilty and fined $600 plus court costs.[23]

The misstep failed to slow him down, however, and in the 1850s McCook was an operative in the Democratic Party, wielding considerable influence in Ohio. McCook's pre-war political activities remained intense throughout the decade. He was a strong advocate of Senator Stephen A. Douglas of Illinois, one of the most powerful and popular men of his time. In 1853, possibly through the senator's influence, McCook landed a position with the Pension Bureau in Washington, D.C. He and Martha lived in Douglas' Washington mansion.[24] In 1858 he was a "subordinate" clerk in the U.S. House of Representatives.[25] Daniel McCook and his sons were strident supporters of Douglas in the senatorial campaign of 1858, when the "Little Giant" defeated Lincoln, following a series of famous debates that showcased the talents of both men. The McCook family backed Douglas when he ran for the presidency in 1860.

Although the McCooks were strongly allied to the Democratic Party, and were suspicious of the new Republican Party, they were only lukewarm in their support of President James Buchanan. A life-long politician with a long string of political offices as good credentials, Buchanan handily defeated John C. Frémont, the first Republican to run for president, in the 1856 general election. Thereafter, because of the sectional crisis over slavery, Buchanan's presidency was beset by problems that he was unable, and unwilling, to address. He was indecisive and weak and both the North and the South knew it. What to do with Buchanan, while the break-up of the Union was imminent, was a dilemma that for some called for desperate measures.

After South Carolina and other states seceded, some Southerners were fearful that Buchanan's lack of strength and leadership might embolden the North to take aggressive measures against the South. It was then that a "few choice spirits" came up with a plan. They would kidnap Buchanan, ferret him away to a hiding place so that the vice president, John C. Breckinridge, believed to be a stronger, more principled man, would be placed in the president's chair. The plotters reasoned this would bolster the South because, with Breckinridge in charge, the "South would feel secure against being 'trapped into a war.'" The plot was never carried into execution because, among other things, Secretary of War John Floyd, despite his Southern sympathies, flatly refused to be a part of something so bizarre, mad and entirely off the wall.[26]

Secession by the Southern states set in motion the guns of civil war, and men from Scots-Irish and Irish Catholic communities in the Northern states eagerly joined the Union army regiments. Some of the new regiments were made up entirely of Irish soldiers. In Ohio, approximately 8000 Irishmen, mostly Democrats, joined the Union army. They proved to be some of the most loyal and patriotic "War Democrats." And because they freely contributed their heroic sons to the war effort, John and Daniel McCook went on to become known as "American Brothers Who Won Fame" as "fathers of the 'Fighting McCooks.'"[27]

Over the course of the four-year war, about 145,000 Irishmen served in support of the Union cause.[28] Among the best known Union Irish-American Civil War generals were Philip H. Sheridan and Thomas Francis Meagher. Patrick Cleburne, born in Ireland, was an outstanding Confederate general. Meagher was the leader of the 69th New York Infantry regiment, consisting of Irish soldiers. It went on to serve with great distinction in many campaigns of the Civil War and acquired a reputation as the "greatest brigade," the one that paved the way for a Union victory over the Confederacy.[29]

The McCook family contributed mightily to the Union war effort. Seventeen members of their extended family—fathers, brothers, uncles and cousins—served in the Union army during the Civil War. They were fiercely pro–Union and believed wholeheartedly that anyone who would secede from the greatest government the world had yet created was a traitor and the only answer to treason was to destroy it. To a man they rejected the ironclad Southern belief that the Constitution guaranteed the right of a state to secede. To a McCook, secession meant treason. A traitor was a man without honor, and he must be struck down and shown no mercy. Armed with these strong beliefs, no other American family contributed as much time, talent and blood to the Union cause as did the McCooks. Theirs is a record of gallantry, pride and honor. Motivated by an innate, Scots-Irish warrior ethic, they earned the honored title "the Fighting McCooks."

This book will feature the illustrious careers of Robert L. McCook and his younger brother, Daniel McCook, Jr., offspring of Daniel and Martha McCook, whose oldest son died in 1841 while serving in the U.S. Navy. Both Robert and Daniel Jr. distinguished themselves in combat and earned the rank of brigadier general. And more significantly, both suffered and died from battle wounds. Their father Daniel McCook, Sr., a strident supporter of the Union, was also killed in the war as was their younger brother Charles. Brothers Latimer, George, Alexander, Edwin, and John, all of whom served the Union they loved, and survived, will also be introduced. As it is with all true heroes, the McCooks' place on the roster of the honored is secure, and their names are indelibly written in the history of the Civil War. Like all brave soldiers throughout all time, they earned it.

The McCooks didn't slip into the war quietly. They were introduced to the American public rather dramatically in an Ohio newspaper article entitled "A Military Family." On May 30, 1861, the *Holmes County Republican* revealed that "among the most startling illustrations of the war spirit roused in the North," the "well-known Ohio family of which Judge Daniel McCook is the head," stands in the front rank of Union supporters. Formerly a probate judge, Daniel McCook, Sr., was 62 years old, an age when many men were looking for a front porch and a rocking chair. But "Judge" McCook, as he was familiarly called, picked up a rifle and volunteered his services as a soldier.

His age prohibited him from serving in a regiment, so McCook found other ways to contribute. He joined up with James H. "Jim" Lane of Kansas, a fiery former congressman from Indiana and a staunch abolitionist. Lane led a group called the Frontier Guard that set up a camp in the White House to protect the president and the capital city until regiments could be organized and put in place.[30] While people were fleeing Washington, D.C., because of the fear of an impending attack by Southerners, Lane, McCook and other veteran fighters, mostly from Kansas, chose the East Room of the White House as a base of operations. On April 18, 1861, a group of 60 well-armed men marched into the White House and made camp in the elegant East Room. In time the roster of men grew to 116, including Edward M. McCook, a nephew of Judge McCook. All were prepared to fight to the last man in order defend the president and the federal government.[31]

Dr. Latimer A. McCook, the second oldest of the sons of Daniel and Martha, joined the 31st Illinois as an assistant surgeon. Latimer had studied medicine at Willoughby Medical College of Chagrin, Ohio, as a student of his uncle, the eminent Dr. George McCook, and graduated in 1845. He began a medical practice and then married Eliza McLain and fathered a boy named Alexander. Unfortunately Latimer's son died in infancy and his wife abandoned him for reasons the family kept from the public. He was thereafter simply referred as a "widower."[32]

In 1861, Dr. Latimer McCook volunteered his services to the Union and set himself to easing the suffering of the wounded, removing bullets, searing wounds, cutting off shattered limbs and dealing with the day to day struggle with death and disease.³³ Although he was given the rank of major, he didn't actually join the army but rather was a civilian contract surgeon, earning $100 per month. At his side were two dogs, his loyal and constant companions as the good doctor moved from place to place. Building a remarkable record of service and devotion to duty, he never took a day of leave and only stopped cutting and bandaging when the war ended.

Latimer's younger brother George Wythe McCook was easily more conspicuous in his personality and lifestyle. A gregarious man large in size and imposing in his intellectual capacity, George loved the classics and the companionship of his fellow Democrats, including Edwin M. Stanton, a native Ohioan and brilliant young lawyer with a dominating personality and an ambitious outlook. The two hungry young lions prowled Ohio and Pennsylvania with a conquer-the-world attitude.

After attending Franklin College in Athens, Ohio, George W. McCook read law in Stanton's office and was admitted to the bar. In 1845, the two men formed a law partnership in Steubenville, Ohio. McCook was thirty-three years old and Stanton two years younger; both were good lawyers. More important, perhaps, the partnership was the beginning of a strong friendship. In the tense and nervy antebellum years, the two men constantly had their sights set on the political and social upheaval going on all around them. They intervened whenever they could and as best they could. They were both too headstrong to sit on the sidelines.

It was their friendship that probably saved Stanton's life, for in his early years he was beset by tragedy that forced upon him a morbid attitude toward life, death and the grave. The sudden death of the daughter of his Columbus, Ohio, landlady from cholera shocked and saddened him so much that he enlisted the help of friends to open the grave to make certain the girl had not been buried alive. Premature burials were known to have happened and were a natural, though usually unspoken, concern. Then, in 1841, the death of Stanton's young daughter, Lucy, caused the distraught father to exhume her body after a year in the ground. Unable to rebury her, Stanton kept her body in a metal casket in his room. When his beloved wife, Mary, died in 1844, Stanton was persuaded to inter both bodies.³⁴

But more family tragedy followed. His brother, Dr. Darwin Stanton, killed himself by cutting his throat. Edwin was inconsolable and in his grief he ran off into a dark, wooded area, vanishing in the cold night. George McCook and others engaged in a frantic search fearing that Stanton would kill himself or die of exposure. They found the grief-stricken Stanton. Over time he regained his senses and powers of intellect, but having survived multiple tragedies he turned "a stern face to the world."

At the outset of the Mexican War, George W. McCook commanded a

Proud father Edwin M. Stanton poses with his young son Edwin in a daguerreotype taken between 1852 and 1855. A stalwart friend and law partner of George W. McCook, Stanton was forced to deal with overwhelming grief as a young man, suffering the loss of his first wife and their daughter, and later the death by suicide of his brother. To keep his sanity and survive the losses, he turned a cold and stern face to the world. This tactic enabled him to coordinate his talent with that of President Abraham Lincoln to hammer out a Union victory in the Civil War (Library of Congress, gift from the James Madison Counsil and George S. Whitely, IV).

company of troops known as the "Steubenville Greys." Stanton wanted to join and fight with his friend, but for health reasons, he stayed home while Lieutenant McCook went to Mexico. The two men kept up a steady correspondence that churned the fires of their friendship. Stanton promised to keep tabs on McCook's fiancée, Margaret Beatty, and was faithful in that regard. After the war ended, McCook returned to Ohio to marry his sweetheart; Stanton was the best man at the wedding.

Stanton and George W. McCook resumed their law partnership in Steubenville, but the former grew restless with the slow pace of professional life. Without breaking up their partnership, Stanton moved to Pittsburgh to practice law and continue his involvement in national politics. McCook chose to stay in Steubenville, a town that would always be home to him.[35] He was elected the attorney general for Ohio in 1853.

In time, Abraham Lincoln would harness the Stanton energy, talent and stubborn brain power. Added to the acclaimed "Team of Rivals," the strong-minded Ohioan would serve as an effective and hard-working secretary of war during the Civil War. His friend George W. McCook was given the rank of colonel and tasked with organizing and training Ohio regiments. Although he never took to the field, his brothers did. In the McCook family, the president and his secretary of war had at their disposal a group of loyal, dedicated and hard-fighting soldiers.

Alexander McDowell McCook was one of those soldiers who unflinchingly stepped up. A graduate of West Point, Alexander was off on a military career that would last to the end of his days. Before the Civil War he had served in the far Southwest fighting Indians. He also did a stint as an instructor at West Point. After the war started McCook recruited the 1st Ohio Voluntary Infantry and was appointed to be its colonel. The 1st Ohio fought in the first battle of Bull Run where Colonel McCook distinguished himself and was promoted to brigadier general for having led and fought with valor and gallantry.

Younger brothers Charles and Edwin were also present at Bull Run, the former a private in the 2nd Ohio Infantry

George Wythe McCook was the politician of the McCook family, keeping active in the Democratic Party's conventions and elections. His political acumen meant that he had opportunities to make friends with other politically-minded men such as Edwin M. Stanton. The two became friends when they were young. Both were lawyers, and while George served in army in the Mexican War, Stanton remained a civilian, practicing law in the firm he and George started together. After the Civil War broke out George organized Ohio regiments and Stanton eventually joined President Lincoln's cabinet as secretary of war. Both were committed to the defeat of the Confederacy and the restoration of the Union (courtesy Ohio History Connection OM 1289_793691_007).

regiment. Edwin was there as an observer, along with his father and John A. Logan from Illinois. It was a short war for Private Charles McCook, for he was shot and killed after refusing an order to surrender. Attended by his father who was serving as a voluntary nurse near the front, Charles died after a few hours of suffering.

It was a bad day for both the McCooks and the Union. The federal army was repulsed by the Confederates, causing soldiers to panic and then retreat in disorder back to Washington. Despite the chaos and confusion both Edwin and Alexander were able to say good-bye to their mortally wounded younger brother. Edwin was not yet in uniform, but having seen the terrible fruits of battle, he went to Illinois and organized the 31st Illinois Infantry Regiment. John, the youngest McCook, was a teenager when the war began, but he would eventually join the Union army, for like his siblings and his father, the cause was just and the need to serve in the military was far greater than any personal ambitions or family considerations. The intensely competitive McCook family, as one, was in it for the duration with only one goal: victory.

In 1850, during a debate in Congress, a man from South Carolina shrieked: "Give us slavery or give us death!"[36] The fiery remark expressed, fully, the heartfelt belief in the legitimacy of slavery by the Southern elite. A decade later, the flames of outrage were out of control, slavery and secession had created irreconcilable differences—North and South; there was nothing left to do but to commence shooting. Both sides understood that there was a war to fight and all other matters were reduced to trivia.

Robert L. McCook

1
Commander of the 9th Ohio Infantry Regiment

> "It really looked just like what we read as having taken place in the days of '76, when men left the plow standing in the furrow, dropped the uplifted hammer and rushed to the defense of their country."—
> *The Wheeling Intelligencer* in the *New York Tribune*, June 1, 1861

Unlike the article in the Wheeling newspaper, the *New York Times* sent a pessimistic message to its readers while the Union and Confederate armies geared up for what many believed would be a great battle at Manassas Gap on Bull Run Creek in northern Virginia. "A feeling approaching a foreboding of evil has for a day and a half been visible among the people," was the message that seeped ominously from an article on July 21, 1861.[1] The *Times* was irrevocably pro–Union but it was not willing to succumb to the war hysteria whipped up in other parts of the North; it waited anxiously, as reports from the battlefield of Bull Run came in. The news was bad.

But while Major General Irwin McDowell's makeshift and inexperienced army was fighting, and losing, the Bull Run campaign in northern Virginia, about 25 miles south of Washington, D.C., another, more successful Union effort was coming to fruition in the rugged mountains and scenic valleys of western Virginia, where disunion was disfavored. Although most of the Old Dominion was solidly Confederate, it was known that the people west of the Allegheny Mountains were leaning pro–Union with economic and social ties to Ohio and Pennsylvania.

The national flag flew proudly in Wheeling, the center of anti-secession feelings where Union men were ready to "throw themselves into the arms of Ohio and Pennsylvania." Western Virginia folk had long complained about being overtaxed and unfairly represented in the state legislature. As a result, they were cut off from the plantation culture of their "aristocratic" eastern counterparts and had little or no sympathy with the institution of slavery.

1. Commander of the 9th Ohio Infantry Regiment

Unfortunately for the mountain folks, they were citizens of a commonwealth that had the dubious distinction of owning more slaves than any other Southern state.

The average western Virginian was probably unaware of this. But in 1859, a *New York Times* correspondent noted that "there was a general unwillingness on the part of the people of Western Virginia to employ slave labor," and that "it [slavery] is rapidly giving way under the influence ... of the free labor system."[2] According to an 1860 census, that portion of the state identified as western Virginia contained 18,371 slaves, a relatively small amount when compared to the 472,494 in the rest of the state.[3]

When the Virginia Ordinance of Secession was put to popular vote, the men of western Virginia voted against it in high numbers. They began organizing with a view of holding their own convention which would include delegates from the counties west of the Blue Ridge. Pro-Union feelings ran high, leading observers to believe that because Virginia, led by the slave holding planters, seceded from the Union, then western Virginia would also secede from the state.[4] It would not be a part of a "Cotton Republic."

Local groups gathered and advocated in favor of staying in the Union. In Hancock County, a group of loyalists passed resolutions lauding the "heroes of '76" and the "star-spangled banner." These Virginians condemned the "East Virginia traitors" and vowed to demand a "division of the state."[5]

In Richmond, the capital of Virginia, the U.S. flag was hauled down and torn to shreds, but the stars and stripes was held in high esteem in western Virginia. The anti-secession sentiment among the people was as strong and pure as the mountain air and fully in accord with the man who said: "The man who is willing that his country should be divided by the sword of treason may have been born in America, but he cannot have an American heart."[6]

President Abraham Lincoln sought to use this proud attitude to his advantage. The president could not coax the entire state back into the Union, but if he could cut off a good-sized chunk of Old Dominion, there would be significant net gain. Tying western Virginia to the Union was necessary in order exploit the mineral wealth that included coal, salt, lead and iron, and also to keep control of the railroad that connected Washington with the west.

To lead this campaign, Lincoln selected Major General George B. McClellan, who at age 34 was an egotistical, unstable, yet thoroughly military man, having graduated second in his class at West Point in 1846. The jaunty "Young Napoleon," as he was called, took command of the newly formed Department of the Ohio on May 26, 1861, just three days after Virginia seceded from the Union. The department included the states of Ohio, Indiana and Illinois with headquarters in Cincinnati. Soon Ohio volunteer regiments were crossing into western Virginia to protect the loyalists and drive out the secessionists.

It was during the western Virginia campaign that another McCook made his Civil War debut. Robert Latimer McCook, like his younger brothers Alexander, Daniel and Charles, answered Lincoln's call for volunteers. Not to be outdone by Alexander—who organized the 1st Ohio Infantry regiment, or cousin Anson G. McCook, who created the 2nd Ohio Infantry—Robert L. McCook offered up a volunteer regiment of his own.

A fully manned regiment contained 900 to 1,000 men divided into ten companies. McCook's regiment consisted of German immigrant volunteers and was formed in April of 1861 under the leadership of the Turner Society of Cincinnati. On April 15, while America was reeling from the attack on Fort Sumter, attorney Robert L. McCook gave a fiery speech at Turner Hall before a predominately German audience, condemning the South and secession while calling on support for the Union. He said, "I know the Germans will fight!"[7] Before long he had his volunteers: a 1,000-man regiment dedicated to the Union cause. Hundreds of disappointed excess volunteers had to be turned away.

McCook—the lone native-born American in the regiment—was elected colonel by the troops, as was the practice during the early stages of the war. This unusual, democratic practice meant that the selection of leaders was often a popularity contest, one that did not always contribute the best qualified officers to the cause. It would eventually be replaced by a system whereby the governors of the various states created military examination boards, staffed by officers, who then examined the qualifications of officer candidates.[8]

Fortunately the election of the well-liked Robert L. McCook would prove to be an excellent choice. His unit of volunteers was called the 1st German Regiment and was later renamed the 9th Ohio Infantry regiment. The proud regiment was mustered in for three

Robert L. McCook as a young man posing in civilian clothes. As a boy, Robert was regarded as serious and studious, lacking the rowdy nature of other boys his age, but the calm exterior belied an aggressive personality. He studied law at the office of Edwin M. Stanton and George W. McCook, his older brother. When the war broke out, Robert enlisted in the Union army with enthusiasm. He recruited the 9th Ohio Infantry Regiment, a unit he led until his untimely and tragic death in August of 1862 (U.S. Army Military History Institute).

months' service in the Union army on May 8, 1861, at Camp Harrison near Cincinnati.[9]

In fairness to McCook, he did not engage in political arm twisting in order to get a command. And yet he readily accepted the honor and took control. He used his political savvy and family connections in Columbus and Washington, D.C., to ensure that the 9th Ohio had the distinction of becoming first three-year regiment.[10] At the outbreak of the Civil War—when brass insignia was available almost for the asking—Robert was given the rank of colonel.

In selecting McCook to command the regiment, a better qualified man was passed over. That man—narrowly defeated in the colonel contest—was Germany native Augustus Willich, who had lived in the United States since 1853. A member of an aristocratic Prussian family, at age 15 he was enrolled in the Royal Military Academy in Berlin. But his military career was short-lived because Willich became enamored with the liberal movement that was sweeping Europe. Because he espoused free speech and a free press, he was forced to resign his commission. He then became active in the communist movement and was involved in two failed armed revolts against the German government, showing leadership and courage under fire. He worked with radical luminaries such as Karl Marx and Friedrich Engels, but soon fell out of favor with them and moved to the United States with hope in his heart and a strong belief in the rights of the workingman.[11]

Before the war Willich worked as a carpenter and later for the U.S. Coast and Geodetic Survey office. The tall, bearded and dignified man was also an editor for a German-language newspaper in Cincinnati. He believed in and strongly supported the U.S. Constitution, seeing it as a model of good government. In short, he was a proud American who saw in secession political folly and a dangerous precedent, if allowed to stand. Following the onset of hostilities, the staunchly patriotic Willich joined the 9th Ohio as a private and became thoroughly involved in the formation of four companies of infantry from among his German brethren.

The German immigrants, an ethnic group that came to America in large numbers in the 1840s and 50s, settled primarily in urban areas. They were repulsed by Southern aristocracy because it reminded them of life under the oppressive German aristocrats. They were also anti-slavery and wanted to stop slavery from spreading, but they feared that immediate emancipation would result in a flood of people looking for jobs, and they didn't want that kind of competition. Above all else they admired the American example and were amazed to see how lightly Americans were governed compared to the hard hand of authority in Europe.

They were outspoken in their political beliefs, and many, like Willich, were steeped in radicalism, so they were looked upon with a fair amount of suspicion and hate. Epithets such as "damn Dutch" or "lop-eared Dutch" were hurled at them. But name calling was not always satisfactory and many Germans were attacked, beaten and killed by mobs.[12] Like the Irish and other immigrants, Germans were the target of anti-immigrant, nativist people from political organizations such as the Know Nothings, who wanted to keep immigrants in a lowly status, or better yet, out of the country. Even when they were in uniform defending the Union, German soldiers, such as those in the 9th Ohio, were often treated badly and called insulting names.

Due to the pervasive anti-immigrant sentiment in the United States, Robert L. McCook was placed in charge of his volunteers despite his lack of military experience, versus the obvious martial skills of Willich. McCook did, however, show an interest in military matters before the war and in 1860 visited Europe, where he studied the European armies, particularly those of Germany, France, Austria and Italy.[13]

As a boy growing up in Columbiana County, Ohio, Robert was a serious, introspective child, with a maturity that overmatched his adolescence. Ohio governor David Tod was struck by Robert's mature "bearing" upon meeting him for the first time more than twenty years before the Civil War started. The governor recalled making the "acquaintance of a lad whose countenance engaged my attention the first moment I looked upon it. He had a bearing that every passer-by would notice."[14]

Nor was Tod the only man who took notice of the moody, young Bob McCook. Others were in accord and concluded that his "grave manners distinguished him from his brothers." People who knew the McCook family called him "an old-fashioned child, sober beyond his years."[15] It would seem that these traits served him well as an adult, for at an early age he was on track to become a well-grounded, solid citizen.

It was understood that McCook's political connections in Columbus, Ohio, and Washington landed him a command. Although a Democrat, he harbored no sympathy for the South and was as loyal to the Union as was any abolitionist. He was introspective and intelligent and seemed destined for the well-balanced life of an intellectual, but the man his family called Bob was shaken by secession. Then, as if breaking out of a shell, he became a hard man of action, driven by a strong desire to lead men against the Confederacy.

Prior to the war McCook had studied law in Carrollton, Ohio, at the office of Judge E. R. Eckley.[16] Next, he joined the prestigious Steubenville law firm that included among its members his older brother George W. McCook and Edwin M. Stanton. After gaining admission to practice law, young lawyer Robert relocated to Cincinnati to work with Judge J. B. Stallo.[17] Stanton went on to fame as Lincoln's caustic and aggressive secretary of war, emerging as one of the key figures in the Civil War.

Despite his status as a "political colonel," Robert L. McCook lacked the shallow arrogance that marked the undistinguished careers of other officers appointed for political reasons. He was not a West Point man and he had no military training, but in the words of an Ohio newspaper, he possessed "natural military genius."[18] Furthermore, he didn't seem to be burdened by feelings of jealousy of West Pointers, unlike many other officers who didn't go to the academy. Still he understood his limitations. And his loyalty to the Union cause was enough to make him realize that the real work of whipping his regiment into shape should be placed in Willich's hands.

Robert L. McCook, who apparently had no ego to bruise and no political career to pursue, jocularly referred to himself as "just the clerk for a thousand Dutchmen." But he was a popular "clerk," for his Dutchmen treated Robert like a brother, and his mother Martha McCook was affectionately called "Mother McCook."[19] The likeable Robert was also a thinker whose actions were the product of a fertile mind.

Colonel McCook was entirely comfortable having "Papa Willich," his adjutant, in charge while he studied the military manuals and learned to be an officer and a leader. There was a practical side of the arrangement too. McCook didn't speak German and the men of the 9th Ohio Infantry didn't speak English. Willich, however, spoke both languages.

Robert's older brother George W. McCook was also instrumental in organizing Ohio regiments. George had some prior military experience, having served in the Mexican War as an officer of the 3rd Ohio Regiment. He could claim political clout too, for he held the office of attorney general of Ohio in 1854–56.[20]

Ohio governor David Tod invited the George W. McCook to lead the 84th Ohio Infantry regiment, called the "best body of undrilled men that has yet been raised in Ohio."[21] George also organized and commanded the 157th Ohio Infantry in the field in 1864. But this McCook—a Democratic Party stalwart of long standing—was not in good health and therefore never took the field as a commander in a combat role.

Not so for brother Bob and his German regiment. On May 16, 1861, the "Niners" were sent to Camp Dennison, 13 miles north of Cincinnati, where the regiment was reorganized for three years' service. McCook got his sword, rifles for his troops, and a 24-piece band. The troops, eager to meet the enemy, were informed they were going to western Virginia to serve under Major General George B. McClellan.[22] On June 13, 1861, while his brothers Alexander and Charles, along with his cousin Anson, were bivouacked with the Union army in northern Virginia, Robert L. McCook and his 9th Ohio were off to deal with the enemy in the western part of the state. On the 18th, the 9th landed at Parkersburg.

Bob was joined in the mountain region by his cousin John J. "Little Johnny" McCook, who enlisted in the army despite the concern of his parents and brothers that at least one of the boys should stay home with their parents. Since Johnny was the youngest of his brood he was nominated for that role, but he thought otherwise and the adventuresome lad soon found himself a second lieutenant in the 1st Virginia Infantry regiment.[23]

The Union objective was the Kanawha Valley, whose residents were about equally divided in political sentiment. The Union held a majority of the people, but the Confederacy was better organized. Newspapers tended to favor the South and most office holders were either pro-secession or neutral. Charleston, the principal city in the Kanawha Valley, took on an air of neutrality where troops from both sides drilled in their respective camps.

The Ohio troops were there to assist and protect the loyalists, but they acquired a bad impression of the mountain people, whom they looked upon as miserable simpletons or wild creatures. It was said that if a "soldier looks at one of them, [a local] straightway he makes out a bill against the Government."[24] They were on the same side of the war but seemingly a world apart.

Boredom was more of a problem for the Federals than encounters with the enemy. While the scenery was pleasing and the berry picking was fulfilling, the enforced idleness gave way to diary entries and letters that bemoaned the lack of action in a war that seemed to be taking place somewhere else. There was little gunfire and no glory in western Virginia, so soldiers turned to drinking, gambling, reading and other *ad lib* activities.

Hunting down civilian secessionists kept the some of the Federals busy. Disloyal men were taken into custody and dealt with harshly, as if trying to disprove the Rebel boast that "one secessionist can whip five Union men." On one occasion, a Southern sympathizer was "tried" and "convicted" of disloyalty. The Union boys forced him to get down on his knees, swear allegiance to the Union, kiss the flag and join their ranks. He was then pardoned.[25] On another occasion, a group of wealthy Kanawha secessionists was captured and put aboard a steamer and sent into Ohio. There they were to be held hostage and later exchanged for Union soldiers who had been taken prisoner by "marauding bands."[26]

If the anti-secessionist sweeps became too heavy handed, the offending Union troops were punished. McClellan, in step with the Lincoln administration, believed that Southern civilians and their property had to be respected and protected. For violating this policy, a company of the 19th Ohio Infantry was "paraded before the regiment ... disarmed and ordered to report at Columbus." Eight privates and a lieutenant were summarily booted out of the army for "disgraced outrages perpetuated on the property of reputed Secessionists."[27] While such action did not please the hardliners, it was still early in the war and at least two years would pass before both sides took on a much less gentlemanly approach to the fight.

General Robert E. Lee, the prototype Southern gentleman, did not favor Southern independence, but was strong on the necessity of defending his home state of Virginia. As such he chose the South when it came time to choose, rejecting Lincoln's offer to command the Union army. Lee disfavored both slavery and secession, but decided he could not raise his sword against his native Virginia. In choosing to reject Lincoln's offer, he placed his love and loyalty for his state above that of his country.

Jefferson Davis appointed Lee to take charge of all Confederate troops in Virginia. Lee then placed a small Rebel army under two brigadier generals, Henry A. Wise and John B. Floyd, and sent them into the western region of the state to confront the Federals. This was an unfortunate circumstance for the South because the two men hated each other intensely and wasted valuable time quarreling, each man trying to undermine the other. Jefferson Davis expected Lee to persuade Wise and Floyd to cooperate, and he tried but to no avail. Both were former governors of Virginia and both had newspapermen on their staffs.

Despite his hatred of Floyd, Wise was unequivocal in his belief in secession and the formation of a separate nation in the South. Before the shooting started, Wise boasted about leading an army into Washington to prevent the inauguration of Lincoln.[28]

Floyd had served as secretary of war in the James Buchanan administration. While all prominent Rebels were deemed traitors, Floyd's treason was considered far more serious than that of ordinary secessionists because of his recent service on the cabinet. According to John C. Nicolay, Lincoln's private secretary, Floyd had planned ahead, anticipating secession, and shipped a large amount of arms and ammunition to posts on the Atlantic and Gulf coasts.[29]

A Union general was of the same opinion, and after watching Floyd for six months, concluded that there was "little doubt" that the secretary was "playing into the hands of the secessionists."[30] Commenting on his clever ploy, the New York Times called Floyd the "artful dodger of the Southern Confederacy."[31]

After Sumter fell, Floyd busied himself by turning over other federal posts to the Confederates and then he became one. Although the switch came as no surprise to the Lincoln administration, taking his scalp became a priority for the Union. Edwin M. Stanton, who had served as Buchanan's attorney general and knew Floyd well, was determined to apprehend and hang him.[32]

Before Robert L. McCook's men were added to the regiments gathering in the mountains, a skirmish at the town of Philippi kicked off the western Virginia campaign. It happened when four regiments of Union infantry came across a Rebel encampment and opened fire at 5 a.m. on June 3. Among the attacking Union troops was Robert's cousin, Lieutenant John J. "Little Johnny" McCook, son of Dr. John and Catherine McCook. Although the youngest of all the McCooks to serve in the war—he was just 16 when he volunteered—to him went the honor of participating in the opening campaign in western Virginia.

Lee had placed the Confederates under the command of Virginia native Colonel George A. Porterfield and ordered him to report to the town of Grafton where it was expected that men would flock to his standard. When Porterfield arrived at the railroad station, he was shocked to find out that he was utterly without volunteers. He did, however, manage to gather about 775 men and set up camp at Philippi.[33]

Porterfield was warned that a force numbering 4500 federal troops were approaching his position, so it was decided to pack the wagons and be ready to move out. They did not move, however, due to the torrential rains that night. So heavy was the rainfall that no one among the Rebel contingent believed that the enemy would make an assault.

As a result the Rebels were caught completely off guard by a two-pronged attack spearheaded by Colonel Benjamin F. Kelley and Colonel Frederick W. Lander. The war correspondent who covered the event noted the "Rebels were sleeping more soundly than usual," having the night before helped themselves to generous amounts of whisky taken from a nearby farm. Once fully aroused by the sobering sound of cannon fire that ripped through their tents, the Rebels scattered "like rats from a burning barn." They left behind a large cache of arms and ammunition and a reported 15 dead comrades, although the actual casualty list was much higher.[34]

Although Philippi was a minor battle, its impact jolted both sides. The fleeing Rebels made their way to Beverly, about 35 miles south of Philippi, where they expected to meet reinforcements. The Union commanders decided not to pursue, but rather to establish a presence in Philippi and they set about occupying the town.

The one-sided fight is considered to be the first land battle of the Civil War, and the actual first shot fired at Union soldiers came from the gun of an irate and determined Confederate woman in an attempt to warn the sleeping Rebels. It was a win for McClellan, even though he was still in Ohio, training troops, and an embarrassment for the South. The "Philippi rout" or "Philippi races" was unfurled in the *New York Tribune* in a manner that reflected a desire by the press to gain some bragging rights in the soon to become state of West Virginia. The victory boosted the pro–Union sentiment in western

Virginia and secured the federal control of the Baltimore and Ohio Railroad, better known as the B & O.³⁵

McClellan was slow to pursue the Confederate troops. But soon after the Philippi rout, additional Ohio units crossed the Ohio River, giving the Union forces superiority as they moved further south, causing the Confederates to backtrack. In some towns, Union troops were hailed as liberators. They were greeted by large, cheering crowds, with sobbing women and flirtatious girls waving hankies.

Buoyed by the minor victory at Philippi, delegates from approximately 40 counties gathered in convention at Wheeling on June 11. They angrily denounced the "treasonable usurpations" of the Richmond Convention and Governor John Letcher, while declaring loyalty to the Union. On the 19th, they set up a "state" government, appointed their own governor, and on July 9 they elected two U.S. senators who promptly reported to Washington and were seated in Congress.³⁶

While the fighting that ensued over the next few months was relatively insignificant by comparison to the blood-soaked battle fields of eastern and northern Virginia, several men of historical importance gained valuable military (and political) experience in the mountains. Among them was Major Rutherford B. Hayes, who commanded the 23rd Ohio Infantry regiment and was destined to become commander and chief of the Union army in 1876. His regiment included another future president, William McKinley, who would be elected 20 years after Hayes. Both men proved to be good soldiers and they made Ohio proud.

Hayes was a volunteer, a civilian

Future president Rutherford B. Hayes shared a tent with his friend Colonel Robert L. McCook during the campaign to drive the Rebels out of the mountains and meadows of western Virginia. Major Hayes was held in high esteem by Americans as a volunteer and a proud citizen soldier in command of the 23rd Ohio Infantry Regiment. He has been remembered for his loyalty to the Union and his love for army life, both which made him a popular leader. Among those serving in the 23rd Ohio was William McKinley, the man who would be elected president 20 years after Hayes.

soldier and proud of it. His letters to his wife Lucy proclaim his loyalty to the Union cause and his love of army life. His temperament, intelligence and political acumen set him apart from other volunteer officers. He possessed an energetic optimism that would carry him through political battles later in life. The studious but high-spirited Hayes—with a keen eye for nature— endeared himself to the western Virginia commanders and wrote with special pride about his camaraderie with Robert L. McCook, with whom he shared a tent.[37] He was the kind of soldier well suited to deal with the special demands of a mountain campaign.

After the debacle at Philippi, Lee recalled Porterfield and ordered him to face a board of inquiry to answer for his misfeasance and blunders. Lee then ordered Brigadier General Robert S. Garnett to take charge of the scattered Confederate forces in western Virginia. Garnett accepted his orders with a fatalistic outlook, believing he had been given a death sentence. He had about 3,000 men at his disposal for the purpose of containing the Union forces and, if possible, to regain control of the B & O Railroad. It was essential that the Union forces be prevented from further penetration into the interior of the state where they could threaten the Shenandoah Valley.

Garnett divided his meager army and placed troops in the mountain passes near Laurel Hill and Rich Mountain, not far from the town of Beverly. While Garnett was inching his way north, McClellan—never known for bold moves—decided on June 21, 1861, to cross the Ohio River and take charge of his army. Robert L. McCook's 9th Ohio and two other Ohio regiments, along with two Kentucky regiments, formed part of McClellan's small army.[38]

McClellan joined his troops at their encampment in the Grafton-Philippi region and began planning his campaign. He organized his regiments into five brigades under Colonel Robert L. McCook, Brigadier General Newton Schelich, Brigadier General Thomas A. Morris and Brigadier General William S. Rosecrans.

Although McClellan was soldierly and expected the same out of his men, he was not an aggressive commander. As a result, the troops were still susceptible to the woes of inactivity. McClellan was not a man to make a sudden move; rather he took his time and preferred to carefully plan every campaign down to the most minor of details. It was with great difficulty that he made a decision, and when he did make up his mind, he never seemed comfortable with his decision. In June of 1861, McClellan decided to go into the wilderness.

When troops were on the march, the spooky environment often overwhelmed and played tricks with the mind. As such, the Union troops looked to well-armed local men referred to as "Snake Hunters" to act as guides and spies.[39] Described as "half horse, half alligator and the rest—snapping turtle-est [*sic*] of human beings," these men were skilled backwoodsmen, accustomed to life in the trackless wilderness.[40] They could survive where even experienced men could get lost in the hazy, thick-wooded maze.

Most of the Ohio boys had seen hills but were unfamiliar with mountains and easily succumbed to their beguiling influence. In one instance of enchantment, a wagon master out foraging rushed into the camp of General Cox to report that he accidentally came upon a Rebel encampment not far away from the federal tent ground. While Cox had his doubts, he nevertheless sent out a woodsman turned soldier, Lieutenant Bontecou, to corroborate the excited wagon master's story. Bontecou returned with a tale of a narrow escape, agreeing that there was indeed an encampment of the enemy close by.

Cox needed no further encouragement or proof. He ordered Colonel McCook to take his brigade out to surprise and capture the camped men. McCook's guide led the colonel and his men in various directions, through thick woods and brush, and after seemingly traveling a great distance, finally coming near the target of their search. McCook himself crawled through the woods until he spotted a group of tents. Then, to his utter surprise, McCook realized that he was creeping up on the rear of his own camp! McCook "convulsed with laughter over the misadventure," and it was several minutes before he could "collect himself sufficiently to explain that he had come out to attack his own brigade." The comic incident became known as the "Battle of Bontecou" after the lieutenant who found the "Rebel campground."[41]

The genial Colonel McCook was liberal in his acts of kindness and consideration toward his beloved regiment. Whenever possible or expedient, he let the men rest and sought to make camp life comfortable. It was said that he always interpreted orders as humanely as possible and still maintained sufficient discipline so as not to jeopardize his mission. He treated his men as equals and they repaid him with feelings of utmost respect and brotherly love. One of his soldiers said, "He [McCook] takes care of his men in a fatherly way and does not rest until he knows everything is in order."[42] The biographer of the 9th Ohio Infantry said "to know him was to respect him," and that McCook's courage, always on display, was cause for his men to follow him "to Hell itself."[43]

Once while on the march during the western Virginia campaign, McCook noticed three soldiers struggling desperately, under the weight of heavy packs, to keep pace with their comrades. The man who was having the most trouble keeping up was sent by McCook to the ambulance. Addressing the other two soldiers, McCook said, "tie your packs together," after which he swung them over the front of his saddle. Freed from the oppressive weight of their packs, the men were able to make it to the bivouac. No one was left behind while Colonel McCook was in charge of the brigade.[44]

Bob McCook's kindness wasn't superficial for he truly cared for his men and saw to it that they were always well-supplied. It was said that no one knew where his wagons came from (and McCook didn't tell), but when they arrived, they usually contained twice as much as did the wagons of other regiments.[45] Truly, McCook was, in many ways, an unorthodox and unmilitary general. He was a combination of big brother, friend and father figure to his men, and while it was unusual, in a military setting, it worked very well and got results.

2

The Union Takes Western Virginia

"If such a thing as a battle takes place, it will be one of extermination on either side. For it will be the great battle for supremacy in the Kanawha Valley."—*The Daily Times* (Cincinnati), November 11, 1861

General George B. McClellan finally broke camp and moved out on June 29, 1861. With a small army at his disposal, he picked his way slowly and extra cautiously over the rough terrain, keeping in mind that he wanted to flank the Rebel force at Rich Mountain. He believed that the Confederates had the bulk of their western Virginia troops there. It took three days to move a mere 25 miles, a pace that irritated many of McClellan's subordinate officers. But he was in no hurry and went into camp at Buckhannon to stage a big 4th of July celebration for his troops including a stag dance. A German soldier complained, in a good-natured sort of way, that the celebration was too dry: no speech, no beer, no schnapps, but "only good fresh spring water."[1]

The spiffy and self-assured McClellan was also dry and unimaginative. But he was fond of military pomp and circumstance and was wrapped up in excessive feelings of self-importance. When he took command, he cleaned up his soldiers, drilled them, put them on display. He liked a nice clean army and didn't seem to want his men to get dirty or bloody. While he was popular with his men, because he made them proud to be soldiers, he drew the wrath of his superiors who wanted action and results even if it meant McClellan would have to tally up dead and wounded soldiers.

General Newton Schelich, for one, was anxious for some action and was upset with the timid nature of McClellan's advance. He sent out a reconnaissance party under Captain O. A. Lawson in the direction of General Robert S. Garnett's Rebel forces at Rich Mountain. A skirmish erupted at Middle Fork Bridge and Lawson's party found itself pinned down by the Rebels and was forced to take cover in the dense brush. One man was killed and five others were wounded. When McClellan learned about this unauthorized sortie, he was furious and relieved Schelich from command and sent him packing back to Ohio. Next, he sent a contingent from the 3rd Ohio under Colonel John Beatty to rescue the trapped Union soldiers.

Schelich's rashness did, however, succeed in getting McClellan to do something besides drilling and marching. Finally, on July 7, he sent a sizeable reconnaissance force consisting of the 4th and 9th Ohio, the Coldwater Michigan Battery and a company of cavalry under Colonel Robert L. McCook toward the Rebel position at Middle Fork. Up at 4 a.m. and on the move, McCook far outnumbered the two companies of infantry he faced, and after a weak effort, the Rebels retreated. McCook pursued but not fast enough to catch up, and the Rebels were able to get back to their Rich Mountain retreat. He did succeed in finding the body of the man killed in Lawson's skirmish.[2]

McClellan augmented McCook's forces with more men and on July 6–7 skirmishes erupted at the Middle Fork Bridge. McCook was successful in taking the bridge with a loss of two men killed.[3] These were the first small battles fought since the arrival of McClellan in western Virginia and were a harbinger of more significant fighting in the days to come.[4] In his report McClellan boasted that "the men are in magnificent spirits for battle. The only trouble will be to restrain them."[5]

Rich Mountain was the next Union target and McClellan began carefully feeling out the Confederate positions there. He was inclined to be over cautious with a penchant for overestimating the size of the opposition, so he believed that he faced 8,000 or 9,000 men when the Rebel force was only about 5,000 divided between General Garnett and Colonel John Pegram. The Southerners were, however, well concealed and dug in. Armed with this intelligence, McClellan decided to attack on July 12, with a combination of artillery and infantry, a total force of about 12,000.

The wary McClellan was the beneficiary of a lucky break in the person of a Union sympathizer named David Hart, who arrived at General William S. Rosecrans' camp on the 10th and volunteered to be a guide. Hart was a young man in his early 20s whose parents operated a tavern on top of Rich Mountain. Since he had tended cattle in the area and was familiar with the terrain and was deemed to be honest, he was recruited by Rosecrans.[6] Encouraged by this break, Rosecrans proposed to do a night march and be in a position to surprise the Rebels, striking their rear, while McClellan attacked from the front. After some prolonged coaxing, McClellan agreed to the plan.

Using Hart as his guide, Rosecrans made his night march through rough, steep terrain in a steady rain, pushing his men hard. His soggy brigade finally reached its destination near the summit of Rich Mountain about noon the next day. The wet and tired men rested for about two hours after which time they were ready to fight.

The Rebels, having captured a Union soldier, learned they were about to have company, but they were entrenched and ready. As they waited for the advancing Federals, a prominent pro–South Virginian appeared on the mountain side. John Hughes, a secessionist member of the Virginia legislature, learned that Rosecrans was approaching with the intent to turn the Rebel flank. He dashed off on horseback to warn the Rebels. Upon approaching Rebel lines, he was stopped and thinking he was facing Union soldiers called out: "Hold, I am a Northern man." A barrage of musket fire in response killed him. For the small Rebel army it was a tragic case of misidentification.

Following the killing of Hughes, Rosecrans took the offensive, but without the services of Hart, who got cold feet and fled the scene. Nevertheless, about three o'clock that afternoon, near the Hart farm, the Federals were met by Rebel fire. Rosecrans, who was involved in combat for the first time, bravely placed himself at the head of the 13th Indiana and led the charge of his brigade.[7]

The maneuver brought the Rebels out of their trenches and shooting began in earnest. The Rebels pounded the advancing Union troops with artillery fire, but the shells, aimed too high, did little else than send timber crashing down and make the mountainside tremble. Although McClellan never made the strong frontal attack as planned, Rosecrans' men out maneuvered and out fought the enemy in a three-hour battle at Rich Mountain, an important victory for the North.

It was important for McCook, too. Over a three-day period, McCook and his men of the 9th Ohio marched, fought, shivered in the wet and cold, and "received its baptism of fire and blood."[8] After the fight was over and the eerie Rich Mountain battleground was examined, a large number of dead Rebels were found shot in the head. This included a dead officer holding a part of his brain in his right hand.[9]

It was with no little pride that the new Union troops claimed victory over the outnumbered and demoralized Rebels. The survivors slipped away, leaving behind approximately 170 wounded men along with some provisions.[10] Another source says Rosecrans captured about 550 Rebels and sent the rest scrambling toward the town of Beverly.[11] McCook was quoted as saying the beaten Rebels were on a "clean trot" toward Richmond.[12]

The victorious Federals went in pursuit of the enemy. Moving southeast, they arrived at Beverly. It was a heavily fortified place but it was abandoned. Huttonsville on Cheat Mountain, another Rebel position, was also found empty and quiet. McClellan gave up the lackluster pursuit, returned to Beverly and went into camp. When asked by an ardent young soldier why he did not

The battle of Rich Mountain in western Virginia resulted in an important Union victory and a big win for General George B. McClellan. At the outset of the Civil War, the mountain folks of western Virginia showed little interest in slavery and had strongly opposed secession. The people of that region cast their lot with the Union. Colonel Robert L. McCook's 9th Ohio Infantry Regiment played a critical role in the running fight that drove the Rebels out of western Virginia and led to the formation of the state of West Virginia.

send the 9th Ohio after enemy patrols "swarming near out outposts," the general simply said: "Our department ends right here, my boy, we have no business over there."[13] The soldier turned away wondering how the North could win the war if it did not take the offensive. It was a question about McClellan's thinking that would be asked over and over again by many others as time went on.

McClellan's work in western Virginia was, in fact, done and he would have no further business in this theater of the war. Putting it behind him, he wrote about the Rich Mountain campaign in glowing terms thereby impressing the administration in Washington. His narrative reeled in Northern newspapers that were wildly enthusiastic in their coverage. McClellan was free and lavish in his praise for Rosecrans' dogged leadership and commended the common soldiers for their bravery. But it was McClellan who emerged from this minor campaign as the coming man, a national figure, trumpeted as a hero by the Northern press. He trotted off the field like a conquering Roman, having made significant strikes toward placing western Virginia in Union hands.

By the end of July McClellan was off to northern Virginia to take command of the army so recently defeated at Bull Run under General McDowell. In Washington, Daniel McCook, Sr., met with McClellan and the general said that he tried to get Robert McCook's regiment transferred to the Potomac. McClellan told a proud father that "Bob" was his "right bower, and he commands the best regiment in the service."[14]

More importantly, McCook proved himself to the men in his brigade. Leading by example, he showed raw courage in the face of danger. One of his men wrote: "In our colonel we have a trustworthy brave leader who will not stand behind a tree or disappear when it is dangerous, but rather will always remain at the head in the fiercest fight."[15]

Rosecrans—who had also proved himself under fire—retained McCook and the 9th Ohio and kept them in western Virginia. On July 23, 1861, General Rosecrans was placed in command of the Department of the Ohio, consisting of western Virginia, Ohio, Indiana, Michigan and Illinois, with his headquarters at Clarksburg, Virginia. Not long after, the machinery to create the new state of West Virginia was set in motion. While the North had yet to win a major battle, it managed to secure important ground for its cause. The Kanawha valley was theirs.

It was at this point that Robert L. McCook parted company with his mentor, friend and adjutant, Augustus Willich. Having experienced combat for the first time in the uniform of an American officer, "Papa" Willich had performed well. Then he said good-bye to the 9th Ohio and left western Virginia in response to a call from the governor of Indiana to come to that state and raise another German regiment. Later on during the war, Willich and his 32nd Indiana Infantry regiment served with another member of the McCook family, namely Major General Alexander M. McCook.

Rosecrans had about 4500 men under his command, divided into three brigades. His brigade commanders were Colonel Robert L. McCook and brigadier generals Henry W. Benham and Eliakim P. Scammon. Throughout the month of August, Rosecrans meticulously planned and fortified various strategic points, preparing to deal with General Robert E. Lee, who was now in charge of the Rebel forces in western Virginia. Never one to stay in one place too long, the energetic and tireless Rosecrans led his small army that he termed "monstrously green"[16] out of Clarksburg in early September 1861, planning to join General Jacob D. Cox and make an assault on Rebel positions at Carnifex Ferry on the Gauley River.

The Rebel forces near the ferry were commanded by General John B. Floyd, assigned by Lee. Rosecrans had no knowledge of the strength or position of the enemy and was essentially going by the seat of his pants. And yet he was beaming with confidence, pumping up his men, saying forcefully, "When we go in, we go in to win."[17]

Benham's brigade was to lead the assault with McCook in support and Scammon held in reserve. Although Benham was ordered to proceed with caution, his men rushed forward in a reckless manner and were surprised by Floyd's well-entrenched troops that opened fire in dense woods at the crest of a low hill. The blundering Benham struck the Confederate left and center with negligible results and called for help. McCook and Scammon hurried to support the inexperienced Benham who in his excitement failed to send skirmishers out ahead of his main body of troops.

Rosecrans was up to handling the emergency. Once he located Floyd's position, fronting Carnifex Ferry, Rosecrans decided to attempt to turn the Rebels' right flank. The 13th Ohio was ordered to assault the extreme right and the 10th Ohio and a portion of the 12th Ohio were directed to attack the enemy center and left. McCook's 9th was soon in the mix as well.[18]

As darkness was settling in McCook was ordered to charge the entrenched Rebels. McCook "waived his slouch hat and roared: 'Forward my bully Dutch! We'll go over their dammed entrenchments if every man dies on the other side.'" McCook was seen running wildly along his lines, in civilian attire, trying to inspire his men to fight hard. The charge by the 9th Ohio was by the textbook, but with no bloody consequences because the enemy had abandoned their trenches.[19]

McCook's official report on the battle of Carnifex Ferry was sedate and businesslike, noting only that the 9th Ohio was "ordered to the junction of the path with the main road near the east side of the corn field, in front of the enemy's works and then halted."[20] As the terrain was rough, it was difficult to make a coordinated assault against an elusive foe. Darkness persuaded Rosecrans to call off further attempts to attack.

An injured General Floyd fled the area with his small force, crossing the Gauley River and burning the bridge at the crossing along with all his boats. While they did not put up much of a fight, they did manage to escape.[21] The aggressive Rosecrans was bitterly disappointed with the bungling Benham and with the results of his campaign and the "battle" of Carnifex Ferry. He so badly wanted to crush the elusive, ragtag Confederate army that was always just out of his reach. The failure to nab Floyd also no doubt weighed heavily on Rosecrans as the ex-secretary of war was a high-profile arch-traitor in the eyes of many Northerners, and his capture and arrest would have been in the headlines of newspapers across the country.

They did locate Floyd's "war chest" that contained about $20,000 in Confederate money. The men tossed it about like so much worthless paper, using some "graybacks" for "spills." They also helped themselves to food and other provisions left behind. After that their diet consisted largely of good-tasting, non-poisonous snakes that were caught in the gullies and trees.[22]

The slightly wounded foxy Floyd having been driven off by Rosecrans did not rush all the way back to Richmond for treatment. He was deemed useful to General Robert E. Lee who still commanded what remained of the Rebel army in the mountains, despite pressure and outright ridicule in the Southern press. He did get a break when Wise was ordered to turn his troops over to Floyd and report to Richmond, thus ending the problem of feuding generals. Still Lee's army was in a miserable condition, with many sick and weak soldiers existing with scant supplies in the mud. At one point, rain continued for 20 consecutive days, definitely not the kind of weather for fostering troop morale.

Nevertheless, Lee—with numerical superiority—came up with a complex plan for attacking the Union forces, but carrying it out would require leadership from his commanders, strong and healthy troops and favorable weather. Lee had none of these advantages. He therefore determined that he was too weak to take the offensive so he took up a defensive stance and waited for Rosecrans to attack him at Big Sewell Mountain.

The two armies faced each other on parallel ridges, separated by a deep gorge, but there was little shooting. The 9th Ohio listed casualties of one man dead and eight wounded, one of whom later died of his wounds. The standoff ended when Rosecrans withdrew his 5,200 men to a place near the Gauley River Bridge at the intersection of the Gauley and New rivers. There he would rest and recuperate.[23] Lee's miserable soldiers were probably relieved that there was a lull in the action as they suffered greatly from rain and sickness. Floyd recalled that the hardships experienced at Big Sewell Mountain "cost more men sick and dead, than at the battle of Manassas."[24]

A determined Rosecrans—who could think and plan no matter what the weather—pushed on down the Lewisburg Road, watching for Rebels to fight and finally joining forces with Cox on September 26, 1861. The combined Union army trudged on through rough mountain terrain, further hampered by steady rain and the resultant mud. Streams were swollen and his troops were suffering from the cold, wet weather, the lack of adequate clothing and supplies. Misery had replaced boredom. The mountains—once looked upon as enchanting—had become oppressive. Recognizing the low morale of his troops, Rosecrans decided to pull back to Gauley Mountain, close to his supply base.

Supplies were what he needed so desperately. In some of the regiments, many men were shoeless, without blankets and, worse yet, "a great many had no pantaloons, and were compelled to do duty in their drawers." While reporters were generally disliked by military men, the suffering soldiers from the Ohio regiments were grateful that news correspondents from sympathetic Cincinnati newspapers publicized their awful plight.[25]

Then—as if their personal hardships were not bad enough—9th Ohio received more depressing news. Colonel McCook tendered his resignation. In a long letter to Rosecrans from Camp Lookout, McCook confessed that he could no longer in good faith act as the commanding officer for a brigade whose subordinate officers refused to obey orders. He pointed out that on a recent march his officers failed and refused to keep their troops in line and marching in good order. He also complained soldiers from the various companies would fall out of ranks and duck into the woods to rest. McCook said, "This I believe is the first time since the organization of the Regiment that ... officers or men have shown any disposition whatever to disobey or evade my orders. However it seemed so general on yesterday that I cannot but believe they have always been ready to do so."[26]

The letter seems to have been written in a fit of anger by the high-strung McCook, who had a bad day on the march and suddenly wanted no more of being an army officer. It was more of an attention-getting complaint than a serious notice of intent to resign, and it appears that it achieved the desired results. When his alarmed and disappointed men learned of their colonel's threatened resignation, they called upon him to stay. The urging had the desired effect; McCook changed his mind and withdrew his resignation.[27]

An Ohio newspaper called the whole thing a "canard," thus downplaying any problems that McCook had with his men, or with Rosecrans. An "informant" reported seeing McCook and Rosecrans at the Gauley bridge "smoking cigars together, apparently on the best of terms."[28]

But it had been a miserable time for the 9th Ohio and for the entire army as well. Then, after a shipment of new uniforms finally arrived for his troops, Rosecrans' rested and revived army was ready for another encounter with the persistent Rebels, still under the leadership of Lee. By mid–October, Lee and Floyd had moved their troops toward the Gauley River, opposite McCook's encampment at Miller's Ferry. Rosecrans ordered McCook to cross the Gauley River, capture or scatter the Rebels and occupy the area, or, at his discretion, re-cross the river.[29]

McCook's men constructed a flatbed rope-pulled ferry, crossed the river and progressed toward Fayetteville. When they arrived they found the Rebels were gone. McCook ordered a search of the town after which several houses and other buildings were set on fire. The principal opposition came from the pro–Confederate citizenry who the Union troops were "permitted to handle, with something other than kid gloves." The men were also allowed to pilfer "fruit and other comestibles."[30]

The burning and plundering of Fayetteville that occurred on October 19, 1861, gave the 9th Ohio a reputation for roughness and an unwillingness to tolerate "secesh." During the early stages of the Civil War, the Lincoln administration took a conciliatory approach to the Rebels, believing that there was not widespread support for the rebellion among the civilians, and that by being magnanimous, they would resume their allegiance to the Union. Robert L. McCook openly resented the conciliatory or a soft handed attitude toward the Southerners, preferring to inflict harsh punishment whenever there was an opportunity to do so. For him the hard hand of war was the only hand that should be used.[31]

After the Fayetteville incident, McCook returned to his camp at Miller's Ferry. He encountered some enemy militia at his front but took no action. Finally, after a week of waiting, McCook attempted to take a small force across the river, but was so harassed by Confederate sharpshooters that he called it off.

Rosecrans was joined by Brigadier General Robert C. Schenck, the well-connected political general who had failed to distinguish himself at Bull Run. Schenck replaced Scammon. Under the new plan, McCook would continue his feints at Miller's Ferry and position himself to meet any force that Lee might throw at him. Schenck would move up the west bank of the Gauley River and attempt to cross at Townsend's Ferry. His task was to strike Lee's flank and rear. Benham, who was stationed below McCook, would move to the Gauley River and cross at the mouth of Loop Creek. Once there, Benham would reconnoiter the roads along the river and be positioned to hit Lee's right flank. If all elements of Rosecrans' elaborate plan worked, Lee would be caught in a pincher.

The plan was set in motion on November 10. In the skirmishing that resulted, only Cox's brigade saw action, pushing the Rebels back. Keeping the grays on the run was fine, but Rosecrans was hopeful of trapping the wary Robert E. Lee along with his troops. A war correspondent from the *Cincinnati Times* was worked up to the point of high expectations. From Camp Loup Creek, near Gauley, Virginia, the reporter was preparing to break a story on the "great battle for the supremacy of the Kanawha Valley." He predicted a fight that would result in the "extermination" of one side or the other.[32]

Rosecrans certainly expected a brisk battle and was anxious for it. He threw himself into the challenge, issuing detailed orders to his field commanders and dispatches to McClellan from his headquarters at Camp Gauley. His troops were dressed like soldiers, well-fed and supplied, and morale was high. But poor coordination, lack of enthusiasm from his commanders and unfavorable weather conditions doomed his ambitious plans.

McCook stayed at Miller's Ferry for 20 days all the while trying to keep his men out of sight of the sharpshooters. Benham turned from rash to timid, fearful of the enemy's strength, which he grossly overestimated. He halted after only a brief skirmish. Schenck's efforts were no less futile, having failed to cross the Gauley River as ordered. Benham and Schenck retreated to Camp Gauley where they were forced to deal with a furious Rosecrans, a man who could work himself into a rage like few other generals.[33]

While he once again put the Rebels on the run, Rosecrans had to swallow a large dose of disappointment over opportunities lost. He could not grasp a sodden enemy that seemed to melt into the mist and mud. His frustration is evident in his wordy official report. At one point he complained that Benham "had been instructed *ad nauseam* to look to that way of cutting off the enemies retreat."[34] It was his gentlemanly way of saying that Benham was incompetent. Still Rosecrans' successes were such that he emerged from the first year of the war with a better record than any other Union general, having played a key role in securing western Virginia for the Union. Despite his hollow victories, he had bested Robert E. Lee, a soldier and Confederate leader who would become a legend, and in the process Rosecrans cleared the Rebels out of the region. Aside from the bushwhackers, that replaced the regular Confederate troops, there would be little effort made by the South to reclaim western Virginia.[35]

Rosecrans' dogged efforts didn't look impressive on paper, but the western Virginia campaign provided a boost to his reputation, despite the fact that he failed to post a major battle to his resume. Mountainous western Virginia refused to yield results of that stripe. If the Civil War had been fought solely in the inhospitable, rain-soaked and unforgiving western Virginia mountains, the end may have come much sooner, and with relatively light casualties.

The significance of the western Virginia campaign cannot be easily slighted. While the battle of Rich Mountain pales in comparison to those fought later at Shiloh or Chickamauga, the Union gained complete control of a large portion of Virginia, humbled and drove the Rebels out and established a military frontier a considerable distance from the Ohio River.

In November of 1861, a constitutional convention met in Wheeling to form the new state to be called Kanawha. This was followed by a popular referendum in which only those who took a Union loyalty oath could vote. The vote among 50 counties, of course, ratified the Wheeling convention. Eventually, to finalize the Union conquest, the new state was admitted to the Union as West Virginia in 1863, without slavery.[36]

Following the failure of his hapless campaign to win back western Virginia, Lee went back to Richmond feeling the pain of disappointment. The unmerciful weather, lack of supplies and squabbling political generals, all contributed to his defeat. The loss of 38 percent of Virginia to the Union was a serious blow to Confederate hopes. This was not only a loss of territory, but it meant that loyalists in other border states would be emboldened to hold out against secession.[37]

It was an inauspicious start for Lee, and while he accepted the failure as the will of God, most of his fellow Virginians were unforgiving. He was pilloried by the Southern press, some newspapers referring to him "Granny Lee."[38] He was castigated for having let western Virginia get away without fighting a real battle. But over time he overcame the failure, regaining his popularity and then going on to a lead the Confederate army until the end of the war. His considerable military skills came to the fore and he earned honors and respect for his leadership, surpassing and outlasting Rosecrans and McClellan.

Much to his credit, Robert L. McCook slogged his way over muddy and sometimes impassable trails through the magnificent mountains, although he saw little action. It is interesting to note that while Rosecrans didn't censure or criticize McCook as he did Benham, neither did he praise the bluff Ohioan or single him out for commendation.

With the western Virginia campaign over, McCook was assigned join General Don Carlos Buell's Army of the Ohio. On November 26, 1861, his brigade was put on the steamboats *Silver Lake, Mary Cook,* and *Glenwood* on the Ohio River. Their destination: Kentucky, another troubled border state.[39] Having served with pride and success, his men were ready to do their duty anew.

The brigade was bound for Cincinnati to enjoy a few hours of reveling among the happy townspeople amid peeling bells and roaring cannons. German and American newspapers of Cincinnati heaped praise on the Ohio regiments, especially the 9th Ohio. McCook was lionized by the press; the *Voklsblat,* called him "the regiment's father" who had "shared and endured every hardship," a view echoed by his men who were not "toadies, lickspittles, or sycophants."[40] A proud soldier wrote: "He stands tall and might soon stand before us as a general of a German brigade" to once again lead the 9th Ohio "against the enemy."[41]

The 9th Ohio arrived in Cincinnati on November 28, marching into the city. McCook granted leave to the regiment until eight o'clock the next morning and then extended the time off for one more day. On the 30th, before the men re-boarded the steamer, many insisted on being paid. A stand-off occurred when McCook insisted that they all get back on the steamboat. All did as told with the exception of one company, causing an indignant McCook to "talk to them rather pointedly."

Suddenly, a soldier "struck at him [McCook] with his musket." McCook unsheathed his sword and "struck the offending soldier a violent blow on the head, cutting the scalp." Another angry soldier pointed his gun at the colonel and pulled the trigger, but McCook grabbed the rifle and "with it knocked the offender down." Following the incident, the recalcitrant company boarded the steamboat. The paymaster commenced paying the troops, the tension was broken and finally the steamer left the dock.[42]

McCook's leadership had been challenged and he did not falter or fail. He met the challenge head on and displayed the hard stuff that made up a McCook. While he would be tested even more severely later in the war, in the summer and fall of 1861, he proved that he was tough, dedicated and passionate. His military skills improving with every skirmish and battle, he emerged from the western Virginia campaign as Rosecrans' efficient and dependable brigade commander. It is significant that by serving under Rosecrans, Robert L. McCook established a family connection with the energetic and erratic general that would blossom and bear poisonous fruit in the years that followed.

3
The Battle of Mill Springs

"Seeing the superior number of the enemy and their bravery, I concluded the best mode of settling the contest was to order the Ninth Ohio to charge the enemy's position with the bayonet."—R. L. McCook, January 27, 1862

Following his impressive service and leadership in the western Virginia campaign, Colonel Robert L. McCook and his 9th Ohio Infantry regiment were sent to Kentucky, a state positioned on an uncomfortable fence. At the outset of the Civil War, Kentucky declared itself as a "neutral" entity, figuratively shaking an angry fist at both North and South. Its fiery, pro-secessionist governor, Beriah Magoffin, snubbed the president's request that Kentucky contribute men to the Union effort. Lincoln showed equal determination, as he believed that it was absolutely necessary that the Union keep Kentucky.

Then, after a few months of struggle, strife and heavy newspaper coverage, Kentucky declared in favor of staying the Union, despite strenuous efforts by secessionists. The "loyal legislature" of Kentucky, in the fall of 1861, declared that "the attempt to destroy the Union of these states we believe to be a crime, not only against Kentucky but against all mankind."[1] An overstatement to be sure, but overall, Kentucky's social and commercial connections to Ohio and other Northern states proved to be stronger than its Southern sentiments. Kentucky would not have to endure the northern taunt that was so freely batted about in the press: "Secesshea."

But that didn't stop the South from trying to take Kentucky away from the Union. On December 10, 1861, in an act of defiance, the Confederates "admitted" Kentucky to the Confederacy as its 30th state. They also "elected" George W. Johnson as the "governor."[2] All this, however, was just for show and of little substance because a strong majority of Kentuckians ignored the gesture.

Colonel Robert L. McCook joined his younger brother, Brigadier General Alexander M. McCook, in the Blue Grass state. Their assignment: check any Confederate incursion into Kentucky. Alexander had recently received his brigadier star as a reward for gallantry at the battle of Bull Run. Although the battle ended in disaster for the Union, "Alex" McCook was recognized by the press and army brass as a leader and an officer of great personal courage. Both he and his brother Robert were deemed men with the potential to lead armies to victory.

The McCook brothers were serving under the command of another Ohio native, Major General Don Carlos Buell, a clear-headed, cautious and thoroughly military man with an abundance of experience, having served in both the Mexican War and the Seminole Indian War in Florida. Buell graduated in the West Point class of 1841 and was considered an officer with great potential. The Lincoln administration had high expectations of Buell.

On November 30, by special order No. 16, Buell was placed in charge of the Department of the Ohio that included Kentucky. He replaced General William T. Sherman who, after several months of nervous and seemingly irrational fumbling and stumbling in a command that he was emotionally unprepared to handle, had all but asked to be relieved. Sherman had served with courage and competence as a brigade commander at the battle of Bull Run and was promoted to brigadier general, but his assignment in Kentucky proved to be his undoing. He had taken the assignment on the condition that he would have at his command a force that he deemed sufficient. "Sufficient" in Sherman's thinking was an army of 200,000 men. This request stunned the War Department and the news media, causing both to question not only his ability, but his mental well-being.

Newspapers from Ohio and Illinois picked on Sherman mercilessly. When it was announced that he was on his way out of Kentucky, the *Cincinnati Commercial* erupted into cheers, noting that Sherman, a "perfect monomaniac on the subject of journalism," was leaving.[3] The mean-spirited criticism cut deep and Sherman would hate and condemn the news media for the rest of the war, but he needed a rest and time to clear his head, and he was ready to turn Kentucky over to Don Carlos Buell, although due to their friendship, the transition was awkward.

Buell seemed to be a good fit, and on December 2, he introduced his "Army of the Ohio" to the nation, dividing his forces into six divisions. Brigadier General McCook was placed in command of the Second Division. His brother, Captain Daniel McCook, Jr., was on the general's staff as an assistant adjutant. Colonel Robert L. McCook was given command of 3rd Brigade in the First Division, headed by Major General George H. Thomas. Colonel McCook's brigade consisted of the following regiments: the 18th U.S. Infantry, the 9th and 36th Ohio Infantry and the 2nd Minnesota Infantry.

Thomas was a Virginia native who could not, in good conscience, draw his sword against the nation he swore to protect and serve. He was a West Point man, devoted to the Union, one of the forty percent of Virginia officers who did not join the Confederacy.[4] Although his connections to Virginia made him suspect in the minds of some high-placed Northern men, in the hearts of his sisters, who were Southern through and through, George was a traitor and for all future purposes he was "dead" to them.

Having carefully organized his army, and sent his divisions to the designated points in Kentucky, Buell turned his attention to the threat posed by Confederates under the leadership of Brigadier General Felix K. Zollicoffer, one of the most ardent and determined secessionists in the Confederacy.

The colorful and popular Zollicoffer, the son of Swiss immigrants, was born in 1812 in Henry County, Tennessee, near Nashville. He was educated as a printer and over time worked in the printing trade, including a stint as the editor of the *Nashville Banner,* a leading Whig newspaper. Journalism led to politics and Zollicoffer represented Tennessee in Congress for three terms ending in 1860. He was active in the 1860 presidential campaign as a strong supporter of the candidacy of John Bell of Tennessee.[5]

As a journalist Zollicoffer was known for his fiery editorials, and after the war commenced he used his rhetorical skills to lure young Kentucky men into the Confederate ranks in order to drive the "Northern hordes across the Ohio River."[6] While he was not a military professional, he had considerable leadership ability. The 50-year-old Zollicoffer shocked both Northern and Southern military men with his bold and successful forays in Tennessee and Kentucky. His primary mission was to take control of East Tennessee, where Union sentiment and resistance to the Confederacy was strong, but he did not always follow orders.

Leading a small, poorly equipped body of troops, the zealous Zollicoffer marched into Knoxville, shut down the pro–Union newspaper of his rival, William G. "Parson" Brownlow, and tore down the American flag in front of Brownlow's house. He then took control of the East Tennessee and Georgia Railroad and arrested the sons of Tennessee senator Andrew Johnson for making pro-union speeches.[7] Loved by his men, the audacious "Pap" Zollicoffer was rapidly becoming a Southern folk hero.

By comparison, the Union forces in Kentucky seemed moribund leaving Lincoln very frustrated and impatient for some action. Lincoln was determined keep Kentucky in the Union at all costs and desperately wanted to send relief to the Unionists in East Tennessee. With Buell at the helm and the able Thomas acting as his second in command, Lincoln was hoping that someone would "do something" toward driving the Rebels out of Kentucky.

But a cautious Buell, seemingly in no hurry to strike a blow, was merely keeping an eye on Zollicoffer while paying greater attention to other strategic points in Kentucky. Buell was a confident man who believed he could see the big picture and was therefore not apt to be drawn away from matters of importance by a pesky distraction.

On December 6, Major General Thomas officially took command of the First Division, Army of the Ohio. Like his commander, General Buell, the thoughtful and steady General Thomas was also unlikely to charge into battle in hot haste. But he was a bit anxious to move against the Zollicoffer threat. He sent a dispatch to Buell, advising that "the enemy [is] encamped at the mouth of Fishing Creek" and "can be captured" if a Union force intercepts at Somerset and "gets in their rear."[8] Buell simply replied: "I am letting him alone for the present."[9]

In a letter to his friend, Major General George B. McClellan, on December 8, 1861, Buell stressed the pressing need to whip his army into shape, "now little better than a mob." While he was concerned with Zollicoffer, Buell didn't wish to "fritter away" his organizational effort by pursuing "these roving bugbears."[10]

Zollicoffer's "bugbears" were settled in at Mill Springs, then a small town near the Cumberland River in south central Kentucky, 90 miles east of Bowling Green. They had dug trenches and built cabins on the north side of the Cumberland River, at the junction of Fishing Creek, with lines of troops strung out along both streams. They were comfortable, well-stocked with food and other provisions, and showed no signs of leaving the state.

And instead of merely settling in for the rest of the winter, the aggressive Zollicoffer continued his belligerence, while urging young Kentuckians to join the Rebel cause. Toward this end, he issued a written "proclamation" on December 16, outlining the causes of the war and the goals of the Confederacy. While his noisy presence and bombastic proclamation failed to stimulate mass support from Kentuckians, it did get Buell's serious attention.[11]

When it was finally decided to move against Zollicoffer, the Federals acted firmly and hit hard. Buell ordered Thomas and Brigadier General Albin F. Schoepf, a native of Austria and in command of Thomas' First Brigade, to conduct a coordinated attack against the Rebels at their Mill Springs works. The decision was made after a reconnaissance by Schoepf revealed the location of the enemy and the extent of his armed strength and fortifications.

The Union attack forces included two of Colonel Robert L. McCook's regiments—the 9th Ohio and 2nd Minnesota—all well-seasoned troops as a result of the successful western Virginia campaign. Thomas' 2nd Brigade, led by Colonel Mahlon D. Manson, was also a part of the Union assault. The plan called for Thomas to move from Lebanon through Columbia, and attack the Rebel's on their left, while Scheopf was striking their front. After a trek of 18 days in bitterly cold, wet weather, over muddy, almost impassable roads, and crossing swollen streams, they reached a stopping point about ten miles from Zollicoffer's encampment called Logan's Crossroads, a fledgling community in western Pulaski County. Troop positions were established in preparation for a fight. Readiness, however, mingled with uncertainty, for except for McCook's regiments, most of the men had not experienced combat.

While Thomas and Schoepf conducted their muddy but coordinated march toward Mill Springs, Zollicoffer was joined by Brigadier General George Bibb Crittenden, who outranked the former printer and therefore took charge of the Confederate forces. Crittenden was the son of the powerful Kentucky senator John J. Crittenden, who had worked feverishly in Congress to forge a compromise that would prevent war. Son George, a West Point graduate, was a heavy drinker and—unlike his famous father—was an ardent proponent of secession. George's brother Thomas was also a general—but on the side of the Union. The war was getting very exciting for the Crittenden family.

The hot-tempered George Crittenden was a less than gifted commander

The decisive and bloody battle of Mills Springs, Kentucky, is portrayed in a picture by Currier and Ives. The fight erupted on January 19, 1862, and resulted in an important Union victory. The picture shows the gallant bayonet charge, directed by Colonel Robert L. McCook, that routed the Rebel ranks and resulted in the death of their commander, General Felix K. Zollicoffer, one of the Confederacy's most ardent and aggressive leaders. McCook was seriously injured but recovered and was lionized throughout the North as a hero and rising star.

of troops. He did, however, correctly ascertain that Zollicoffer had hemmed himself in to the extent that, if attacked, there was no means of escape, because the Cumberland River, at their rear was too deep and swift to cross. Sensing the urgency, Crittenden quickly came up with a plan to hit Thomas before the Union troops were fully in place and ready to strike.

Crittenden and Zollicoffer were aided by a "secession spy" who came into the Rebel camp with intelligence about Thomas' advance. They were eager to strike at what they believed was a much smaller force.[12] Starting at midnight on January 18, the Rebel troops marched in darkness through the cold rain over muddy roads for nine miles when they finally met the Union pickets.

The battle commenced early in the morning of January 19, 1862, on grounds known as the "Old Fields" in Pulaski County,[13] with the Rebels opening fire against the Yankees before Thomas had all of his troops in line. Crittenden's plan had worked up to this point, but the Yankees were quick to respond, getting out of their tents and forming lines of battle. They had marched to Mill Springs fully expecting to fight so they were not really caught off guard.

In his official report on the battle, McCook stated that after he was informed of the enemy approach, he formed his two regiments and marched them "to a point near the junction of the Mill Springs and Columbia roads ... the Ninth Ohio on the right and the Second Minnesota on the left of the Mill Springs road." As he moved his brigade forward, he had to go around the 10th Indiana and 4th Kentucky, as these two regiments had already engaged the enemy and were falling back. Then, following orders from Thomas, McCook placed the 9th in cornfield on the right side of the Mills Springs road and positioned the 2nd Minnesota in the spot vacated by the 4th Kentucky and 10th Indiana.[14]

A fierce firefight was maintained for about a half an hour while rain, smoke and rough, wooded terrain hampered both armies. At times the opposing lines were so close that soldiers from the 2nd Minnesota were poking their rifles through one side of a fence while the Rebels were sticking their rifles through the other side the same fence. This competition ended when the Confederates "retired in good order to some rail piles, hastily thrown together."[15]

The arrival of 12th Kentucky and the Tennessee Brigade overwhelmed the Confederate right flank, causing it to fall back.[16] Then with the 2nd Minnesota pouring galling fire against their center, McCook ordered a bayonet charge. McCook's 9th Ohio—his "Bully Dutchmen"—forthwith conducted a spirited bayonet charge that turned the enemy's left flank. The order to charge was given by Major Gustav Kammerling, who called out to his men, "if it gets too hot for you, shut your eyes, my boys—forward!"[17]

The men of the 9th, with gleaming bayonets and their distinctive Teutonic battle cry, powered forward on the double. Apparently their eyes were wide open, for in the vernacular of the age, the disciplined charge was "handsomely done." Thomas' civilian quartermaster, John W. Scully, said, "a more splendid thing I never witnessed." And it had the desired effect, as the Rebel flank was disrupted, causing them to turn and fall back with the Yankees in determined pursuit. McCook described the charge in his report, saying, "This broke the enemy's flank and the whole line gave way in great confusion, and the whole turned into a perfect rout."[18] The coordinated and combined tactics of the 2nd Minnesota and 9th Ohio, for all practical purposes, won the day.

Colonel McCook was severely wounded in his left leg during the attack, but stayed in the fight. He was heard to say to the quartermaster, "Scully, I'm shot in the leg, but I'm good for the day anyhow." And he was good for the day. Scully recalled that McCook was as "cool as a cucumber."[19] In his report dated January 27, 1862, McCook states that "at the time of the first advance of the Ninth Ohio I was shot through the right leg below the knee. Three other balls passed through my horse and another through my overcoat. After this I was compelled to go on foot until I got the hospital of the enemy."[20]

The battle continued throughout the day in the rain, as Union forces pushed closer to the entrenched enemy camp, with a deadly artillery fire coming from the summits, wreaking havoc on Confederate defenses. The poorly led and badly outgunned Rebel forces fought back as best they could, many of them using old flintlock muskets dating back to the War of 1812. The bad weather made things worse as the antique guns misfired or didn't fire at all. About 1,000 troops had no weapons at all. Crittenden's game soldiers were overcome by a much better equipped and better led Union force.

A painfully wounded McCook stayed with his troops while they pursued the retreating Rebels. When he did pull himself out of the action, it was at Zollicoffer's abandoned headquarters. There his leg wound was dressed by army surgeon Dr. W. W. Strew.[21] The wound was later described by his brother George W. McCook as painful but not dangerous. In a letter to his father, Daniel McCook, Sr., George cautioned: "Don't start West. Three balls through his [Robert's] horse, one through his coat, the fifth struck him. Heard from himself."[22]

America's newest hero, the gallant Ohio colonel, "best known to Cincinntians as Bob McCook," telegraphed his friend Judge J. B. Stallo, from Somerset, Kentucky, to allay fears as to his condition. "Telegraph my friends they need not be uneasy about me. I will write."[23]

During the night the defeated Rebels evacuated the area as best they could, crossing the Cumberland River on a barge, leaving behind badly wounded men, artillery pieces, ammunition, and over a 1,000 horses and mules, along with food supplies. After the last man crossed, the barge was burned to deny the Yankees the ability to use it. The cold, battle-weary Rebels made their way toward Nashville.

Although there was some concern that the food left behind might be poisoned, victorious but hungry Union soldiers invaded the camp and enjoyed a tasty breakfast. In the Civil War, it was the winners who were in a position to indulge, while the losers lumbered off in a sullen retreat with growling, empty stomachs arguing with them. Another plus for the Union was that their losses were relatively light, with Thomas reporting 39 dead and 207 wounded.[24]

The Rebel losses were greater and, strangely, many men were found with fatal bullet wounds in the head. "A surprising number were shot in the forehead and eyes." In their haste to escape, the Rebel officers left behind their "heavy leather" trunks. Rummaging Union soldiers helped themselves to "fine clothes, love letters and trinkets," among "an unmilitary assortment of superfluous baggage."[25]

In his official report, McCook gave credit to his men and officers for the victory. "Notwithstanding they had been called out before breakfast and had not tasted food all day, they conducted themselves throughout like veterans, obeying each command and executing every movement as though they were on parade."[26] First western Virginia and now Mill Springs, Kentucky: with each terrible event of war, Robert L. McCook and his gallant soldiers forged in fire, a camaraderie that only combat soldiers understand.

The victory was just the tonic that McCook's Dutchmen needed for it turned complaints into cheers. One happy German soldier declared that Mill Springs "was one of the most glorious and important battles … and the Battle of Bull Run was atoned for." He couldn't resist saying that the "brave Southerners have demonstrated that they also could run very far."[27]

Immediately following the battle, an article in a Washington, D.C., newspaper reported that the "9th Ohio is badly cut up."[28] True, the 9th suffered casualties. But the men of 9th Ohio also suffered from the cold, wet monotony of the winter campaign coupled with the lack of pay and the raging nativist anger directed against the regiment of proud Germans. After months of harassment and ridicule leveled at their ethnicity, their morale was low. Some of the German soldiers questioned their participation in a badly managed war, under the control of men who—by open expressions of hate—failed in every way to appreciate the dedication and sacrifice of the immigrant regiment. And yet it was their firm dedication to duty and overriding loyalty to the Union that resulted in an inspirational victory at Mill Springs.

Among the 125 dead Confederate soldiers was General Felix K. Zollicoffer, killed by a pistol shot fired by Colonel Speed S. Fry, commander of the 4th Kentucky Infantry regiment. Bursting out of the bushes, clad in a white raincoat, on horseback, Zollicoffer blundered too close to the Yankee line, thinking that men of the 4th Kentucky were Rebels. Another officer called out, "General, it is the enemy!" but it was too late.[29] The gallant old civilian solider fell dead from a bullet in his heart. Zollicoffer's horse was taken captive by the Union army and later sent by Colonel Robert L. McCook to the Ohio home of a brother, probably George.[30]

The general's death not only denied the South the talent and dedication of a zealous officer, it meant that the six-story Zollicoffer block under construction in Nashville, would remain unfinished. But he has, nevertheless, been long remembered. The tree under which he died was called "the Zollie tree" until it fell in 1895.[31] A Zollicoffer monument was later erected at the Mill Springs battle site, designated as Zollicoffer Park. It is also the site of a mass grave of the Confederate dead, all of it steeped in legend and lore because of the death of "Zollie," forever a hero in the minds of many Southern Civil War history buffs.

George Crittenden's small army, consisting of ten regiments of infantry, six big guns and an estimated two battalions of artillery, as well as some independent companies of infantry, was defeated by Union troops of about equal number. It was one of the few times in the Civil War that both sides were about evenly matched in terms of troop numbers, approximately 4,000 on each side. Thomas led eight regiments of infantry, two batteries and less than a full cavalry unit. The battle of Mill Springs, also known as the battle of Logan's Crossroads, was won without any wasteful and foolish frontal assaults into a well-protected enemy.

It was hailed as a decisive, complete and important victory in the Kentucky theater of operations, a welcome reversal of fortunes after the disaster at Manassas Gap six months previous. The victory opened the way to East Tennessee and the Union loyalists there desperately waiting for help, and it was the cause of great rejoicing throughout the North. The president sent a note of congratulations to Buell who passed it along to Thomas, praised for his great skill and efficiency at the lowlands of Mills Springs.

High praise also came from the newly appointed secretary of war, Edwin M. Stanton. While he seldom displayed any excitement in a positive way, he praised the "brilliant victory" of Union troops "over a large body of armed traitors." Stanton said that America would "rejoice to honor every soldier and officer who proves his courage by charging with the bayonet and storming intrenchments [sic] in the blaze of enemy fire."[32]

The 3rd Brigade was ordered to proceed to Somerset where it was to go into camp and await further orders.[33] But McCook and his soldiers didn't stay there very long. The brigade's popular and courageous colonel was happy to come home to Ohio at the head of his troops. There he could rest and heal and receive the accolades of Americans of every stripe, knowing that his services toward the Union cause would be called upon again. Thanks in part to Robert's heroics at Mill Springs the McCooks were already known as the "Fighting Family."[34]

Robert L. McCook, who was soon thereafter awarded a brigadier star, was widely commended in the battle reports of other officers for his gallantry in the face of danger. Colonel Manson offered "feelings of gratitude and admiration for the prompt manner in which he sustained me in the hour of trial."[35] General Buell commended McCook for "efficiency and gallantry on the field, and though severely wounded early in the action, continued in his command until the engagement closed."[36] The army granted him furlough from February 1 to February 26, 1862, to recover from his wounds.

The news of bravery and success in battle was the cause for a minor celebration. Marching through Louisville, the "Niners" were cheered loudly, so much so that the soldiers forgot their sore feet. People shouted: "Hurrah for the Ninth Ohio! Bully for the hero McCook."[37] A group of ladies presented "two splendid flags" to the 9th Ohio and 2nd Minnesota to commemorate the victory at Mill Springs.[38] It was "thumbs up" for the German soldiers too, and the 9th Ohio was hailed as one of the "best disciplined" units in the western theater.[39] The uplifted public recognized that everyone, from McCook on down, had performed admirably, giving the North a much-needed decisive victory.

In Columbus, the Ohio General Assembly passed a resolution of thanks for their hero, a true "Fighting McCook."[40] Addressing the assembly, Ohio governor David Tod praised McCook's bravery and leadership under fire. Then, while introducing the colonel, Tod declared that since McCook was a good fighter, he could not possibly be a good speaker for the two were incompatible, and of the two the role of a fighter was far more important and noble than that of a mere talker.

McCook would have certainly agreed that action speaks louder than words, nevertheless he gave a wordy and forceful address to the assembled legislators. Among the many "sharp points" he made, the one directed against the War Department was like a dagger. He was harshly critical of the federal government for the way the war effort was being handled, claiming that the war policy was too soft on the rebellion. He wanted hard blows struck, and "the sooner we do so, the sooner we will have the Government restored."

McCook's speech coincided with a major shakeup in Lincoln's cabinet as Simeon Cameron had been replaced as secretary of war by Edwin M. Stanton. McCook must have sent shivers of unease through many of the legislators when he called Cameron "the prince of thieves." While Cameron was inefficient and ill-suited for the position, he was still a popular man in some circles, so McCook's scathing criticism undoubtedly raised some eyebrows. As for Stanton, his friend, the colonel praised the decision to make him the new war secretary. "I felt like a new man," said McCook, after learning that the "man who had been brought up among the hills of Ohio where I was raised, was appointed." With Stanton at the helm, McCook said he was "not only fighting for my country but also for my friend."[41]

Robert L. McCook was still recovering from his wounds at the time of his fiery speech. Like the other heroes among the casualties, he was a statistic, added to the growing pile of statistics. The Union losses at Mill Springs amounted to 39 dead and 207 wounded. The casualties were relatively small when compared to other battles, and in some respects, a small price to pay considering the magnitude of the victory and its timeliness. Nor was Colonel McCook the only one of his family recovering battle wounds. His brothers, Dr. Latimer McCook and Captain Edwin S. McCook, were wounded in battle at Fort Donelson in northwestern Tennessee.[42]

But despite examples of individual suffering, the impressive and decisive win at Mill Springs in January, combined with the ousting of the Confederates at Fort Henry and Fort Donelson in February by General U. S. Grant, was positively uplifting to the North, and caused the South to change its plans in favor of another offensive strategy. Having met with defeat in Kentucky, and having failed to recruit sufficiently, there was no choice but to abandon the Blue Grass state as well as Nashville, Tennessee. The demoralized and diminished Rebel forces under the command of Major General Albert Sidney Johnston retreated south intending to gather at Corinth, Mississippi. The little known railroad center would soon find itself in the national spotlight.

4

Trouble on the Road to Corinth

"He [General Halleck] has literally crawled, inch by inch, from Pittsburg Landing, with his immense army, right up to the enemy's breastworks [at Corinth]."—*New York Times*, June 2, 1862

Although history records that General Don Carlos Buell's Army of the Ohio helped to turn the tide of battle in favor of the Union at Shiloh on the Tennessee River, not all of his troops arrived in time to participate in the epic struggle. Among the units that missed the fight was the 3rd Brigade, Colonel Robert L. McCook commanding. Colonel McCook had been granted leave to recover from his January wounds and was on the sick list for most of February. Because of his heroically led bayonet charge at Mill Springs, Kentucky, people both inside and outside of the army were taking notice of the young colonel.

A bayonet charge was likened to rushing headlong into the teeth of hell—a feat worthy of only the bravest of brave men. It was the ultimate test of courage and, once experienced, elevated a mere soldier into the company of immortals. In a time when military men were important role models and celebrities, Robert L. McCook, a "Fighting McCook," became a star in the theater of war. He had his moment at the doorway to death, shed his blood and came through alive. He proved his worth; he was a hero and inspirational leader, and the press, public and other military men toasted his bravery and sacrifice.

In March of 1862—feeling well enough to be in the field, but not yet completely healed—Bob McCook and his brigade marched with General George H. Thomas' division. Having recently fought a battle at Mill Springs, Thomas' division was allowed to be the last to arrive in Nashville. McCook's brigade was the tail end of the Army of the Ohio.

Among the men of McCook's brigade were two battalions of the 18th

4. Trouble on the Road to Corinth

The town of Corinth, Mississippi, was one of the most important railroad centers of the Confederacy. Following the battle of Shiloh, in southern Tennessee, a massive Union army under the command of Major General Henry W. Halleck inched and trenched its way toward Corinth with the goal of conquering and controlling the town. When the overly-cautious Halleck finally arrived with his forces he opened up his big guns. But he soon found there was no enemy to attack, for the Rebel troops had been taken away by rail under the cover of night.

U.S. Infantry regiment, made up of 16 companies of regular army troops, commanded by Lieutenant Colonel Oliver L. Shepherd. These men were not volunteers; they were men who chose the army as a career. They reflected "old army" values and were subject to much stricter discipline than their volunteer counterparts. A trooper from the 18th recalled that the regulars were "somewhat sensitive on account of the 'sheep's eye' look we would receive from the volunteer element as though we were no good."[1]

Volunteers and regulars wore the same uniform with pride and dedication, but they faced military life with different attitudes and expectations. On the line of march to Pittsburg Landing, and in the campgrounds along the way, men of both stripes got to know one another and soon learned that in Lincoln's army all privates were not treated equal.

It was widely known that volunteer officers, such Colonel McCook, were lax in matters of discipline and allowed their soldiers get away with violations of military protocol, whereas most regular officers would not tolerate indiscipline, drinking, disrespect and straggling. Military rules and regulations were strictly enforced by the regular officers. Although regulars made up less than 3 percent of the entire Union army, these bluecoats were court-martialed and punished at a much higher rate than were volunteers.[2]

Lieutenant Colonel Shepherd had been suffering from typhoid fever and was so sick that McCook thought he was risking his life by accompanying the brigade out of Nashville on the road to Pittsburg Landing, where the Army of the Ohio was ordered to rendezvous with General U. S. Grant. But Shepherd believed a major fight was in the offing and insisted that he make the trip, and he was hauled in an ambulance much of the way. He was thoroughly regular army and no form of sickness was going to keep him out of the fight.

Since Shepherd was prostrate for much of the journey, he was unaware that his regulars were coming under the undesirable influence of the volunteers. Although Shepherd was too sick to catch and punish malefactors, his subordinates stepped up and dished out hard discipline on the march. Among them, Captain David L. Wood was only too eager to punish. Wood was a sadist in an army uniform and used his position to carry out the cruelty that he craved. Soldiers of the 18th Infantry wrote letters to their families and newspapers describing the cruelty of Wood and others. One soldier recalled seeing a white-haired, 70-year-old enlisted man tied up and in pain, whose crying could be heard throughout the camp. Another soldier recalled seeing a man hung upside down with blood spurting out of his nose and mouth.[3]

Wood's favorite target was a trooper named Henry Tank, a man whose propensity to drink often and excessively landed him in the dog house on many occasions. Private Tank was a problem drinker and Captain Wood knew just how to deal with a man with that kind of problem.

Alcohol consumption was, of course, the norm in the Civil War for men and officers of both sides of the war. It relieved boredom, produced episodes of euphoria and provided a temporary and much-needed respite from the presence of fear that stared a soldier in the face or lurked in the back of his mind. Booze was lovingly called "courage water," and when a large shipment showed up in camp, the troops knew that a battle was in the works.[4]

Tank was the kind of man who dipped his cup into the devil's vat too often for his own good. He and others whose conduct, including lack of sobriety, did not measure up to Wood's standards were subjected to treatment that can best be described as torture. First the man's hands were tied at the wrists and then he was suspended by a rope tied to his feet and drawn over a tree branch so that the man hung upside down, just above the ground, but unable to touch it. The unfortunate soldier could remain hanging in that position for as much as two hours. While Shepherd condoned this type of punishment, to his credit he did not order it carelessly. But due to Shepherd's long bout with typhoid, Wood had the opportunity to inflict punishment almost at will.[5]

4. Trouble on the Road to Corinth

A Civil War soldier's life was strangely episodic, unpredictable, edgy and dangerous. A volunteer accepted stress when he enlisted, believing in his personal capacity for courage and his devotion to the cause. But notions of glory and heroism were often diminished and dirtied by the terrible realities of war. One day it was filthy and boring and the next day exciting and violent in the extreme.

The only consistency was inconsistency. Men had to endure harsh weather, long, taxing marches, poor medical care, bad food or the lack of food. When relationships with family members soured, a letter from home with bad news could send a man into the depths of despair. Dramatic mood swings were common; one day a soldier could revel in the sweetness of victory and the next day be wracked by the pain of defeat, surrounded by dead and wounded friends. With all this to contend with, the last thing men needed was irrational or brutal treatment by ranking officers.

Colonel McCook believed that men who served under him were entrusted to his care and deserved respect and fair treatment. Like his brothers and cousins, he had a hard-edged personality, and demanded loyalty and obedience. But this trait was tempered by a sense of decency and fairness. When McCook's 3rd Brigade was encamped beside the Duck River, near Spring Hill, Tennessee, en route to Pittsburg Landing, he learned that some officers did not share his attitude toward common soldiers.

A detachment of the 18th Infantry pitched its tents next to those of the 9th Ohio and 2nd Minnesota volunteer regiments. While the men waited for the engineers to construct a bridge over the raging river, a wild and violent incident occurred that became known as the "Spring Hill Riot." When it was over the volunteers could not be faulted for thinking that certain regular army officers were the meanest men on Earth.

Captain Wood, the self-designated tormentor-in-chief of the 18th Infantry, put on a show that would long be remembered by the volunteers. On March 26, two men came under Wood's cruel hand. With men of the 9th Ohio and 2nd Minnesota regiments looking on, one of the men, accused of drinking on duty, was staked out, spread-eagle on the ground. This was too much to tolerate for the volunteers whose army life was influenced by the high-spirited, friendly and genial character of Colonel McCook, the founder of the 9th Ohio. Wood's actions were unacceptable; they could not bear to see soldiers like themselves being subjected to such cruelty.

When the angry volunteers invaded the 18th Infantry camp area, they discovered that Wood and his minions had two men tied to trees with their hands over their heads, stretched out so that their toes barely touched the ground. Thinking this was an outrageous way to treat men who were willing to fight and die for the Union, the volunteers moved forward and cut the suffering men down. Officers of the 18th Infantry resisted the volunteers and a scuffle quickly evolved into a brawl.

Lieutenant Anson Mills, the adjutant for the regular battalions, characterized the volunteers' action as those of a howling mob. He was hooted and cursed by the volunteers as were other officers and Lieutenant Colonel Shepherd. Mills gathered some of his troops that regained control of the area and re-tied the prisoners. Mills then rushed over to Shepherd's tent to inform his bed-ridden commander of the rowdy behavior of Bob McCook's volunteers.

An outraged Shepherd immediately rose from his sick bed and weakly made his way out to confront the "mob." He stiffened up as best as he could and told the volunteers that they were disgracing the uniform and the honor of the U.S. Army. His pleas were met by shouts of anger, including one man who said, "tie the officer of the day up by his privates!" This verbal projectile was followed by a piece of wood tossed toward the sickly Shepherd. Fortunately, it failed to hit its mark. At that point the outraged regular army officer ordered his men to disperse the volunteers, yelling, "leave my camp you sons of bitches!" That outburst served as a signal for a general out all brawl, resulting in a volunteer victory over the outnumbered regulars, leaving many of them with bumps and bruises. One man was rendered unconscious.

The grave of Civil War veteran F. A. Van Fleet, Company A, 2nd Minnesota Infantry Regiment. Under the command of Colonel Robert L. McCook, the 2nd Minnesota marched and fought in many great battles of the Civil War, including the Corinth campaign. When the war ended, Van Fleet went west, settling in Lincoln County, southeastern Dakota Territory, to explore opportunities offered by the frontier. He is buried in the Forest Hill Cemetery, at Canton, South Dakota. His grave is marked by a simple gravestone that reminds visitors that here lies a soldier who served in the American Civil War, the war that restored the Union and ended slavery. It was due to the efforts of men like Van Fleet that a strong, united America set it course toward becoming one of the great nations of the world (author's collection).

4. Trouble on the Road to Corinth 59

Shepherd managed to break away from the melee, and with his anger nearly out of control, he ordered Mills to find Colonel McCook, for surely a brigade commander worthy of the rank would restore order and punish his unruly volunteers. Mills recalled that he had "run the gauntlet," so to speak, dodging sticks, stones and other missiles along with assorted curses and other verbal barbs. Mills escaped with his dignity barely intact and went to McCook's headquarters but the colonel was absent. Finding only a foreign officer who chuckled, "vell, vell," when he told his story, Mills left in a huff and stomped back to the camp of the 18th Infantry.[6]

Once there, he joined Shepherd in an effort to restore order. Shepherd ordered his men to fix bayonets and charge the rioters, who were unarmed. The men of the 9th Ohio and 2nd Minnesota wisely moved back to their campground. Shepherd then ordered his men to load their rifles, perhaps expecting, or hoping, that the volunteers would come back so he could order his men to shoot. But the Ohio men kept their distance, while a few Minnesota troops lingered close enough to the 18th to maintain a war of words.

Shepherd was livid over the incident. As a veteran of 22 years he had never once witnessed such a display of disrespect and violence by enlisted men against officers. In his anger, he wrote a letter to Colonel McCook setting forth his grievances, and with considerable detail, he complained about the conduct of the volunteers. Since the 9th was McCook's original regiment, surely he would want to take action against his unruly men.

But McCook ignored the letter and did not respond. Shepherd, however, would not let the matter rest and decided he would personally address the 9th Ohio. That evening, while his own troops were conducting a dress parade, he turned his two battalions so that they were facing the 9th Ohio. Although he was weak from sickness, Shepherd mounted his horse, and, with Mills beside him, faced his men. Then Mills read a "general order" from "Camp Charlotte," dated March 26, 1862, in a voice loud of enough for all to hear.

> I. A crowd of men belonging to the 9th Rgt of Ohio Volunteers and the 2nd Minnesota Volunteers assembled this afternoon as a mob in front of the Guard Tent of this Command, one of them first cut the rope of a man who was under confinement and tied up, the Guard was neglectful of its duty in suffering such a mob like a gang of rowdies to assemble so close to the camp of this Command.
>
> II. The Non Commissioned Officers of the Guard and the Officers of the Rgt were hooted and hissed and groaned at by this crowd. All this was so great an insult to every soldier of the Regiment, who should be proud to call themselves Regulars, that every man should spurn such characters and deny all measure of association. The man himself who was undergoing the punishment which his officer had ordered, should feel pride and satisfaction that he does not belong to such a class of rowdies and contemptible wretches.

Fortunately, the volunteers absorbed the insult and did not retaliate with more hoots, hisses or groans. But Captain Wood seemed inspired by the order and was heard to say, "I'm going to tie Tank up by his heels!"[7]

True to his word, the following day Captain Wood charged Private Tank with drunkenness and the luckless soldier found himself in an all too familiar predicament. This time, however, Wood did his dirty work far enough away from the volunteers and with several men standing guard. He also requested the presence of a surgeon who told Wood that Tank should be released immediately, as suspending a man upside down for any length of time was extremely dangerous. The surgeon also declared that although Tank had been accused of being drunk on duty, he could detect no smell of alcohol on the soldier's breath. Tank was promptly released.

Although Tank apparently had no serious adverse reaction to the punishment, word of Wood's cruelty made its way to the volunteers and Colonel McCook picked it up. McCook observed that his men were upset over what they perceived to be cruel and unusual punishment and sent his adjutant, Captain Andrew Burt, out to gather some facts. Burt went directly to Shepherd and reported what he knew of the incident. The lieutenant colonel decided that, though he was a regular and a believer in discipline, Wood had gone too far.

Short of charging Wood with a court-martial offense, as he should have done, Shepherd made it clear to the other officers, including Wood's immediate commander, that all further requests for punishment must be made directly to him (Shepherd). Interestingly, Shepherd failed to involve (at least openly) the regimental commander of the 18th Infantry, Colonel Henry B. Carrington, who was not traveling with the 3rd Brigade.

Shepherd's actions did not sit well with Colonel McCook, who had been hearing rumors of excessive punishment by the officers of the regulars since the Mill Springs, Kentucky, campaign, including a sword injury incident. McCook may have been a cordial man and easy on his men, but damn it, he was battle tested and so were his volunteers. They had served and fought with distinction in western Virginia and Mills Springs, Kentucky. McCook no doubt believed he was the equal of a regular army officer like Shepherd; he had earned respect. Now his brigade was fighting a war within a war and his leadership and direction were needed.

Yet instead of meeting in person with Shepherd, McCook sent a short letter on March 28, inquiring about cruel treatment to soldiers from the battalions of regulars. In an obvious reference to Wood, McCook told Shepherd that an "officer in you [sic] command, had another soldier tied up by the heels for some time." He closed by asking, in a respectful manner, that Shepherd provide an "official statement" with details including names, places and forms of punishment.

4. Trouble on the Road to Corinth

The letter rubbed Shepherd the wrong way, and sick or not, he was greatly offended at what he deemed interference in the affairs of his command. How could McCook—a political appointee and a colonel in name only, with no military training—question him and his actions when the volunteers were allowed to behave in a manner that offended the honor of every good soldier? But instead of going to see McCook in person, Shepherd put his anger in writing. In a letter he downplayed acts of cruelty and explained that those punished were deserving of punishment because of violations of military regulations. As for Tank—a man of bad and worrisome character—Shepherd admitted that the upside down treatment took place but only for a "few moments" and that Wood was forbidden from carrying out such punishments in the future.

The exchange of testy letters continued. The next volley was a letter on March 28 from Shepherd to Captain G. E. Flint, Adjutant General, First Division, Army of the Ohio. Intending that General Thomas should be notified of irregularities occurring within the 3rd Brigade, Shepherd essentially "tattle tailed" on McCook. His military sensibilities raging full flame, Shepherd seemed to grow angrier with each word. He suggested that McCook and the other officers in his regiment could be charged with a violation of the "8th Article of War, which is a capitol offense." The 8th Article decreed that any officer who failed to put down a mutiny was to be punished by death.

While he never used the word mutiny, and didn't demand that McCook be shot, Shepherd did dredge up details of the brawl between the volunteers and his men, stating "a more disgraceful scene and one more destructive to good order & military discipline, was never exhibited by a mass of men who are called soldiers and so mustered into the Service of the United States." He closed by asking that his regiment be removed from McCook's brigade, lest the negative influence of the volunteers degrade the good character of his regulars.[8] Then, finally, as if he wanted to drive his point home, on March 30, 1862, Shepherd issued a written order reminding his own troops of the necessity to obey orders, unless "they are manifestly against Law and Army Regulations."[9]

The timing of Shepherd's pen and paper onslaught worked against him, and if Thomas had the inclination to investigate and take action, he was just then too busy to act on it. He had much more pressing matters to deal with. For just then August Willich's 32nd Indiana, a part of Major General Alexander M. McCook's division, was working hard to complete the rebuilding of the bridge over the Duck River. Anxious to see his old colleague Willich, Colonel McCook brought his 9th Ohio over for a visit. General McCook joined the group. The surprise visit turned into a happy reunion of comrades, complete with music and a speech by Willich. After dinner, brothers Bob and Alex McCook were serenaded in camp as the day ended.[10]

When the bridge was completed, the delay was over and General McCook's division crossed the Duck River. From there they continued their march to Savannah and finally, to Pittsburg Landing, in time to participate in the fight. While McCook's division fought with gallantry and success, Thomas and his men did not, for according to orders, they waited three days in the rear. By the time of their arrival at the landing, the two-day battle of Shiloh was over. The combined armies of Grant and Buell had beaten back a Confederate attack that began on Sunday, April 6, 1862. There was bad luck in it from the start for the South, as there was a belief among soldiers that when an army starts a battle on a Sunday, defeat will be the result.

When Colonel McCook's 3rd Brigade with its regulars—and irregulars—disembarked at Pittsburg Landing on the Tennessee River, they learned that the combined armies of Grant and Buell had been placed under the command of Major General Henry W. Halleck. Nicknamed "Old Brains" because of his academic record at West Point and his reputation as a strategist, Halleck left a desk job in charge of the Department of the Missouri in order to take a field command. In doing so, Grant was shoved aside, because Halleck was unimpressed with his performance at "bloody" Shiloh. Furthermore, Halleck determined that Grant had "resumed his former bad habits," meaning, of course, drinking.[11]

Although the Confederates had retreated, anyone looking around the landing would not think that the Union won the battle. Death, despair and destruction were all too evident, and Colonel McCook and his men found that their new campground was anything but hospitable. Amid the smoke and carnage of battle, the area around little Shiloh Church was immersed in the sad atmosphere of a charnel house, and the woods around it had become a ghoul-haunted woodland. It was as if the ghosts of the recently killed soldiers were lingering among the twisted, broken and smoldering trees.

Casualties on both sides had been very high and evidence of death was everywhere. Pale and bloated, partly buried or unburied bodies of soldiers and piles of amputated arms and legs were among the nightmarish sights and odors that greeted the troops who, but for being the last in line, missed the terrible fight. More than one man was transfixed by the awful atmosphere of death. The night before Robert McCook's arrival, a drunken soldier mistakenly had lain down to sleep in the company of dead men that were lying in a depression, waiting to be buried. The grim task of interring all the dead would take nearly five days.

Robert's brother, the major general, complained about the dismal and unhealthy campground, saying his "troops suffered severely in this camp from sickness, occasioned by bad water and the stench arising from the unburied carcasses of horses."[12] It was a filthy place made even filthier by the presence of soldiers who lacked clean uniforms because the baggage trains were slow in arriving.

Nevertheless, when Shepherd's column arrived in camp, General McCook was there to greet the soldiers. He asked Shepherd where he could find his brother Robert. Next he called out a friendly greeting to Captain Henry Douglass of the 18th U.S. Infantry, his classmate at West Point. When McCook saw Douglass, he called him by his West Point nickname, "Topdog," and Douglass responded with a hearty hello to "Guts." General McCook then launched into an enthusiastic explanation of the fighting that occurred just the day before, telling "Topdog" about seeing the Rebel leader, General P. T. Beauregard.[13]

Several days later, on April 24, the 18th U.S. Infantry was involved in a skirmish that resulted in another unfortunate quarrel with the volunteer regiments. It began when the 18th and 35th Ohio of Robert McCook's brigade were assigned to scout the area along with three other volunteer regiments from the division of Brigadier General Lew Wallace, namely the 8th Missouri, 11th Indiana and 76th Ohio. General Halleck sent the five regiments on a reconnaissance mission to check out the enemy and determine what the Rebels were up to. The detachment was under the supervision of Brigadier General Andrew J. Smith, a member of Halleck's staff. General McCook's division went forward to support Smith. They were on reconnaissance only and were not to engage in an all-out fight.

Near Lick Creek they came across pickets from a Mississippi brigade. Some shots were fired and the pickets retreated to Pea Ridge, minus a few men taken prisoners. As the Rebels drew back, the 8th Missouri and 76th Ohio started advancing. A quizzical Shepherd held his men in place believing he was following orders. Not knowing why the volunteers were advancing and thinking that Smith gave the order, Shepherd and his men began fuming over feelings of being ignored in favor of volunteers. When the 8th Missouri formed a line directly in front of the 18th, Shepherd could stand it no more and ordered his men out in a line next to the 8th Missouri. The advance continued until they came across a Rebel camp and surprised some men eating breakfast. A soldier recalled that the Rebels "got up and left without ceremony, and the breakfast they prepared was very acceptable to us." After eating a second breakfast, General Smith led his contingent back to the main Union line near Lick Creek.[14]

The Pea Ridge incident did nothing do dampen the hard feelings among the men of the 3rd Brigade. Memories of the "Spring Hill Riot" were fresh in the minds of the volunteers and regulars and many of them began a letter writing campaign explaining, in graphic detail, the horrors of the punishments inflicted by officers of the 18th U.S. Infantry. Letters poured into newspapers and politicians' offices and the soldiers' grievances were given a glitzy showcase.

The *Cincinnati Daily Commercial* came out with a big spread on April 7, a lengthy detailed article that sided with the soldiers and screamed for an investigation. These boys, said the article, were from some of the best families in Ohio, sent to serve their country, "little dreaming that they were sending them to everlasting destruction" at the hands of "heartless and drunken commanders." The reporter omitted the names of the alleged malefactors, saying only the officers were charged with "cowardly abuse of their men." It was feared that naming the accused officers would result in retaliation. And for that reason, the names of the soldiers who sent the letters were also omitted.[15] It was a good start for the men who sought to expose what they believed to be a serious problem.

The article did mention the name of an officer without accusing him of anything. That officer was Colonel Henry B. Carrington, the commanding officer of the 18th U.S. Infantry. After three other papers printed letters of complaint, Carrington was jolted into action, believing his regiment was being portrayed falsely, and that he must act to preserve its reputation.

From his headquarters at Camp Thomas, Ohio, Carrington wrote to Shepherd, calling his attention to "alleged violations" of regulations, including "degrading punishments." Carrington made it clear that he was ignoring the newspaper reports, but he was nevertheless ordering Shepherd to give him a full report, based on information received from other "gentlemen of the highest standing." Stating that he would see that any offending officer was punished, Carrington closed saying: "I shall be most happy to hear that I am misinformed."[16]

Shepherd jumped on the issue and responded in a manner that was calculated to ease his colonel's concerns and counteract the "scurrilous" newspaper articles. It was, after all, the ugly influence of the volunteers—that "infamous horde of Ruffians"—that started the trouble that resulted in accusations. The 9th Ohio, he said, "was a disgrace to our or any service." Next he turned on Colonel McCook, who up to this point had taken a back seat in the controversy. McCook, Shepherd iterated, was trying to stay popular with the "Germans" of the 9th so that they would vote for him when he ran for sheriff of Hamilton County, Ohio. Then he admitted that one officer (undoubtedly Captain Wood) had engaged in a "few indiscreet judgments in punishment," but that had been "corrected."[17]

Unfortunately for Carrington and Shepherd the "scurrilous" articles had hit their mark. Serious retribution came in the form of a letter from U.S. senator Benjamin F. Wade of Ohio, a powerful man with the clout to reach out and sting. In a letter to Carrington dated April 14, Wade, a member of the

Committee on the Conduct of War, ordered Carrington to "lay before the committee," an accurate report of the "brutality practised [sic] on some of the men of your regiment." He mentioned Captain Wood and a heel-hanging incident that resulted in the death of a soldier, and wanted an answer without undue delay.[18]

The Minnesota boys were busy too, and before long Congressman Cyrus Aldrich was weighing in on what was becoming a major military scandal. The Minnesota congressman wrote a letter to General Lorenzo Thomas, the adjutant general of the U.S. Army, with the now familiar hue and cry about brutality and flogging. He said, with no little indignation, that "we are unused to witnessing such barbarity toward White Men, let alone slaves."

Ohio congressman Sidney Edgerton added his own measure of outrage, based on a letter he received from a prominent Ohio man who was involved in recruiting for the 18th Infantry. This man claimed to have received letters from four men of the 18th who complained about brutal treatment from "drunken officers." Edgerton forwarded this information to Secretary of War Edwin M. Stanton. Edgerton pleaded with the secretary to take action for "God pitty [sic] this nation, if this government has got to [be] bolstered up by God forsaken, drunken tyrants."[19] The scandal had reached the top of the heap and those on the lower rungs of the ladder would have take cover.

Carrington and Shepherd could ignore and scoff at letters that appeared in the newspapers, for the press was seldom taken seriously by military men, but with members of congress and the secretary of war involved and demanding answers, there was no escape from having to respond to both the public and the authorities. An angry and frustrated Shepherd, who just wanted to command his battalions, had no choice but to request an inquiry and get all the facts on the record and out in the open. He sent a letter to General Buell asking for a hearing.

While Shepherd may have wanted to get a board of inquiry seated and taking testimony, he had to wait. Buell and the Army of the Ohio were finally headed to Corinth, Mississippi, the object of Halleck's mission. After a lengthy deliberation and methodical planning, Halleck decided it was time to move out, and on May 3, he telegraphed Stanton: "I leave here tomorrow morning and our army will be in Corinth tomorrow night."[20] In actuality, "tomorrow night" would be about a month in coming, for Halleck was in no hurry.

And yet all the military commotion at Pittsburg Landing signaled to the press that a major clash was in the offing. When it was learned that Daniel McCook, Sr., "father of the fighting McCooks," was passing through Louisville on his way toward Corinth, a newspaper in that city declared that the determined old man's presence was "a sign of battle."[21]

The goggle-eyed Halleck was talking and acting the same way. But before he ordered a forward march, Halleck reshaped one of his three large armies. While Grant still headed the Army of the Tennessee, General George H. Thomas was placed in direct command. This meant that Robert L. McCook and his 3rd Brigade would get a new commander. That man was Brigadier General Thomas W. Sherman, recently assigned to the Army of the Ohio. Thomas W. Sherman was no relation to General William T. Sherman who commanded a division in the Army of the Tennessee.

Robert L. McCook's new boss could not have been a worse choice, for "Old Tom" Sherman was a strict disciplinarian in the mold of Lieutenant Colonel Shepherd. He was a regular army West Point man who took a hard line in matters of army regulations. Seen as a martinet, he stood in sharp contrast to the vibrant and unmilitary McCook who scoffed at the spit and polish attitude of men like Sherman. McCook expressed his disappointment over his new commanding officer by purposely disregarding orders whenever he could. For example, McCook disliked Sherman's policy of holding roll call three times daily with full field pack. To avoid this and other "old army" formalities, McCook would take his troops out of camp. He once told the 9th Ohio that having to stand for roll call was "nonsense."[22]

Colonel McCook hated Sherman with a virulence that equaled or exceeded the hate he felt for Shepherd. His men called Sherman the "old woman Sherman," probably because he fussed so much. It was one thing to have an "old army" man as a subordinate, but a much worse burden to have such a man as a commander. For McCook, however, the shoe was on the other foot.

Since he couldn't take his brigade away from Sherman, McCook tried his best to get Sherman removed. He consulted with his brother Alexander, the major general and highest-ranking McCook in the Union army. Robert told Alexander that his men "were so angry with Sherman that he might meet with violence from their hands."[23] Sherman was hated "more than a snake, more than a fever, more than a coward, more than a spy."[24]

There was nothing the young colonel could do, however, for while his internal problems simmered, the Corinth campaign was at last launched. Halleck started to move, albeit very slowly. Thinking in terms of concentration, communication and coordination, and leaving nothing to chance, the thoughtful general—his 111,000 man army divided into three wings—inched its way toward Corinth.

The army was so big that it would have been impossible to keep its movement a secret, and yet Halleck banned all reporters, as if he thought he could stop reports of the march. A reporter for *The Daily Times*, a Cincinnati newspaper, was comfortable with Halleck's wish to keep "his counsel to himself," but he apparently believed the mission was a fool's errand. In an article from "Camp Shiloh," where the army waited for the order to march, he blithely suggested that the maneuver was a waste of time, saying, "If I am not most greatly mistaken we will have no serious conflict with the enemy at Corinth."[25] Halleck, of course, believed otherwise, and like most generals, disliked reporters and would have spurned any advice from them.

The right wing of the military behemoth of 111,000 men was formed by the Army of the Tennessee, now under the direct control of General George H. Thomas, the center was Buell's Army of the Ohio, including the division of Major General McCook which was held in reserve, and on the left marched John Pope's Army of the Mississippi. Grant tagged along, officially the second in command to Halleck, and, on paper, still commander of the Army of the Tennessee. But Grant had little authority and "Old Brains" ignored him for the most part. The result was that Grant felt insulted and useless like a "the fifth wheel to a wagon."[26]

The large mass of men moved at what can best be called a snail's pace, as Halleck was as cautious as any general in the Union army. The men marched through rugged, wet terrain, complicated by bad weather, only to be halted and ordered to dig complex entrenchments. Day after day it was more of the same irksome routine: march, stop and dig.

On the right of Halleck's legions, Colonel McCook's brigade marched in step with the rest of the massive, slow-moving army. The brigade had trekked about a mile and half when an incident occurred that must have reminded everyone of disciplinary problems, both real and imagined. Several drunken soldiers of the 18th Infantry, held as prisoners, were part of the march; two of them were so belligerent that their hands were tied. When the brigade halted at the edge of a timberline, one of the prisoners bolted into the trees with his guard in hot pursuit. The running man managed to make it to the ranks of the 35th Ohio where he frantically, and falsely, called out for help because the regular officers were killing soldiers.

This set off another round of pushing and shoving as approximately 200 Ohioans, including some officers, confronted the men of 18th. As a result, two Ohioans, a lieutenant and private, were arrested by a captain of the 18th. Hearing the shouting and fighting, Colonel McCook rode up and demanded to know the reason for the commotion. Everyone started talking at once which only added to the confusion causing a frustrated McCook to side with his Ohioans. He ordered Shepherd to have his men stack their arms while he tried to sort things out. In short order the lieutenant and the private were released and sent to their units and calm was restored. Once again, however, the regulars got the worst end of it, their pride suffering another wound.[27] Soon the brigade was moving forward with the rest of the army. The slow-moving mass of men halted about three miles outside of Corinth, where Halleck decided to close up all three wings and make a united front.

The evacuation of Corinth by the Rebel army led by General P. T. Beauregard. The Confederate general known as the "Creole" led his army away from Shiloh after being defeated by General U. S. Grant and his Union army. The Rebels fortified at Corinth, but believing it could not be held, Beauregard erected some "Quaker Guns," logs made to look like cannons. Then he loaded his soldiers aboard trains and escaped. When the Union troops under General Halleck arrived and entered the city gates, they were greeted by a devastated town that contained some wounded Rebels soldiers, lying the midst of filth and vermin. Truly, Corinth was not a noble trophy of war.

But instead of making a massive assault on the Rebels' works, Halleck and his generals found there was nothing for them to do except inspect the ruins of the vacated city of Corinth. It was an empty fortification manned by "Quaker Guns," that is, logs positioned to look like cannons. During the night Beauregard's Rebel army departed on a southbound train, leaving behind a massive, putrid mess. For what it was worth, Corinth was in Union hands and Halleck felt like a winner.

With the Corinth campaign over, Lieutenant Colonel Oliver Shepherd looked forward to an inquiry and a chance to vindicate his much maligned 18th U.S. Infantry. He must have been pleased when, on June 15, Halleck ordered the creation of a board of inquiry to "examine into certain charges of brutality or undue severity on the part of the Officers of the 18th U. S. Inf. towards their men."[28]

About that same time in mid-June Major General Alexander McCook, still in Corinth, rode into brother Bob's camp with a copy of *Harper's Weekly* dated May 31, 1862. Alexander bounced off his horse and handed the periodical to his brother, saying: "How's the Dutch, Bob, have you seen the news?"

Bob could hardly believe what he was reading as he scanned an article by J. F. Gookins of the 8th Missouri about the Pea Ridge skirmish that occurred before the Corinth march. The article, accompanied by a graphic drawing, explained that the 8th Missouri had to literally walk over the 18th U.S. Infantry and take on the Confederates at the "Battle of Pea Ridge." Gookins told a huge *Harper* readership that the volunteers were forced to take the initiative because the regulars, "composed of raw recruits," were unwilling to "charge."[29]

Having dealt with the incident at the Duck River crossing, and the flare up while on the march to Corinth, this was the last thing Colonel McCook needed on his plate. Once again it was the regulars versus the volunteers, and in the public eye, the later emerged triumphant. The false article was taken at face value and Shepherd's regulars were made the laughing stock of the Union and Robert McCook's brigade became nationally known as the "Pea Ridge Brigade." Volunteer regiments picked it up and rubbed it in.

While McCook most certainly disliked Shepherd, he was concerned with the truth and wanted refute the fanciful fabrication. After all, the 18th U.S. Infantry was an important part of his brigade. While he had a certain affection for the 9th Ohio, he was enough of a commander to know that all of his men were worthy of respect and fair treatment. Taking up pen and ink, he sent a letter to the *Cincinnati Gazette*, which had also printed the false story. McCook dismissed the *Harper's Weekly* story and stated that the regulars, men and officers alike, acted with "coolness and bravery," obeying all orders.

This assessment is consistent with the recollection of D. M. Price, Company "F," 2nd Battalion, 18th U.S. Infantry. He harbored no hard feelings against McCook or the volunteer regiments. In a letter to *The National Tribune*, after the war was over, Price said nothing about the flare-ups and friction among the officers. Instead he wrote with obvious pride and camaraderie about his service, saying, "we always filled our place in the program, and when the corps had anything to do, Bob McCook's brigade was always ready."[30]

General Alexander M. McCook's division, along with other elements of Buell's army, moved east into Tennessee, but Colonel McCook's brigade did not. The colonel had some unfinished business to attend to. He would soon have ample opportunity to expand on his brief statement to the *Gazette*, for Halleck's three-man board of inquiry, headed by Brigadier General John B. S. Todd, convened on June 17 and began taking testimony. The hearing proceeded at a brisk pace, with Robert L. McCook testifying in a manner that put the 18th on a pathway to vindication. Aside from mentioning that Captain Wood practiced a "most rigid method of enforcing discipline," he could find no other reason to criticize or condemn the officers of the 18th. He also testified that contrary to reports, Private Tank did not die as a result of being hung upside down. McCook said he recalled seeing Tank "a month after running around drunk at Pittsburg Landing with a canteen of whiskey in his hand trying to create another disturbance."

Next, General Todd—who was Mary Lincoln's cousin—called on volunteer soldiers to testify. They spoke rather timidly about what they recalled seeing and hearing, and no harsh or damning testimony was offered and after two days of questions and answers, Todd, having heard nothing that impressed or excited him, called on the regulars. Summed up, their testimony pointed out that there were examples of harsh punishment but all for legitimate military reasons, none of it unjust or cruel, with the exception of the actions of Captain Wood.

Todd closed the proceedings and issued a brief statement of findings and facts. He concluded that there were a few incidents of "tying up" soldiers after the 18th joined McCook's brigade and that the morale of the 18th was negatively affected by the presence of the volunteers and by irresponsible newspaper articles. For that reason, Todd decided, it was unnecessary to impose harsh disciplinary measures. He commended Lieutenant Colonel Shepherd who, despite his illness, did his best to prevent "all undue severity of punishment in his regiment." He castigated the newspaper articles and those who sent letters to be published in them, and closed by stating that no further action be taken—except for Captain Wood. Because of the cruel nature of the punishment meted out to Private Tank, Todd recommended that further action be taken against Wood.[31]

On June 13, Brigadier General Thomas W. Sherman was relieved and Major General George H. "Pap" Thomas was placed in charge of the First Division. This was good news for Colonel McCook and the 3rd Brigade. But even better news came in the form of a "full load of beer" from Cincinnati, along with assorted snacks, thanks to the sutler for the 9th Ohio.[32] Then, on June 24, the 3rd Brigade with the regulars marching with volunteers was sent on a new assignment. The brigade left Corinth with the rest of General Thomas' division heading east to Tuscumbia, Alabama, where it was to secure the Memphis and Charleston Railroad. Having been unable to extricate his battalions from the 3rd Brigade, a sullen Shepherd dutifully carried on while his opinion of the volunteers grew worse.

But things got better for Robert L. McCook. On March 22, 1862, while the Corinth controversy was unfolding, Congress approved the appointment of McCook to brigadier general.[33] Then, in July, McCook was presented with a brigadier's star, a promotion and an honor that surely did not sit well with Shepherd and other regular army officers.

It would have no doubt raised the morale of both sides had Shepherd's regulars been sent to another brigade, for the volunteers were unwilling to accept the judgment of the court of inquiry and continued to view regular officers as tyrants. It was a wound that refused to be healed. As they entered the land of the bushwhacker, however, events would influence an end to the uneasy alliance and bring about an unexpected and tragic conclusion to the volunteer versus regular army quarrel.

5

The Killing of Robert L. McCook

"A brave officer and congenial friend is lost to this division, and the country has been deprived of a general who was firm and devoted to its interests."—George E. Flynt, Assistant Adjutant General and Chief of Staff, Army of the Ohio, August 7, 1862

In July of 1862, Brigadier General Robert L. McCook was in command of the 3rd Brigade in the division of Major General George H. Thomas and was posted at Tuscumbia, Alabama. There, General Thomas, his men and officers celebrated the 4th of July with a national salute, patriotic speeches and a reading of the Declaration of Independence. Soldiers from the 9th Ohio were upset and angered because the speeches tended to go easy on their "southern brothers." General McCook also found the speakers' remarks too soft. When it was his turn, McCook said: "The Union must be preserved, and the rebellion crushed. The secessionists are our brothers no more, they are enemies: ours and the nation's. If they will not submit peaceably, they must be exterminated. My men and I are ready to do just *that*, even if it means the South must be laid to waste."[1]

A fired up McCook, sounding like an abolitionist, placed special emphasis on the duty of the Union army to free every slave.[2] He was followed by other colonels who spiced up the celebration with more "fire and sword" rhetoric. McCook and other soldiers proudly aired their heartfelt belief in the cause of the Union and its virtuous representative government, grounded in a Constitution that was the model of the world. They believed the South was solely at fault for the secession crisis and the war.

The South was seen as a decadent, pseudo-aristocratic society, modeled after old style, authoritarian regimes. The Confederacy was established to prop up the wealthy planter class whose need for slaves was absolute. In the summer of 1862, a writer for the *New York Times* called out the South by declaring that "slavery is so wrought into the texture of [Southern] society ... that it cannot be rudely modified or interfered with without destroying every ramification of Southern life."[3] To the high-minded, patriotic Union soldier, like Bob McCook, the South was ripe for the destruction it so richly deserved and he ripped into the Confederacy when he spoke to his fellow soldiers.

After a while, Thomas, who listened quietly and patiently, decided the tone and content had reached a boiling point so he called a halt to the proceedings and sent all the soldiers back to their camps.[4] But he had to feel good about the outpouring of loyalty coming from his men. It was a force he could harness and put to good use in the weeks to come.

On July 19, McCook received orders to move his brigade across the Tennessee River at Florence, Alabama, and on the 23rd, to march to Huntsville, with five days' rations for each regiment.[5] The troop movement involved the entire division and was in response to intelligence that indicated Major General Braxton Bragg's Rebel army was forming in large numbers with designs on taking all of Tennessee or possibly even Kentucky.

The chess match was on and General Thomas directed McCook to move his brigade again. "You will leave your present camp on the 3d instant and follow the road taken by the cavalry and artillery to Decherd, Tenn."[6] Once there he was ordered to halt his brigade, make camp and await further orders. Sadly for Robert L. McCook, the orders unwittingly led him along a pathway to his untimely and tragic death.

In 1965, the Alabama Historical Association erected a small marker along Limestone Road in Madison County entitled "Old Limestone Road Skirmish." The very brief text of the marker explains that on August 5, 1862, General Robert L. McCook was killed by Confederates. To a casual observer, the marker does nothing other than single out a casualty of the Civil War. And yet the actual manner of the general's death, along with his rank, reputation and the prominence of the McCook family, created a national sensation. While other officers fell in battle causing hardly a ripple, the death of Brigadier General Robert L. McCook became a media event of long duration.

While on the march toward the Tennessee state line, McCook became ill with dysentery, the scourge of the army. With the bulk of his brigade marching as ordered, its commander rode in advance, in an open carriage, lying on a bed in the company of a small detail of men. Driving the wagon was McCook's personal servant, John Vincent, a free black man from Cincinnati. On August 5, 1862, near the town of New Market, they were overtaken by Rebel cavalry, shots were fired and General McCook was mortally wounded, the second McCook to die in the Civil War. He was 35 years old. It was an ugly death in an ugly war. But no one—not even a McCook—was promised a glorious, soldier's death.

The official account of Robert L. McCook's death is contained in a brief report by Colonel Ferdinand Van Derveer, commanding officer of 35th Ohio Infantry regiment, Third Brigade, Army of the Ohio. Because of McCook's illness, Van Derveer was temporarily in charge of the brigade.

According to Van Derveer's melancholy account, on August 5, 1862, McCook was traveling on a road from Athens, Alabama. He was about three miles in advance of the main body of the 3rd Brigade, accompanied by Captain Hunter Brooke, a member of his staff. Major Boynton and nine other soldiers made up the rest of the party. About noon the convoy was approached suddenly by fast-moving horsemen estimated to have been between 100 and 200 men. As they were not in army uniforms, it was assumed that they were guerrillas, or "partisans," the name given to such men by the Confederate government.

Just before the attack, Boynton and three others had been sent to the rear, and a sergeant was ordered ahead to locate a camping stop, leaving the rest to fend for themselves. Captain Brooke, unarmed, was in the carriage attending to the ailing McCook when the Rebels started shooting. An alarmed Vincent turned the carriage around in the direction of the main body of Union troops, and with the horses running at full speed, they were overtaken by the mounted Rebels. Someone in the Rebel party yelled, "stop! stop!" McCook replied, "don't shoot; the horses are running; we will stop as soon as possible."[7]

Despite his attempt to surrender, a rider within a few feet of the side of the carriage fired two shots directly at McCook. One bullet passed through McCook's hat and the other struck him in the abdomen. Brooke later recalled that there was no order to halt, insisting the only words he heard were "Yankee sons of bitches."[8] John Vincent fled, having been ordered by McCook to leave the area, fearing that if he were caught, the Rebels would summarily kill the "Yankee negro." Vincent ran for his life and freedom; disappearing in cornfield, he stepped away from the pages of history.[9] Brooke was made a prisoner and McCook was taken to a nearby house, the home of a widow and her family. McCook's sword was kept by the officer in charge of the Rebel party as a trophy of war.[10]

It was first thought that McCook should be housed in the "negro quarters," for "should he die on their hands their premises would be burned." Nevertheless, he was taken into the widow's house. When the Union doctors arrived, a suffering McCook was spitting blood. An examination by Dr. Gordon and Dr. Boyle of the 35th Ohio revealed he been struck by a single shot "in the bowels," the bullet having entered his left side, coming out "between the 9th and 10th ribs" on his right side. Someone counted 11 bullet holes in the wagon that had carried McCook.

5. The Killing of Robert L. McCook

Realizing his grave condition, McCook made out a will with the assistance of Colonel Van Derveer. He bequeathed his favorite horses to his brothers Alex and Dan and the rest of his property to his mother. Bob McCook was cared for and made comfortable by those present. The doctors did all they could to try to save him but he died the next day. It was said that his last words were "tell Alex [his brother General Alexander M. McCook] and the rest that I have tried to live like a man and do my duty."[11]

In another account it was claimed that McCook died in the presence of a friend, saying: "I am done with life, yes this ends it all. You and I part now, but the loss of ten thousand such lives as yours and mine would be nothing, if their sacrifice would but save such a government as ours."[12] If someone had wanted to create an epitaph for the fallen general, these high-sounding words would have been more than appropriate.

As if competing for attention, other versions of the tragic event entered the picture. An unnamed officer interviewed by the *Cincinnati Commercial* recited a version of the attack and McCook's last hours that differed from the official record. This informant claimed that the attack was the result of a planned ambush and that the Rebels learned of McCook's presence in the area after talking to "citizen spies." The Rebels had decided to lay in wait and kill McCook when his wagon passed by. The officer informant chastised the men of the 1st Ohio Cavalry whose duty it was to guard the sick general, for when the shooting started, all but one acted like "craven cowards" and fled the scene, thereby sacrificing their general.

According to this account, upon hearing gunfire, McCook shouted, "The bushwhackers are upon us," and ordered Vincent to turn the team around. McCook got up from his bed to assist in turning and controlling the team. More shots were fired and one of them struck McCook, tearing into his intestines. The informant said the shooter was a "cowardly murderer" named Charles Wood.

After the team was stopped, another Rebel approached the wounded general and was about to shoot when McCook said: "You needn't shoot, I am already fatally wounded." The officer claimed that the general died while the men of his brigade, his "faithful soldierly [sic] were grouped about the house, waiting to bid a last farewell to their commander." The dying general remained calm and "the last moments found him as firm and calm as ever he was in the face of death."[13]

The Confederate version of the shooting was, understandably, different than Van Derveer's report that went into the official records of the Civil War. The pursuit of McCook and his men was prompted by a report that a party of Union foragers was in the vicinity of New Market, about 15 miles northeast of Huntsville, Alabama. A detail of cavalry under Captain Joseph M. Hamrick galloped out to intercept the foragers. When they spotted McCook's wagon and military escort, Hamrick ordered a charge. The cavalrymen guarding McCook rode away, abandoning the ailing general. His wagon struck a tree branch, tearing the canvass and sending it into the ditch. Instead of surrendering, McCook "grabbed the reins and tried to escape." For that reason, McCook was shot, although his identity was unknown at the time.[14]

In addition to shooting McCook, the Rebels captured some of his wagons along with horses and mules and a few prisoners including Captain Brooke, who was released after 12 days in captivity. They also took the sword that Congress presented to McCook, bearing an inscription on its blade that memorialized his gallantry in battle.

Van Derveer concluded that the sneak attack was made for the purpose of capturing or murdering General McCook. He said, "the condition of General McCook could not but have been known to the attacking party, as he was on his bed, divested of all outer clothing except a hat used as shade, and the curtains of the carriage raised on all sides." It was called a "cowardly assassination," and caused many soldiers from McCook's brigade to retaliate.[15]

Before they could be brought under control by Van Derveer, the angry soldiers, especially those from the 9th Ohio, completely destroyed the plantation of the man they believed had led McCook into the death trap.[16] Then they went on a looting, shooting, hanging and burning spree. At one house put to the torch, the woman resident begged the men to spare her home but her pleas were ignored. Instead the captain said: "Madam, for the first time in this war an American General has been cowardly murdered.... I give you 15 minutes to get out your things."[17]

Several men suspected to have been involved in the shooting were hanged on convenient tree branches. Having lost their beloved leader, the angry Yankees killed livestock and put the torch to all Rebel property they could find in the vicinity of the attack, including the house of the widow who cared for McCook during his last hours.[18] They also shot a Confederate lieutenant out on furlough, assuming he was connected to the "gang."[19]

The undisciplined and outrageous behavior occurred only about four weeks after Major General U. S. Grant had issued Special Order No. 133 in response to recent "irregularities." Among other things, the order specifically forbade trespassing, "marauding, pilfering" and "destruction of private property." Violators were subject to "the extreme penalty imposed by the laws of war, which is death." The order was published "for the locality of Memphis" and was to be "rigidly enforced."[20]

General Thomas sympathized with McCook's brigade but he understood the importance of keeping focus on the mission and therefore intervened. In a written order, he said he could understand the sorrow of the men and their desire for revenge, but he said that it would be better to express that revenge in battle. He reminded the men that they were soldiers and had accept the loss and move on. He wrote, "Without discipline ... no happy result can be expected from an enemy who could use the helplessness of the grievously mourned colonel to murder him." Thomas ordered 30 days of mourning for the dead officer.[21]

The angry assumption among people of the North was that the men who overtook and shot Robert L. McCook were not soldiers but rather guerrillas or murdering thugs commonly called "bushwhackers." The Union army, from private to general, had a low opinion of this species of fighters. They were seen as sneaking, low-life, back-shooting cowards who struck from ambush and therefore deserved no respect.

Bushwhackers and guerrillas were often lumped together, and while their tactics were similar, they were not fighters cut from the same cloth. Some guerrillas were actual soldiers or "partisans," sanctioned by the Confederate government. Partisans, while not always in uniform, were expected to follow orders from their commanding officers. Usually on horseback, their role was to do scouting, raiding and reconnaissance. They differed from "regular guerrillas" who fought according to their own initiative. Both types were useful to the Rebel command.[22]

While all Rebels were enemies, the bushwhacker was an enemy in its lowest, most degraded form, inspiring universal hatred. The circumstances of McCook's death excited the North in the extreme and the "dirty fighter" came under special scrutiny. An Ohio newspaper captured this scalding anger in an article, saying "The blood of this murdered officer [McCook] cries out from the ground for a war policy that shall exterminate the whole guerrilla system."[23] An angry soldier from the 3rd Ohio Cavalry bemoaned guerrilla tactics, writing "Rebels won't stand and fight." Instead he said, they "lie behind bushes and murder."[24]

McCook, no doubt, felt the same way before he was "bushwhacked." Once when his regiment was engaged in bridge repair at Columbus, Tennessee, his men were fired upon by civilians in hiding. He sent word to the town that unless the sniper fire ceased, he would retaliate. The fighters failed to heed the warning and true to his word, McCook turned his artillery on Columbus and shelled it for two to three hours without interruption. The shelling had the desired effect and the work on the bridge proceeded without another shot fired on his men.[25]

Now Robert L. McCook was dead and the outrage and sadness experienced by soldiers from his brigade was soon felt throughout the Union states and among his many friends in the army. Lieutenant Colonel John Beatty, who served with Robert L. McCook in the West Virginia campaign, lamented the loss of the man he respected. He remembered McCook as a "brave, bluff and talented man and his loss will be sorely felt."[26] When news of McCook's death reached Secretary of War Edwin Stanton, he was grief stricken and angered at what he believed was a brutal murder. The secretary was a friend of the fallen general, who studied law at Stanton's office before the war.

The newspapers accepted Van Derveer's version of the tragic event, agreeing the attack amounted to a cowardly assassination of a man so sick and so unprotected that he was barely able to resist. An emotional editorial in the usually sober *New York Times* called the killing "one of the most melancholy and disastrous events of the war." Because McCook was "a helpless invalid" in an ambulance, there was "not a single circumstance to redeem it from classification among the most wanton and savage butcheries that ever occurred in a civilized country." It was a "national disaster," beyond the pale, because it would likely trigger outrage and "a series of retaliations ... of rapine and slaughter at which humanity will shudder."[27]

An illustration in a popular publication falsely portrayed McCook on his knees begging for his life as he was shot. *Frank Leslie's Illustrated Newspaper* incorrectly reported that McCook's wagon was turned over and he was shot while on his hands and knees on the road, unable to get to his feet. The paper later issued a correction, informing readers that McCook was shot while in his conveyance.

Years after the tragedy, Hunter Brooke was interviewed by a newsman who pumped him for details. Brooke said the official report, submitted by Van Derveer, was right in most respects, and then went on to reveal additional and tantalizing information. Brooke confirmed that he was with McCook in the wagon, caring for the ailing general, who chose to ignore the advice of his doctor and instead travel with his brigade. He said that McCook established the direction of travel through an area that he knew quite well, and then turned command over to Van Derveer who was to direct the troop movement. Due to extremely hot temperatures during the day, they set out at 3 a.m., with a view of resting during the afternoon hours.

Brooke said that Van Derveer became confused and veered from McCook's route, taking a turn in the wrong direction. The brigade was on the Fayetteville road instead of the Dercherd road. When McCook realized they had strayed off course, he sent a rider off to find Van Derveer. Expecting that Van Derveer would backtrack and correct the line of march, McCook and Brooke set off to find a place to camp, preferably with shade and water. Brooke recalled that McCook "frequently halted and talked with people, white and black," asking about campsites.

About midday, McCook halted his conveyance and sent messengers out looking for water. One of the messengers came "rushing back, bareheaded and in great excitement," said he had been fired upon by Rebels. McCook expressed great surprise as he had no intelligence of any enemy force north of the Tennessee River. McCook shouted, "Get in quick Brooke, we've got to get out of here." In an instant the wagon was going full speed while horsemen were rapidly approaching and shooting.

With bullets "whizzing ... about our ears," they feared that capture or worse was imminent and yet on they went. McCook looked back at the pursuers and yelled, "Where in the hell is Van Derveer?"

Brooke recalled, "Well, we ran at full speed full three-quarters of a mile, and finding that we had no friends in front and an abundance of enemies in the rear," the decision was made to surrender. McCook ordered the driver to halt the team.

Brooke told the journalist that they held up their hands in the universal gesture of surrender but the Rebels continued to shoot, despite "every assurance that we had measured our helplessness and were willing to surrender." Thus Brooke concluded that General McCook was murdered.[28] It was a conclusion shared by most people in the North.

The death of Robert L. McCook meant that his long-running quarrel with Lieutenant Colonel Oliver L. Shepherd was at an end. Far from expressing sympathy, however, Shepherd used the occasion to renew his request to detach his battalions from the 3rd Brigade. In a letter to the headquarters of the Army of the Ohio, Shepherd complained that due to McCook's demise, he now had to serve under Van Derveer, a fate worse than serving under his now deceased nemesis. Shepherd pleaded for headquarters to sever his ties with the brigade so he and his fellow regular army officers could be freed from the "malignant conduct of Volunteer Officers." The letter went to Van Derveer who ordinarily would have forwarded it to headquarters, but he was so insulted by its contents that he did not send it on.

Once again it seems Shepherd put his foot in his mouth, for his letter drew the wrath of Van Derveer and essentially stoked the fires of the old feud with the volunteers. Van Derveer returned it to Shepherd with an angry retort, objecting to the "false and slanderous charges against the volunteer officers and soldiers of the brigade." Shepherd's constant harping at the volunteers had earned him a reputation as a meddlesome and unsuitable subordinate. Using the occasion of McCook's death to launch yet another complaint was in poor taste and viewed as unworthy of an honorable man.[29]

When Robert's brother Major General Alexander M. McCook received the tragic news, he immediately requested Major General Don Carlos Buell's permission to take his older brother's body home for burial. Buell responded promptly, expressing his shock and sympathy but denied the request. Buell said, "it is painful to be compelled to refuse your request, but I feel that your services at this time are most important, indeed indispensable."[30] Buell was just then gearing up to meet a new Confederate threat in the form of General Braxton Bragg's Army of Tennessee. As a major battle was expected; General McCook could not be spared. He understood and accepted Buell's decision with soldierly grace and stoicism. If he complained, he did not do so publicly or in his official capacity.

General McCook met with the men and officers of the 9th Ohio and offered to attach the regiment to the brigade of August Willich. The 9th could march along side of the 32nd Indiana, also a German regiment. The general offered to care for the regiment "as well as his brother cared for it." The men were largely in favor of joining General McCook's division, but the officers disagreed, believing it better in the long run to stay with General Thomas.[31]

The immediate concern was the burial of Robert L. McCook. Union troops placed his body aboard a train and sent it to the Commercial Hotel in Nashville, where it was laid out for public viewing. Among those who viewed the body was Tennessee governor Andrew Johnson, who "was visibly affected by the sight of the corpse of his late friend." Nashville was in "a perfect uproar of excitement over the details of the death of brave Gen. Robert McCook of Ohio."[32]

After the Nashville viewing the body was taken by train to Louisville. It was attended by captains Andrew Burt and Fuchshulter along with 11 enlisted men from the 9th Ohio. The soldiers escorted the coffined remains to the Galt House, a prominent Louisville hotel.

In Cincinnati, the city council appointed a committee of three men to escort McCook's body to that city for a funeral service befitting a hero. When the committee arrived in Louisville, it was escorted by a guard of infantry and cavalry from the depot to the Galt House, to receive McCook's coffin. Then, in a military show of respect, the body was carried home to Ohio by boat. When his body arrived in Cincinnati on August 9, the mood was appropriately somber and reverent; the city was draped in mourning with flags at half-mast. With bells tolling throughout the city, McCook was carried to the Hamilton County Court House and placed in the rotunda where the remains laid in state all afternoon. A long line of people walked by slowly and paid their respects.

The funeral service was solemn and patriotic, as a family, a city, a state and a nation were all doing their duty to a fallen hero, the gallant soldier familiarly known as Bob McCook. With a team of six white horses pulling the hearse, a band played the "General Robert L. McCook's Funeral March," composed for the occasion by Cincinnati composer F. W. Rauch. The funeral procession was the largest in the city's history. Trailing the hearse, the grieving family and some 2,000 mourners, some walking, some in carriages draped in black, gently escorted the fallen soldier to his place of burial.[33] Robert L. McCook, Ohioan, soldier, lawyer, beloved son, brother and cousin—the second of his family to be killed in the Civil War—was buried at the Spring Grove Cemetery in Cincinnati.

The death of Robert L. McCook was the cause of great sorrow, and intense anger, in his family. No one felt the impact of the volatile combination of emotions more than his younger brother, Colonel Daniel McCook, Jr. When Colonel McCook received written confirmation of Bob's death, he read the dispatch in the presence of a reporter. The sad event was remembered by the reporter who took note of Dan's "agony of bereavement" and the self-evident expression that some "wreaking of terrible vengeance" was about to happen, when, through "gritted teeth," the Colonel said, "I'll never take *another rebel prisoner* as long as God gives me breath."[34]

Robert's cousin, Colonel Anson G. McCook, was unable to "refrain from expressing" his "sorrow and condolences" to his grieving aunt in a heartfelt letter. Understanding the grief Robert's mother, Martha, was experiencing, he wrote: "But one short year ago you were called upon to mourn the loss of one loved son, [Charles] and now, when time has but partially healed the wounds, another as brave and as noble and good a son as ever spoke the name of Mother has fallen for his country and the right." He gently reminded his aunt that Robert's death was "glorious, that he died full of honor and has left you as a legacy a name that will be cherished by his countrymen as long as worth and manly virtues are recognized and appreciated."[35]

In a letter to his cousin Mary Sheldon, Anson took a different tone, expressing great anger over the death of Robert, "as good a soldier as ever drew a blade … and another victim of the cursed rebellion." Anson confided that he could accept the death of his cousin had he died in battle. But Robert was denied that elevated form of death and instead was "shot like a dog in an ambulance." Lashing out at the assassin and his ilk, Anson condemned the South, cursing the "day when their unholy, causeless and ungodly rebellion reared its devilish head." In a state of intense anger, Anson was ready to throw himself into the struggle to defeat the Confederacy with even greater determination though it might mean his own death.[36]

George W. McCook wrote a tender, heartfelt letter to his mother, offering comfort and expressing his sorrow over the loss of his brother. Having just found a picture of "dear Robert," George wrote, "when I wrote you last year, I spoke of poor Charlie's death and how long it had been since your family circle was broken. Now another year has taken away still another of your children, and it rests with the good Providence of God, how many will be left to comfort your old days."[37] The war was well into its second year and the astute George W. McCook had accepted that it would be a long and costly fight.

Outside of the McCook family, the loss of Robert fell especially hard on the men of the 9th Ohio, Bob's "bully Dutchmen." A prominent member of the 9th, William Stangel solemnly declared: "McCook's memory will never disappear. When we are all dead and gone history will assert itself, and among the heroes of this war and this land he [Robert L. McCook] will assume a prominent place."[38]

The men of the 9th Ohio Infantry would never forget their leader. Held in high esteem while he lived, General Robert L. McCook's stature had, in death, risen to new heights of greatness. A Tennessee newspaperman expressed the opinion of many when he wrote: "He [Robert L. McCook] was one of the stars of the celebrated fighting family of McCooks."[39]

In the meantime the war went on and the search for the perpetrators, now believed to be regular Confederate cavalry, progressed and more details of the incident were made known. General George H. Thomas ascertained that McCook's escort stopped at a house of a "man named Petit to inquire about water and camping ground."[40] A short time later, the attack occurred.

General Thomas was ordered to take steps to find and punish the "guerrillas" and "no pains must be spared" to accomplish this. He was instructed to arrest all "men of bad character in the vicinity where General Robert L. McCook was shot, and let them see such outrages cannot be unnoticed." General Buell wanted the arrest of "every able bodied man of suspicious character or suspicious disloyalty or hostility within a circuit of 10 miles around the place where McCook was shot." All such men caught in this sweep were to be brought to Huntsville and there dealt with by military authority. Short of ordering summary executions, Thomas was told that "bushwhackers actually caught in arms should not be leniently dealt with" as the object was to "destroy them."[41]

A soldier from the 29th Indiana Infantry regiment expressed the views of the majority of Union men in uniform when he wrote to his mother: "The time for milk and water manner of doing business is past. This war has gone far enough and if it requires a half a million more men let them be had."[42]

An angry soldier from the 2nd Minnesota Infantry harbored the same sentiments. Under the name "Uncle Tom," in a letter to a Minnesota newspaper, he insisted that the loss of McCook was greater than losing "any other commanding officer in the department." Casting blame on the Lincoln administration, he declared that McCook was a victim "of the stupendous folly of our Government" and demanded to know when "the Government will take the necessary steps to put a stop to such atrocities?" He called on the government to "stop *playing* war and go at it in earnest." Foreshadowing the policy that in two years would be pursued by Lincoln and Grant, the soldier wanted to "desolate the entire South, and make it a howling wilderness."[43]

5. The Killing of Robert L. McCook

The McCook family was in the mood for a crackdown, for they concluded that Robert was not just a casualty of war, but a murder victim. The hot-tempered Colonel Daniel McCook, Jr., was over-anxious to join the search for the culprits. On August 25, 1862, while his regiment, the 52nd Ohio Volunteer Infantry, was being mustered into service in Cincinnati, Colonel McCook accepted a battle flag in a ceremony dedicated to the memory of Robert L. McCook. As the flag—inscribed with the words "McCook's Avengers"—was presented to Daniel McCook, Thomas J. Gallagher, friend of the family, said: "Colonel McCook, it is my pleasant duty to present to you and your regiment, the 'McCook's Avenger's—these flags."

In the presence of many "friends and intimates of your murdered brother," Gallagher said, "to your hands, and to the keeping of the 'Avengers,' I commit this banner of beauty." Gallagher went on to praise the late Robert L. McCook, whom he knew well in life, saying, "in his death, our country has lost a useful citizen, a brave soldier, and a gallant gentlemen."[44] After the solemn proceedings concluded, Colonel McCook's regiment marched off and boarded a train for Kentucky. The 52nd Ohio Volunteer Infantry became known as the "McCook Avengers," their dark blue banner, so dark that it appeared to be black, fluttered with special pride and purpose. It became known among other Union regiments as the "black flag."[45] Daniel McCook was especially proud of the banner, and seeing it no doubt reminded him of his oath of vengeance against the Southern prisoners that might fall into his custody and control.

Colonel Edward M. McCook, a cousin of the late and lamented Robert L. McCook, was fully involved in the hunt for bushwhackers. He sent a note of congratulations to Colonel L. D. Watkins who was pursuit of the raiders that attacked his cousin's convoy and a note to General Alexander M. McCook with a progress report. Edward's correspondence to General James A. Garfield indicates that 11 prisoners were taken one day, "among them some of the band engaged in General McCook's murder."[46]

Cavalryman Edward M. McCook was just then beset by problems with bushwhackers who burned bridges and otherwise annoyed his brigade while he was operating in northern Alabama and Tennessee in the summer and fall of 1862. At an inquiry McCook recalled that he received orders General Buell to hang a man in connection with acts of destruction. McCook turned the man over to the 17th Kentucky Infantry, but before he could conduct a hanging, the man escaped.

There were more problems for "Horse Ed" McCook to contend with. While on the march, one of his soldiers left the column, entered a field, "unbuttoned his pantaloons and sat down to relieve himself when he was shot out of a house." McCook found the dead body and in a fit of anger ordered the cornfield burned as punishment after a slave told him that his "master" had shot the unlucky soldier. McCook would have burned the house itself had it not been for women and children present.[47]

Eventually, however, the demands of war stalled efforts toward finding and punishing bushwhackers, and besides, these hideout men would remain a problem without a solution throughout the war. After the war, some such men formed gangs of outlaws that continued to plague Yankee interests, among them the James-Younger gang, directed by the politically motivated and unrepentant Missouri rebel Jesse James.

Guerrillas were often just angry civilians whose lives were disrupted by war. They were also soldiers gone feral and were subjected to a special breed of contempt because they lacked the soldierly discipline of an infantryman fighting in line. They were, however, still merely cogs in the war machine, engaged in killing the enemy. But when a victim was a well-liked general from a prominent family, the man who did the killing would have to be blessed with extraordinary luck in order to escape the pursuing hounds of vengeance. And the Union army would never stop trying to find the man who killed Robert L. McCook.

6

Frank B. Gurley: Soldier or Murderer?

> "A more cold-blooded and fiendish murder was never perpetrated … than these guerrillas of Northern Alabama have been guilty of, and it is not surprising that the most intense excitement is stirred up in the West."—*New York Times*, August 9, 1862

While the Union army was searching for the man who shot and killed General Robert L. McCook, a Rebel doctor languishing in a federal prison sent a letter to his congressman blaming the late Ohio general for his imprisonment. Joseph E. Dixon of Tennessee was among the Rebels captured when Fort Donelson surrendered to General U. S. Grant on February 16, 1862. After it was learned that Dixon was a surgeon he was released. On his way to rejoin his unit, he was intercepted by McCook's men and brought before the general. McCook indicated that Dr. Dixon would be allowed to continue on his way, but changed his mind and arrested the doctor.

After seven months of confinement Dixon was extremely bitter and made it known that he blamed Robert L. McCook for his dilemma. He tasted some relief, however, when he learned of McCook's death. In his angry letter to H. S. Foote, a member of the Confederate congress, Dixon said his treatment would have been "intolerable did I not have the pleasing satisfaction of knowing that General McCook who ordered my arrest has gone to reap the reward of his doings—a reward richly deserved by him and all others engaged in this unholy nigger war."[1]

Dixon savored his revenge behind bars, while high ranking Southerners worked to free him. The business of handling, housing and exchanging prisoners was something that taxed both sides throughout the war. Prisons tended to be filthy hell-holes where caged and ragged men existed like wild beasts. As time went on and prison populations increased, officials were pressured to find ways to exchange prisoners to relieve crowding. Since men were often arbitrarily herded together, it was not always possible to distinguish between those ordinary soldiers who deserved to be released and others who had committed crimes and needed to remain incarcerated. Dixon was caught in this shuffle and his hatred of Robert L. McCook—whom he blamed for his suffering—was a natural consequence of the unfortunate chain of events.

Finding McCook's killer quickly became a needle-in-the-haystack exercise for the South was awash with guerrillas and bushwhackers, all of whom were constantly on the move. But so strong was the desire to hang the crime on someone that the search continued in one form or another. Then, suddenly, on December 11, 1862, an Ohio newspaper published a small notice on the bottom of a page. It said simply: "It is ascertained that Capt. Gourly [sic] of Alabama, murdered Brigadier General Robert L. McCook."[2]

Time and investigation would eventually uphold the truth contained in that small nugget of news, but following the third day of the terrible battle of Gettysburg, on July 4, 1863, suspicion was focused on one of Robert E. Lee's brigade commanders, namely Colonel Birkett D. Fry. Fry had performed with gallantry during the ill-fated "Pickett's charge," and he was wounded and taken captive. While incarcerated, rumor had it that Fry was the killer of Robert L. McCook. It was a short-lived rumor, however, for Fry was cleared by Union general John Gibbon, who knew Fry while the two men attended West Point. Gibbon's persuasion silenced suspicious tongues and Fry was exchanged and released.[3]

It wasn't until October 13, 1863, that a man was arrested and locked up in connection with the death of Robert L. McCook. That man was Frank B. Gurley, at one time a trooper in a Confederate cavalry unit led by the skillful and notorious General Nathan Bedford Forrest. Born and raised on a plantation near Huntsville, Alabama, Gurley enlisted in the Confederate army in August of 1861, although he was not a fire-breathing secessionist. In the summer of 1862, Gurley was involved in guerrilla operations against the Union throughout northern Alabama.[4]

Having served well under Forrest, General Braxton Bragg appointed Gurley to the rank of captain with orders to recruit a company of cavalry whose mission it was to raid and harass Union supply lines, while the main body of Rebel troops made their way to Kentucky. Gurley gathered together some men from the mountains of Madison County, Alabama, calling the group "Gurley's Company." They were later augmented by a company of horse soldiers under Captain Joseph M. Hamrick, 4th Alabama Cavalry. Altogether, Gurley's force consisted of about 150 men. The Rebels were kept busy harassing the enemy, raiding and destroying Union property. It was while on this assignment that Gurley and his men encountered and killed General Robert L. McCook.[5]

For more than a year following McCook's death, Gurley was a hunted and hated man, having in the public mind of the North committed a cold-blooded, cowardly murder. Finally, on August 26, 1863, some encouraging news surfaced. Troops under Colonel Edward M. McCook, a cousin to the late General McCook, rounded up 11 guerrillas near Larkinsville in northeast Alabama. During the night, they snared a man named Ragsdale who was identified as one of Gurley's men who was with him when Robert L. McCook was shot. Edward immediately sent a dispatch to General Alexander M. McCook, announcing the good news.[6]

Then, on September 5, 1863, while the brigade of Colonel Daniel McCook was marching toward Chattanooga under the command of Major General William S. Rosecrans, they camped on Hurricane Creek, near Huntsville, Alabama, within a "mile of Frank Gurley's farm." The area had been "laid to waste" at the order of Rosecrans. Later that day, they passed by "old man Gurley's farm," presumably the father of the alleged murderer. After passing the farm, Colonel McCook ordered Colonel J. T. Holmes and 50 soldiers from the 52nd Ohio to go back and burn all the buildings with the exception of one or two "negro shanties." Holmes recalled that he was "ordered to deaden the fruit trees and fire the fences." Daniel McCook said, "make it an utter desolation."

Holmes and his detail moved toward the farm by quick step and went to work, carrying out their orders with enthusiasm. They burned about 25 buildings, including the house where Frank Gurley was born. Holmes recalled seeing no white people on the plantation. The McCook "avengers" struck a terrible blow against the Gurley family.[7]

Not long thereafter Frank Gurley was captured by a Union force led by Captain Lawson Kilborn. It was learned that the fugitive was holed up sick at his brother's house near Brownsboro, Tennessee. On October 13, 1863, the Union troops arrived at the house. Captain Gurley's brother surrendered without a struggle while Frank attempted to escape through the back door. But Kilborn had posted guards at the rear of the house, and when Gurley made his exit, they fired upon him, hitting only his clothing. Wisely, Frank B. Gurley surrendered and was taken to Brownsboro with his brother, where he was placed under heavy guard.[8]

Captain Kilborn had been leading a scouting party under the orders of Brigadier General George Crook, who proudly circulated a dispatch applauding the capture of the "notorious Captain Gurley ... who murdered General McCook." Crook affirmed that he had caught several of Gurley's men and hoped to "clear the country of guerrillas before long."[9]

The Union men at Brownsboro wanted no part of waiting for a court to convict and hang Gurley. The excitement and threats of mob violence was such that Gurley was taken to Stevenson, Alabama, on October 29, 1863, and from there by train to Nashville. A dispatch from C. Goddard, Assistant Adjutant-General of the Army of the Cumberland, to Brigadier General Gordon Granger in Nashville, advised the latter to "keep him securely; we may be able to convict him of murder. Report his arrival."[10]

However, he almost didn't arrive at all, for while en route, Gurley thought about trying to escape after the train was bombed and derailed, but he was too sick to make the effort. At Nashville he was chained and stuck in a small, cramped, dungeon-like military prison cell. A long, hellish ordeal was in the works for Gurley. Conditions were so bad that he wrote to the Union commandant asking to be shot rather than wait for trial.

Because he was in the clutches of the Union, and Northern sentiment was dead set against him, Southerners were certain he would not get a fair trial. Still Gurley had competent legal representation. His lawyers were dedicated to proving that their client was merely acting as an enemy combatant and not a murdering marauder. Yes, he killed McCook; in fact, he admitted it. But at the time he opened fire, he had no way of knowing that he shot a general, for McCook was out of uniform and therefore had no brigadier star on display. And furthermore, Gurley said that after the chase he returned to the house where McCook had been taken, introduced himself as a Confederate captain with Forrest's cavalry and apologized. McCook accepted his fate like a soldier, expressing no bitterness or anger. The general died as a casualty of war, not unlike so many thousands of others who were shot or succumbed to disease.

In a strange twist of fate—that had negative forebodings for the accused—the acting judge advocate for the Department of the Cumberland was none other than Captain Hunter Brooke, the same man who was attending to the ailing McCook at the time of the killing. Brooke issued a written statement to Colonel Joseph Holt, judge-advocate general of the U.S. Army, on November 3, 1863, saying, "I can positively swear that he [Gurley] was a guerrilla acting without authority from the Confederate Government."[11] Gurley, he said, was not a commissioned officer. He was the leader a band of murderers that used the war as an excuse to rob, kill and destroy property. This, of course, was a critical factor in the case. If Gurley was not an officer acting under orders, it would be easier to convict him of murder.

Secretary of War Stanton and others pressed hard for a trial and a conviction. Brooke's letter to Holt was referred to Stanton who agreed that Gurley was to be tried for the murder of Robert L. McCook. Holt made this known in a letter to Brooke and added that Gurley should be tried for any other crime he may have committed "without a commission from the so-called Confederate States." Holt closed his letter with a postscript, noting that while Congress gave field generals authority to carry out executions, in the case of

Gurley, "political considerations may be involved," and recommended that should he be convicted, the president would have the last word.[12] Thus it appears that Holt had a preconceived notion of guilt, but for "political" reasons, he was not anxious to have some general immediately order Gurley's execution.

No doubt Holt and the rest of the Union army brass were concerned that should they hang Gurley, then the Confederates would feel justified in retaliating by hanging some captured Union officer. A hanging contest was psychologically distasteful; it was something that both sides would want to avoid.

Confederate brigadier general Nathan B. Forrest wanted to prevent this sort of thing from happening. In a gentlemanly letter to Union general Stephen A. Hurlbut, Forrest—upon learning of the opening of the trial of Gurley for the "so-called murder of General McCook"—calmly explained the Southern view of the matter. Captain Gurley, he said, "was then, and is yet, a Confederate soldier and officer, and that he should be treated and regarded as such." As if his word could be persuasive, Forrest pointed out that Gurley had been "regularly mustered" in to the Confederate army in July of 1861, and from that time, served as officer under his command.

Forrest was angered that generals from the other side could be so easily seduced by prejudiced newspaper reporting and biased popular opinion. He urged Hurlbut to look at actual facts and muster records and ignore the falsehoods and exaggerations in the newspapers. Hoping to convince the Union brass to look at the matter in light of reason, Forrest acknowledged that guerrillas were bad men and he too wanted to drive them from the country. A man who burned houses was unworthy of any consideration and he would shoot such a man, whether he was from the North or South. Captain Gurley, however, was not such a man and deserved to be treated as a prisoner of war and nothing more.[13]

Gurley may have been just a captain among many captains, but his cause gathered a great deal of support. The Confederate secretary of war, James A. Seddon, intervened. In a letter to General Joseph E. Johnston, Seddon called Gurley a "gallant partisan," who was captured while lying ill in Alabama. Seddon said that Gurley had killed Robert L. McCook, and for that he was about to be tried as a "bushwhacker or an unauthorized insurgent." He wanted Johnston to "take proper steps to warn against and prevent such outrage."[14]

The governor of Alabama sent a letter to Jefferson Davis, beseeching the president of the Confederacy to protect Gurley by "the most prompt and stern retaliation." Gurley, he said, was known to him to be "an honorable, high-toned gentleman, modest, unassuming, and universally popular both as a citizen and soldier." As tension mounted, a letter made its way to General U. S. Grant, making it known that the South was prepared to do all it could to "secure the safety of Captain Gurley or to vindicate his memory and its indignity to our Government if his life is taken."[15]

Despite the insistence of General Grant that Gurley would get a fair and impartial trial, no one in the South expected that he would be acquitted. But they could not stop the trial, and on December 2, 1863, a five-officer military commission was convened in Nashville, by order of Major General George H. Thomas, charging that Frank B. Gurley, "citizen," a man "not being lawfully in the service of the so-called Confederate States ... did feloniously shoot with a revolving pistol and kill Brig. Gen. Robert L. McCook ... lying sick and helpless in an ambulance."[16] Captain Hunter Brooke appeared as a witness.

At the trial two versions of the incident were presented. The Union version had McCook murdered while he rode in an ambulance, in a sick and helpless condition, leading to the unavoidable conclusion that "Gurley had no thought of capturing prisoners, but was determined on nothing less than taking life." McCook's attempt to surrender was rudely ignored. Gurley was just an outlaw riding with outlaws, "for the purpose of killing, robbing, and plundering Federal soldiers and loyal citizens of the United States."

The Confederate stance was that Gurley was a commissioned officer doing his duty as a soldier. Riding in civilian clothes didn't make him a civilian. If he had no uniform it was because the South couldn't afford to provide them for all of its men. He was made a captain under a law that allowed the president of the Confederacy to appoint bands of "partisan rangers." It was pointed out that Union general Lovell H. Rousseau, a friend of the McCooks, testified that he believed Gurley was an officer and not a guerrilla.[17]

Gurley was ably defended by two lawyers who produced compelling evidence from credible witnesses. They argued that Gurley's case was given high priority because of the "victim's influential family."[18] They insisted that had Gurley killed a lesser known man, he would not have been charged with murder. All of this was unavailing, however, for on January 11, 1864, the commission unanimously decided in favor of murder and death by hanging.[19]

The sentence, of course, surprised no one because the Union, from the War Department on down, was determined to have its revenge. Anger and indignation steam from much of the Army correspondence on the subject. Letters and reports indicate that the McCook killing and its aftermath were used to emphasize the illegitimacy of the Confederacy. Gurley was often referred to as a "so-called" captain in the "so-called" Confederacy. Jefferson Davis was called the "so-called President of the rebel Confederacy."[20]

While Gurley languished in a hellish prison, waiting for his date with death, the case moved up the chain of review. General Thomas agreed that the verdict was just, but then he strangely suspended the hanging and recommended the sentence be reduced to five years in prison due to the unusual nature of the incident. It appears that Thomas had softened and was now looking at the shooting as an act of war, despite popular belief and desire. His recommendation was sent on to Washington, D.C.

Thomas' recommendation of a reduced sentence was ignored, and Lincoln ordered the sentence be carried out, even though he was warned that the Confederates would retaliate with their own hangings of Union officers. Perhaps understanding the risks involved, Lincoln "pigeon-holed" the verdict. Captain Hunter Brooke declared that threats to retaliate "saved his neck" until "President Lincoln, with his usual kindheartedness," ordered Gurley held in Nashville.[21]

While observers on both sides waited to see what would happen next, Gurley remained confined, believing that at any day he could be executed. Then, strangely, after nearly a year in prison, he was transferred to Louisville along with a group of prisoners to be exchanged for the release of Union captives. Because he was under a sentence of death, Gurley probably did not think he was among those who would be released.

The select group of prisoners was moved by rail to Pittsburgh where an angry mob had gathered, hoping to treat themselves to a lynching. The mob was left disappointed as the train moved on to Baltimore. Then, on March 17, 1865, just a short time before the war would end, the unexpected happened. Due to an army mix up, a sickly Captain Gurley and the other prisoners were exchanged and he was allowed to go free. In a weakened condition, but feeling good about being free, he went on his way toward home.[22]

Apparently all this transpired without direction from the War Department for some weeks later Secretary Stanton ordered that Gurley be put in irons and sent to Washington. He learned, however, that it was too late for that, for the resilient prisoner—so recently under a death sentence—had been processed for release.[23] Other official correspondence makes it clear that Gurley's release was the direct result of an order from General Grant dated February 17, 1864, that "all prisoners, without exception, who were or had been in close confinement or in irons," were to be exchanged. The general in charge of the prisoners followed the order to the letter and later admitted that he had no knowledge that Gurley "was charged with the murder of General McCook" until after the exchange.[24]

During the summer of 1865, a letter surfaced that injected some new and startling information into the Gurley/McCook story. The letter, dated July 25, 1865, was sent by A. L. Brewer to Dr. John McCook, uncle of the late Robert L. McCook. Pointing the finger of guilt in another direction, the letter explained that the "notorious Capt. Kirk, who had charge of the gang that murdered the General," had been killed. Kirk was taken prisoner after the war ended, and in an attempt to escape, he was shot dead. "There can be no mistake in this matter," concluded Brewer.

This letter was printed in the *New York Times*, in connection with an article that outlined the villainous career of Captain Kirk, strongly asserted to have been the killer of Robert L. McCook. It describes Lewis Kirk as a mean, illiterate, intemperate blacksmith who had been taken into the Confederate army, having been pardoned for killing a man in a drunken row. He once killed a man simply for refusing to "hurrah for Jeff Davis," and was also credited with killing "refugees and contrabands," the latter a reference to runaway slaves. Although he was a "cold-blooded murderer," he was nevertheless promoted to Captain by General Braxton Bragg upon the recommendation of General Forrest and "placed in command of a gang of desperadoes."

If some people were unconvinced that the *Times* had named the killer of McCook, it was also mentioned that a belt belonging to the late general had been recovered. It was in the possession of Lieutenant Lamb who got it from Rebel general Gilbert when the later was captured at Lamb's Ferry on the Tennessee River. The *Times* article reads: "Gilbert, on handing his sabre-belt to Lieut. Lamb remarked that the belt belonged to the Yankee General McCook, who was killed by Kirk, and that the belt had been given to him by Kirk, who stated that he had taken it from McCook after he had been shot." The belt was in the possession of Major Brewer (probably the A. L. Brewer who wrote Dr. McCook) who was going to send it to the mother of Robert.[25]

While this revelation adds some intrigue to the story, it is uncorroborated and flies in the face of official records of the confession and conviction of Frank B. Gurley. The man who shot McCook was not the dastardly described "Capt. Kirk." Importantly, Gurley made no effort to deflect the crime toward Kirk or any other person. He killed him, but in his mind, the killing of McCook was simply an act of war, for which there was no punishment.

After the surrender of General Robert E. Lee at Appomattox, Frank B. Gurley, the true and apparently repentant killer, took the oath of allegiance to the Union and received his parole. He then indulged in the pleasures of the flesh for a couple of months in Gallatin, Tennessee, after which he went home to Huntsville, Alabama. On November 6, 1865, the staunch defender of slavery, who lynched at least two black men during his army days, was elected sheriff of Madison County, perhaps thinking his past was safely behind him.

Gurley—with his Houdini-like talent for escaping death—had captured the imagination and respect of Huntsville folk. Upon entering that city following his election as sheriff, he was given a hero's welcome. All this was too galling for Northerners. A reporter for the *Cincinnati Commercial*, who witnessed the spectacle, said the convicted "murderer" of "one of the noblest men and one of the best Generals ... that the late war produced," was "literally covered with flowers." The reporter was shocked over the way, "women, many forgetting their sex in their eagerness to greet him, made their appearance upon the streets in garments I had never before seen." Expressing the opinion of his Ohio readers, the reporter fumed over "this pet" Gurley's election victory over a "good Union man."[26]

The war had ended but Gurley's troubles were not over yet for the War Department wanted him re-arrested, imprisoned and expeditiously hanged. Brigadier General Joseph Holt, the judge-advocate general, was outraged over Gurley's impromptu release. In a communication to the secretary of war on September 8, 1865, Holt wrote: "The murder of General McCook by this man [Gurley] was one of cowardly and cold blooded atrocity, and no pains should be spared for enforce the forfeiture of life which the sentence has declared."[27]

On November 24, 1865, Gurley was re-arrested, placed in irons and cast into a Huntsville prison. He was to be hanged on the 30th. President Andrew Johnson ordered the execution to be carried out and the War Department sent word to General George H. Thomas to execute the sentence of death on the prisoner. Then, on the 28th, Johnson ordered that the execution be suspended until further orders.[28]

The year ended, war was over and Gurley was still alive. People continued to rally to his side. One of them, Joseph C. Bradley, wrote to President Johnson from Huntsville, Alabama, on November 27, 1865. He claimed he was in a unique position to recommend clemency for Gurley, for he (Bradley) and others were once arrested by the condemned man in 1862 for being disloyal to the Confederacy. Instead of being hanged as a spy, Bradley and the others were well-treated by Gurley, earning their lasting respect. Furthermore, Gurley had conducted himself as a "good and loyal Citizen of our Government" up to the time he was re-arrested.[29]

This infuriated Joseph Holt, who sent a letter to President Johnson, dated January 5, 1866, demanding that Gurley be executed. Holt outlined the case against Gurley and noted that Lincoln approved the death sentence on May 11, 1864, and on August 29, 1865, Johnson also approved the execution, although due to some "misapprehension" the condemned man had been released.

Holt angrily dismissed a petition sent to the president by "many citizens of Alabama" and their claim that "Gurley did not in fact commit the murder," and, further, that since the war ended, he had been a loyal and law abiding citizen. Holt urged the president to reject such false sentiment and reflect on the evidence presented at the trial. "This was murder," said Holt. "A Major General [McCook was actually a brigadier general] of the United States service" from a "family of heroes whose conspicuous ability and ardent patriotism have illustrated the annals of the war," while in the act of surrendering, "was

From left to right: the Honorable Joseph Holt, General Robert S. Foster, Colonel H. L. Burnett and Colonel C. R. Clendenin. Joseph Holt was determined that the death penalty handed down in the Frank B. Gurley case be carried out. He was the judge advocate general of the Union army, and from the outset of the case, Holt wanted Gurley tried for murder, ignoring Southern pleas that Robert L. McCook's death was merely an act of war. Holt had been a key player in the prosecution and execution of the Lincoln conspirators, and he threw his energy into putting into action the hanging of Gurley. But the execution that had been approved by Lincoln was postponed for what Holt called "political reasons."

shot down like a dog." To pardon Gurley under such circumstances, Holt said, would be "disrespectful to the claims of the living and to the memory of the dead."[30]

When Holt wanted something, he wanted it desperately, and he usually got what he wanted. He was one of the legal architects in the arrest, trial, conviction and execution of Lewis Powell, *aka* Payne, David Herold, George Atezrodt and Mary Surratt, who, along with John Wilkes Booth, conspired to assassinate President Lincoln. As the principal prosecutor at the conspiracy trial, he could boast that he put in motion the legal machinery that resulted in the hanging of Mary Surratt, the first woman executed by the federal government. Johnson did not stand in his way then, so why was he doing so now?

Despite Holt's adamant arguments for death, President Johnson did not order the execution to proceed. Seventy-four of Gurley's friends and supporters, some of them Unionists, sent a letter to the president, asking for mercy, stating that Gurley was a wronged man and not "an original secessionist."[31] Johnson may or may not have been moved by the letter and the soft image of the man that it conveyed, but he ordered the execution be suspended after learning that—due to Gurley's popularity—locals threatened to kill Yankee officers stationed in northern Alabama.

Due to the reluctance of the government to hang him, Gurley remained in prison until April of 1866 when he was released for good. The angry, wild publicity that surrounded the killing of McCook seemed to have dissipated over the years as Gurley's release was announced rather unceremoniously in the press. A small article in the *Nashville Union and American* simply said that he had been released by order of the president, upon the recommendation of General Grant.[32] There was no pardon; Gurley was simply another ex–Confederate soldier.

The game-changer was undoubtedly a letter from Grant to Johnson, dated April 10, 1866, recommending that Frank Gurley "be released as having been duly exchanged." Grant noted rather forthrightly that when it was decided to exchange prisoners, even those Rebels who deserved death, the Union did so because the deal provided relief for a "class of union prisoners undergoing the severest suffering." Having gained the desired benefit of the exchange agreement, Grant wrote, "we cannot honorably avoid fulfilling our part of the contract." Johnson endorsed Grant's recommendation and Frank Gurley was set free.[33]

Having gained his freedom a second time, Gurley returned to his home near the town of Gurley, Alabama. He was emaciated and bore the mental scars of a long and harsh ordeal, but he was lucky to be alive, having survived two dates with the hangman. He went on to become one of Alabama's most respected citizens and was involved in organizing the Ku Klux Klan in Madison County.[34]

Not long after Gurley's second release a mysterious letter appeared in the record, authored by James M. Mason, a Confederate trooper who rode with Gurley and was one of four men who were actual eyewitnesses to the shooting of Robert L. McCook. By June 10, 1866, when Mason wrote a curious letter to Gurley, only the two of them were left alive.

Mason's letter expressed great and lasting friendship for Gurley and coyly suggested that it was he (Mason) who shot McCook. Choosing his

President Andrew Johnson was forced to deal with the Gurley matter after the assassination of President Lincoln. Johnson was stubborn by nature and his hatred of the Southern slave-holding aristocracy was well-known. Therefore he could not be expected to show any sympathy toward Frank B. Gurley, the man convicted of murdering General Robert L. McCook. And yet when faced with ordering the execution, Johnson wavered and suspended it. Johnson was soon put under pressure to order the hanging, but General U. S. Grant intervened, insisting that Gurley be released in order to facilitate the release of Union prisoners, suffering in Confederate prisons. Johnson endorsed Grant's recommendation and Gurley was, at long last, a free man.

words carefully, Mason wrote that his name had "been used in the affair" and that "if it was any manner an advantage to you, I was glad it was used." As if writing about a secret that only he and Gurley knew, Mason claimed an unselfish motive, for he "believed that if the guilt could be shifted from yourself to me, the thing would go much easier with me that it would with you."

The "thing" was the shooting death of Robert L. McCook, a matter that apparently haunted both men, neither of whom wanted to be known as a soldier who killed a sick and bedridden officer from the other side. While generals were fair game, it was far more "honorable" to shoot one who was in a position to shoot back. Mason asked Gurley to preserve the letter, probably thinking it might come in handy at some future time. "I believe we understand each other in this matter."[35] Apparently they did understand for the two remained friends for the rest of their lives. Mason went on to become a minister and died in 1909.

In 1880, a second mysterious letter appeared in newsprint, having been obtained by the *Stark County Democrat* of Canton, Ohio. That newspaper received the letter from H. W. Gunnison, who had served in the war with General Alexander M. McCook, brother of Robert L. McCook. Gunnison said that he got the letter from Edwin S. McCook, another brother, who said that he (Gunnison) could use it "as he might deem proper."

The letter—allegedly written by Gurley and addressed to Edwin S. McCook—dated June 8, 1866, is soft and apologetic in its tone and content. Gurley not only denied killing Robert L. McCook, but contended that he was "not nearer than three hundred yards, and really I did not know that he [McCook] was wounded until six or eight hours after it was done." He denied having any knowledge of anyone else shooting McCook. Furthermore, on the day in question, Gurley insisted that his mission was to capture a herd of cattle "the federals were driving to Winchester, Tennessee." Gurley also tried to put to rest the old rumor concerning Captain Kirk, insisting that no man by that name ever rode under his command.

Gurley expressed regret over the death of McCook, saying, "I hope the impression will be erased from the mind of yourself and the balance of the relatives and friends of General McCook, that I was the man who killed him." In closing he wrote: "You can do with this letter as you like best."[36]

The letter is suspect for a number of reasons. First of all it contradicts the official record of the trial which contains Gurley's admission that he fired the fatal shot as an act of war. The official record also says nothing about the federals having a herd of cattle with them, nor do any contemporary newspaper articles mention cattle. Second, it seems odd that Edwin S. McCook, who was shot and killed in 1873, would have kept quiet about the letter, for being a brother of the slain officer he would have no doubt harbored strong feelings against Gurley. More likely, had the letter been genuine and received by Edwin, he would circulated it in the press as a means to denounce the hated Rebel. Finally, the date of the letter dampens its credibility, because Gurley was a free man in June of 1866, and he had no reason to stick his neck out again in a public way by composing such a letter less than two months after re-gaining his freedom. It makes no sense that he would want to swing a careless branch at a hornet's nest when simply living out his years quietly would better serve him.

But that wasn't the end of it. In 1910, another Gurley statement surfaced in *The National Tribune*. This one repeated the assertion that the Rebel cavalry was after a herd of cattle that Union soldiers were driving on the road to Winchester, Tennessee. Gurley recalled that a firefight started and after the Rebels proved to be "too strong," the Federals retreated. The Rebels then came upon "wagons all running back in the road." One wagon struck a branch "hung low," causing the top to come off, revealing three men, "one in full uniform and one in shirt sleeves." Gurley stated that he shot three times at the man in the full uniform, and one shot hit the man in "shirt sleeves," meaning McCook. "I was not closer than 50 yards to him when he was shot."

In this version of the tragic incident, Gurley insisted that McCook was "not sick but was in command of his brigade." Furthermore, McCook was not riding in an ambulance but rather in a "school wagon, as it was more comfortable."

Perhaps to give the story more credence, the article in the *Tribune* featured a statement by Alabama judge, David D. Shelby, who "personally knew Captain Frank B. Gurley," a "regularly enlisted soldier and commissioned officer." The judge averred that in 1876 or 1877, he "came into possession" of the sword worn by General McCook on the day he was fatally shot. The judge gave it to a Chicago man who in turn presented it to John J. McCook, the brother of the late lamented general. Judge Shelby concluded his statement by saying that the "fight between Gurley's company and the squad of General McCook's command" was "not unlike a thousand skirmishes that occurred ... during the civil war."[37]

All this was too much for Union veterans to take, and less than two months later, the McCook supporters fired back, calling Gurley's story of the general's death a white-wash of the truth. Ohio veterans vehemently denied there were any cattle on the road that fateful day, and furthermore, they insisted that any man who claimed he put together a military unit by enlisting "sick soldiers" and "little boys" was not a commissioned officer but rather a common guerrilla. Their harshest criticism, however, was to rebuke the claim that McCook was not sick and that both sides had engaged in a firefight. "Not a shot was fired by our side at this time, for the attack was an unexpected one" that occurred when a party of about 50 armed men "sprang from the thick brush by the roadside and began firing."[38]

The story about the death of a popular and gallant Union general seemed destined to swirl dreamily, endlessly, without settling into a pillar of truth that satisfied both sides, not unlike the countless other Civil War stories about the exploits and misadventures of men unwittingly drawn into the complex and tragic tapestry of war. But if there was a measure of truth, it was that Brigadier General Robert L. McCook would forever be numbered among several other illustrious generals in the Ohio "galaxy of stars."[39]

Frank B. Gurley lived quietly and peacefully in Alabama, faithfully attending reunions of the 4th Alabama Cavalry regiment. To ordinary Southerners he was a good man and a good citizen. To those who wrote about the Civil War from a Southern point of view, General McCook and all the other Union soldiers who were killed got just what they deserved. In 1909, a writer from Huntsville, Alabama, blithely concluded that McCook was killed by Gurley in a skirmish with Rebel cavalry while trying to escape, and that the Federal report that the general was sick and riding in an ambulance was false and made for the purpose of inciting hate and violence against the people of Alabama.[40]

Vindicated by his fellow Southerners, Gurley—having twice escaped the gallows—eased into old age while memories of August 5, 1862, continued to shift in an old whirlwind that, like the war itself, would not easily settle into dust. But the post war years saw some strange magic at work and Gurley became a good friend of someone who knew the McCook family well. And as a gesture of good will, Gurley returned the sword of Robert L. McCook to the slain man's survivors.[41]

Despite the time spent in prison, the years of suffering and mental anguish, Frank B. Gurley lived to be an old man, dying on March 29, 1920, outliving many of the men who so eagerly sought to end his life at a much earlier age.

Daniel McCook, Jr.

7
A Fighting Lawyer in Kansas

"Here's for a Colonel's epaulets or a soldier's grave..."
—Daniel McCook, Jr., 1861

Of the many McCook men who willingly, and with great pride, joined the Union army, none did so with more boyish enthusiasm and mature determination than Daniel McCook, Jr. Existing photographs reveal the image of an intense man of ambition and energy, traits that Daniel displayed throughout many campaigns of the Civil War. While his eyes are soft, his gaze is strong, indicating an inner strength and a singular sense of purpose. He was studious, ambitious and goal directed toward success for himself, his family and his country. As was the case with so many young men of his time, it was the Civil War that shaped his personal destiny and put to good use his aggressive nature along with his talent and courage, for when he volunteered, he became a soldier in earnest.

Born in Carrollton, Ohio, on July 22, 1834, Daniel was the eighth child of Daniel Sr., and Martha McCook. In childhood, his physical condition was considered delicate, and he spent much of his time indoors. But he was endowed with sufficient inner strength to overcome the common maladies that cut short the life of many vulnerable youths, and he grew into a six-foot tall, thin man. Described as "overstudious," and a lover of poetry, he attended LaGrange University at Leighton, Alabama, because his family thought that a warmer climate would be beneficial. He graduated in 1857, having studied forensics and debate.[1] And importantly, Southern culture failed to ensnare him, for he remained true to his family's anti-secession, pro–Union beliefs.

He returned to Ohio in good health and studied law at the firm of his brother, George W. McCook, and Edwin M. Stanton in Steubenville. Dan was in some very heady company. His brother George was not only an outstanding and influential lawyer, but one of Ohio's leading political figures in the Democratic Party. Stanton, also a Democrat and a brilliant lawyer, dropped the law in favor of politics and served as the attorney general on President

James Buchanan's cabinet. After the war was well underway he signed on as the secretary of war in the Lincoln administration, replacing Simon Cameron.

A letter from George W. McCook, written November 2, 1857, says, "Daniel is doing well, and is drinking in the law every day, but he has had recently *a shake* or two. He thinks he will have no more and I trust this may be a farewell to the fatal old legacy of his residence in Illinois."[2] The emphatic mention of "a shake or two" possibly means that Dan was afflicted by epilepsy.

If so, it was something that neither conquered nor controlled him, for after "drinking in" a healthy measure of statutes and cases, he was ready to be a lawyer—but not in Ohio. Instead he traveled to Leavenworth, the largest city in Kansas Territory with a view of practicing law there.[3] On January 1, 1859, Daniel McCook, Jr., a studious lover of poetry, books and military history, became the fourth partner in a new law firm. It was made up of fellow Ohioans turned westerners, William Tecumseh Sherman, known as "Cump" to his family, and his step brothers, Hugh and Thomas Ewing, Jr. The Ewings had settled in Leavenworth in 1856 where they established a law practice along with a land speculation business.

Their decision to live and work in Leavenworth is a curious one. The new town seemed unlikely to attract educated and sophisticated people, and yet the population growth was quite fast and vigorous. Founded mainly by slavery men, anxious and determined to spread the "peculiar institution" further west, Leavenworth became the headquarters for a number of pro–South, militant organizations. But they would not have the field to themselves, and before long the abolitionist opposition arrived. After that, tension and violence increased as the two groups squared off in a life and death struggle. The great slavery debate had once again grown legs and in Kansas found new ground ready to be bloodied.[4]

It was in this strange place that four transplanted Buckeye lawyers, young, eager and confident, and all destined for the history books, decided to settle. But they were quite uncertain where their legal business would come from in a town peopled by men seeking to make a fortune, but with little money to invest or pay lawyers. Seemingly undaunted, the firm of Sherman, Ewing and McCook opened an office on Main Street, between Shawnee and Delaware streets, in the second story of "a shabby looking, tumbling, cotton wood shell," fronted with a "dingy sign." The office was reached by walking up a "crazy-looking stairway" on the outside of the building. It was so treacherous that "none ever went without dread of their falling."[5] It would seem that the young lawyers were set up to attract only the bravest of clients. But such was the state of affairs in the rough, frontier boom town of Leavenworth, Kansas Territory, in 1859.

In those days there were no rigorous bar examinations to pass and often little or no law schooling, especially in the West. If a man wanted to be lawyer, he usually read law in some law office, absorbing as much of the Blackstone treatise as he could, and then applied for and was admitted to the bar. For example, Sherman had no legal training at all, but was an exceptionally bright and aggressive fellow, so he was admitted to the practice of law in Kansas by Judge Samuel D. Lecompte based on "general intelligence."

Never at a loss for self-deprecating words during his pre–Civil War days, Sherman sent a letter to his wife, Ellen, saying, "If I turn lawyer it will be bungle, bungle from Monday to Sunday."[6] Nevertheless he "turned lawyer," and with a mental shrug, accepted his fate, while believing that there had to be some calling that would bring him success. A graduate of West Point, and a former army officer, the self-conscious and highly intelligent Sherman had tasted too much disappointment in his young life, and therefore, hated to look foolish when he tried something new.

When the law practice consisted of just Sherman and the Ewing boys, business was rather scarce, so with the addition of a fourth partner, there was even less work to pass around. A small population meant a paucity of clients, and having set up shop way out west, the chance to land a well-heeled client was slim at best. And to make matters worse, the frontier was papered

A proud, youthful Daniel McCook, Jr., in the uniform of the Union army. He was the eighth child of Martha and Daniel McCook, Sr., and as a boy, he experienced bouts of weakness and otherwise bad health, but he was mentally strong and intelligent and eager to learn. After college in Alabama, he read law in the office of his brother, George W. McCook, and his brother's friend, Edwin M. Stanton. For a short time in the late 1850s, Daniel practiced law in Leavenworth, Kansas, in partnership with William T. Sherman and Hugh and Thomas Ewing, all of whom were destined for fame and success. The arrangement was short lived, however, because at the outset of the Civil War, Dan joined the Union army in an outburst of patriotism. He became a leader and served with dedication and determination until he died from wounds received at the battle of Kennesaw Mountain in Georgia in 1864.

with lawyers and would-be lawyers, all hoping to make a buck. Many had something going on the side such as surveying, writing deeds or washing dishes. Sherman sensed the futility of it all when he quipped, "business must swell considerably before we have work for us four."[7]

Daniel McCook, Jr., came to Leavenworth with good legal credentials and strong family ties to the Democratic Party and to Illinois senator Stephen A. Douglas, one of the nation's most powerful and prominent politicians. Dan was a political animal too, but he threw himself into the practice of law, showing considerable ability. In a western town with too many lawyers, McCook more than held his own. He loved the courtroom dueling as it matched his aggressive personality. Among his projects was a "high profile murder case."[8]

McCook was a hard and willing worker, once traveling to Colorado to collect fees owned to the firm's creditors. In court, he was an ambitious and "intense partisan," sparring freely with the judges, always, it seems, finding ways to criticize them. It was a time when court work was conducted in an off-the-wall, circus atmosphere, featuring a mixture of rough humor and sarcasm, with little of the dignified decorum found in the big city courts. The rules either went out the window or were made up on the way to a resolution of the case. To be a successful frontier lawyer, one had to be a verbal bulldozer.

Socially, Dan McCook was remembered in Leavenworth as "one of the best of the 'good fellows.'" He delivered the 4th of July oration in Leavenworth in 1859. Kansas was just then a hotbed of dissension, with anger and hate flowing to and from both pro-slavery and anti-slavery groups, but it was fertile ground for someone like Dan McCook, who might want to flex some political muscle. "Bleeding Kansas," as it was called, was a dangerous but ideal place for men of strength and ambition. An outspoken Democrat, young McCook fearlessly attacked the new Republican Party, although its strength in Kansas was growing.

The Ewing brothers were definitely politically ambitious, and, like McCook, eager for success. They were members of a wealthy, prominent and politically connected Ohio family. Hugh and Tom were described as men of high culture, "considerable natural abilities, cold and impassive temperaments."[9] Their father, Thomas Ewing, Sr., a very successful Ohio attorney, had been elected to the United States Senate in 1831 as a member of the Whig Party.

William T. Sherman—who hated politics and politicians—was just nine years old when his father died. Fortunately, Billy grew up in the Ewing family as a step-brother to the Ewing boys, and in 1850 he married their sister Ellen. Thus he had strong connections and from time to time he relied on those ties, however reluctantly, as he was constantly dogged by disappointment and failure in the business world. He had failed in the banking business in San Francisco, but he liked the solitude and newness of the frontier and was not a quitter.

A Kansas newspaper said that Sherman had lived on a farm near Topeka before moving to Leavenworth, where he apparently acquired some interest in real estate for a city plat map displayed a "Sherman's Addition." His neighbors remembered his "abrupt manner; reserved, yet forcible, speech and character." A writer for a Leavenworth newspaper said this of Sherman: "He sphered [sic] himself to our perception as the most remarkable intellectual embodiment of *force* it had been our fortune to encounter."[10] To state it another way, Sherman—like a rocket—might go spiraling into the unknown, but he would never be a sputtering mediocrity.

Always an assertive man and never at a loss for words, Sherman's legalistic pontificating irritated his partners, all of whom decided that Cump should have his day in court, and, if need be, take his lumps. It was not long before Sherman had to take a case to trial. In a panic because he had no trial experience, he sought out his partners who were nowhere to be found. He was forced to plead to the judge that he was merely an office lawyer, that his trial partners were absent, and requested a continuance.[11] This the judge refused, causing Sherman to lose his composure. He was then verbally attacked by opposing counsel and lost the case. An article in the *Leavenworth Conservative* states that Sherman "had been pettifogged out of the case by a sharp, petty attorney ... in a manner that offended his intellect and convictions."[12]

The disconsolate lawyer tramped back to the dingy office in a foul mood, "swearing to have nothing more to do with the law." McCook, "appearing innocently and smiling secretly," intervened and rescued the beleaguered client, but Sherman was finished as a trial lawyer, thereafter devoting himself to real estate.[13] He had more than enough intellect to be a lawyer; what he lacked was the temperament and the willingness to be a punching bag.

In his *Memoirs of W. T. Sherman*, Sherman wrote about a case involving real estate. The client, whom he called an Irishman, came to the office one day in need of a lawyer to represent him in a squabble with his landlord. The client had rented a lot from a fellow Irishman and built a small shanty on it. The rent was five dollars a month. The tenant added a lean-to to the shanty that extended onto an adjacent lot also owned by the landlord. As a consequence, and to his tenant's utter surprise, the landlord raised the rent to $7.50. The tenant fell behind and was sued. Sherman took careful notes and, after collecting a five dollar advance fee, placed the file in McCook's hands.

Thinking he was done with the case, Sherman was surprised when about a month later the client came rushing into the office, saying that he had to be in court that very day and, of course, needed his lawyer. Sherman could not locate McCook so he went to court and asked for a continuance. This the judge refused and the case went to trial with the landlord plaintiff winning. The victorious landlord was then in a position to execute on the judgment by taking the shanty.

A down-on-himself Sherman and his equally chagrined client explained the dilemma to McCook who immediately came up with a plan to thwart execution of judgment and save the shanty. McCook suggested that the client get a few of his neighbors together and move the shanty off the landlord's lot and onto a lot owned by a non-resident. This was done and "the grasping landlord, though successful in his judgment, failed in the execution, and our client was abundantly satisfied." Thus ends a tantalizing little anecdote that, like countless others, suffers from lack of detail. But then writers of autobiographies always choose to leave out some facts.[14]

Probably because there was a shortage of clients, politics offered an alternative. While the anti-political Sherman took no position in the great slavery debate, just then plaguing Kansas, his law partners, Tom Ewing and Dan McCook—aggressive and outgoing men—had no such scruples against getting their hands dirty in retail politics. Both were showing a greater interest in politics than in the law. Tom was a Republican candidate for a seat on the state constitutional convention and Dan for the same office as a Democrat.[15]

As for Sherman, he had had enough of Kansas and the shaky law partnership. He inquired of his friend General Don Carlos Buell about an opening in the army, and upon learning that no position was available, Sherman took a job as the superintendent of a military college in Louisiana.[16] But after a relatively short time on the job, his tenure was interrupted by the secession of several Southern states. Although Sherman was fond of the South, and had no quarrel with slavery, his true devotion was to the Union. And after collecting his pay, Sherman returned to the North, perhaps with the anticipation that he would soon be back in the army. The firm of Ewing, Ewing and McCook continued without him.

Sherman's friend Dan McCook entered the ranks of married men on December 5, 1860, marrying the lovely Julia Tebbs, a Southern girl from Leesburg, Virginia. Her family had relocated in Kansas where her father, Algernon S. Tebbs, practiced law and ran a plantation. She met Dan and he was smitten "beyond hope of redemption." The gala wedding took place in Platte City, Kansas.[17]

Dan had entered a relationship that was destined to be placed under stress because of his wife's ties to the South.[18] And not long after Dan and Julia tied the knot, South Carolina severed its connections with the Union. America had entered into the secessionist winter, a season that wore a mask of death. Changes were erupting with alacrity, and within two months of the McCook wedding, Kansas was made the 34th state in the Union, on January 29, 1861. It entered the Union slave-free. The "free-state" movement had prevailed after a long, intense struggle against the pro-slavery element.

Dan had very little time to enjoy his marriage, nor was he able to devote his talents to politics and the law, as secession followed by war intervened and rearranged the lives of the young lawyer and his companions, insuring that each would occupy a unique place in American history. With the winds of war blowing, lawyers McCook, Sherman and the Ewing brothers redirected their energy. Personal goals could wait; their country needed them. One apocryphal source says they nailed a sign to their office door that said: "This office is closed." The same source proclaims that the three men sent a telegram to Edwin M. Stanton containing the terse message: "We are yours to command—Sherman, Ewing and McCook."[19]

The foregoing quotes, however, echo with a fanciful ring, for when the war began, Stanton was not part of the Lincoln administration. He was appointed secretary of war in January of 1862. Nevertheless, the Leavenworth law partnership was, in fact, history, and before long the partners would be wearing the Union uniform. All would eventually earn the rank of general.

Daniel McCook was in no hurry to leave Kansas, but he stopped looking for clients. Instead he sought out soldiers for the cause, despite Julia's urging that he not be rash. Non-action, however, was impossible for McCook, a man who never saw a challenge that he could let pass by.

A veteran recalled many years later that a young Dan McCook went directly to the governor of Kansas and asked: "'Governor, do you want recruiting officers?'" After the governor replied in the affirmative, McCook said: "'Well, I want a commission as captain.'" The governor sized up the bold young man and decided then and there that he had the makings of captain and the request was granted. Then, shaking the commission as he departed, McCook said: "'Governor, that means a yellow sash or six feet of earth.'"[20]

The war had not yet begun, but McCook was already gung ho. Like many others, he believed that because of secession, it was only a matter of time before the shooting started. Although he had no military training or experience, he was willing to learn the skills of soldiering as he went along. Along with other willing volunteers, Dan McCook and his friend Jim McConigle created a Leavenworth militia made up of several companies of troops.[21] McCook was made captain of one of the companies, the "Shield's Guards," later the "Leavenworth State Guard."[22]

On February 20, 1861, young Daniel McCook wrote to the secretary of war, Joseph Holt, offering to the government "the services of the volunteer militia company, consisting of sixty rank and file infantry, which I at present

7. A Fighting Lawyer in Kansas 109

command." He and his men were willing to serve "against any powers which the public need may require."[23] Daniel McCook, captain of the Leavenworth State Guard, asked only for an "equal chance" for his men and himself to serve.[24] His tender of troops on the eve of war was the second on record, behind only that of Charles H. Volk, from Elk County, Pennsylvania.[25]

Secretary of War Joseph Holt was a Democrat serving on the cabinet of President James Buchanan. Holt would go on to serve in the Lincoln administration as the judge advocate general and would prove to be a staunch and effective supporter of the war. But when he received McCook's letter, Holt could do nothing but file it away for Buchanan was not about to take action toward addressing the threat of secession and war. The president's inclination was to sympathize with the South, and struggling with divided loyalties, he spent his final days as commander in chief floundering, vacillating—probably cursing his fate.

Daniel McCook, Jr., the would-be soldier, seemingly in hot haste to enlist, paused to reflect on the hostile developments in the South. Then he seemed to draw back a bit. Despite his patriotic gesture, an uncertain McCook turned to his brother George for answers to questions that burned in his psyche. In a letter dated March 10, 1861, Daniel asked for George's "superior wisdom" about where the country was "drifting" to; everything "seems dark to me." He expressed some uncertainty about his priorities when he said that he knew "not whether to support the Administration or oppose 'coercion.'" Daniel had attended college in the South and was living in Kansas, next to the Missouri powder keg, so a moment of hesitation is probably consistent with his conservative background. But the pace of events caused his "army fever" to rise with the "war clouds." He closed his letter to George by saying that his wife married a lawyer, not a soldier, and if he became a soldier, he would be guilty of breach of contract.[26]

Julia, of course, wanted Dan to stay neutral and probably influenced him to look with sympathy on the Southern ideals, for, after all, he was a Democrat, the party of the South. But all equivocation ended with the firing on Fort Sumter. It was then that Julia must have fully realized that she had married a fighting man. The entire McCook family was fired up and ready to fight against what they deemed treason. The South had attacked the lawfully constituted federal government and that was treason. It would be impossible for Dan McCook to be neutral or favor the South and still stay in the good graces of his pro–Union family.

When Lincoln called for volunteers in April of 1861, Kansas had little money and no state militia. Nevertheless, following the fall of Fort Sumter in Charleston harbor, the desire to enlist among Kansas men was great. In less than a week more than 60 companies were forming.[27]

The timing was good because on April 20, 1861, during the early stages of the rebellion, a rumor circulated through Leavenworth that Rebel raiders from Parkville and Independence, Missouri, were planning an attack. The mayor took the lead in forming a militia consisting of the Leavenworth Light Infantry, divided into the Union Guards and the Shield's Guards. Daniel McCook commanded the latter unit. Ten days later, however, the arrival of regular army troops led to the disbanding of the guard units, with letters of thanks to McCook and the other leaders.

McCook and his fellow volunteers were far from being finished as soldiers, for by May 20, 1861, the strong, pro–Union town of Leavenworth had organized 18 companies of infantry. The new Kansas soldiers were ordered to Missouri—one of the border-states that President Lincoln was determined should not secede.

Missouri had been admitted to the Union in 1820 as a slave state after protracted debate led to what became known as the Missouri Compromise. Before the historic compromise was reached, the House of Representatives sought to restrict slavery in Missouri by prohibiting the further introduction of slaves and by requiring it to grant freedom to the children of all slaves once they reached the age of 25. The Senate, however, would not agree with the House and ultimately Missouri was created as an unrestricted slave state, but with the proviso that slavery would not be allowed north and west of the new state.[28]

Largely agricultural in its economy, Missouri was dominated by small family farms instead of large plantations. As such, the number of slaves per household was small compared to the Deep South where "slaveocracy" was firmly entrenched. In 1860, slaves consisted of 9.8 percent of the total population of Missouri.[29] In the years leading up to 1860, slave holders were constantly coming into conflict with those who disapproved of the practice of owning another human being. St. Louis, the leading city of the state, was industrial and cosmopolitan, more Northern than Southern, thus bearing small resemblance to other Confederate cities.

As the growing population of St. Louis and state was increasingly made up of large numbers of easterners, along with German and Irish immigrants, the relatively small number of black faces might have caused a visitor to think that slaveholders were in the minority. And in fact the number of slaves decreased from 1850 to 1860. Yet those who were wedded to the "peculiar institution" were not concerned with statistics and not about to cave into pressure from abolitionists. Like the country, Missouri was divided north and south, meaning the Northerners generally preferred to stay in the Union while the Southerners favored secession.

Led by South Carolina, Southern states, one by one, seceded from the

Union, causing Missourians to face the vexing question: to secede or not to secede? While Missourians were not a part of the planter aristocracy, many had strong personal or economic ties to the South. These people had a Southern identity and outlook. But there was another vocal element composed of members of the old Whig Party that believed secession was not the answer.

While many of the Whigs refused to follow their colleagues into the Republican Party, they held firm to the Union, thinking that remaining loyal was the best way to ensure the future of slavery. The rising controversy is reflected in emotionally-charged rallies and mass meetings by "unconditional Unionists" and "Southern Rights" groups. Hard-nosed secessionists not only had to deal with abolitionists but also with pro-slavery anti-secessionists.

On March 4, 1861, as Abraham Lincoln was taking the oath of office, Missourians met in St. Louis to debate secession. With both sides engaged in plotting and dark intrigue, and were ready to explode into violence, Missouri congressman Francis P. "Frank" Blair, a strong Unionist, and his allies persuaded the delegates to oppose secession. After the vote taken on March 22, the result was 98 to 1 against secession. Missouri had declared its loyalty, deciding that there was no "adequate cause" to leave the Union. But the overwhelming pro–Union vote did nothing to blunt the anger and energy of the die-hard secessionists, so when soldiers started shooting at one another, Missouri was still a hotly contested prize, with both sides exerting energy and determination, struggling to gain majority approval.[30]

No one understood this volatility better than the new president. At first he seemed to ignore Missouri and allowed the commander of the Department of the West, Brigadier General William S. Harney, to run things. But Harney had a distinct liability: he was a Southerner and his wife was a member of a pro-secession family. While Harney was entirely loyal, he was relieved at the urging of the Blair family. This left Frank Blair and Brigadier General Nathanial Lyon in charge of the Union fortunes in Missouri.

Fortunately for the president, he had a capable general at St. Louis in the presence of Brigadier General Nathaniel Lyon, a West Point graduate with impressive academic credentials. Lyon—a friend of Frank Blair—was in charge of the arsenal located on the outskirts of St. Louis. In May of 1861, the arsenal was under the curious and envious eye of Confederate supporters, led by the secessionist governor, Claiborne F. Jackson, a true "son of the South," and an energetic opponent of the Lincoln administration.[31] In response to Lincoln's call for troops, Jackson wrote that the president's request was "illegal, unconstitutional and revolutionary in its objects, inhuman and diabolical...."[32]

While he would provide no troops for Lincoln, Jackson threw himself into preparing secessionists to resist Union efforts toward keeping Missouri out of the newly formed Confederacy. He came to St. Louis for that purpose, meeting with General Daniel M. Frost, the officer in charge of a volunteer militia. The volunteers were gathered at "Camp Jackson," on the west side of St. Louis. They were drilling, oddly enough, under the Union flag, while poised to make a run at the arsenal on behalf of the Confederacy, when the opportunity presented itself.[33]

The St. Louis arsenal was, at that moment, the key to holding the state of Missouri for the Union. Within in its confines was the largest stock of weapons and ammunition in the country, and should it fall into secessionists hands, the balance of power would tip dramatically in their favor.[34]

Lyon, a Connecticut Yankee and a decorated veteran of the Mexican War, was known for his fiery red hair and angry, aggressive manner. Lyon also served on the Plains in the 1850s at remote outposts in what later became Dakota Territory, namely Fort Pierre, Fort Lookout, Fort Randall, all near the Missouri River, and at a cantonment at the mouth of the Big Sioux River.[35] Called "Daddy" by his men, Lyon was a strict disciplinarian. He stood opposed to everything Southern, including slavery and states rights, making him the ideal specimen for leading the Union charge in Missouri. He understood the gravity of the situation and after sending some surplus munitions into Illinois decided to do a pre-emptive strike on Camp Jackson.

General Frost, in command of the militia at Camp Jackson, was a native of New York and a graduate of the U.S. Military Academy, where in 1844 he finished fourth in his class. Frost was brevetted for gallantry in the Mexican War, and after leaving the army in 1853, he became a wealthy St. Louis businessman engaged in manufacturing. Among his other ventures was an interest in a series of fur trading posts on the upper Missouri River in Sioux Indian country, soon to become Dakota Territory.

Frost's partner in the fur trading business was John B. S. Todd, the leading political figure from the newly-created Dakota Territory. A Kentucky-born West Point man, Todd was a cousin to the president's wife. Although he ranked only 39th in the class of 1837, he was skilled at using political leverage, and he re-entered the Union army with the rank of brigadier general. Born into an aristocratic, slaveholding family, Todd was, nevertheless, a motivated pro–Union man with more to gain from his connection with Lincoln than from his frontier enterprise with Frost.

Severing ties with Todd meant Frost was giving up the lucrative fur trade in order to support the Confederacy. He made a bad decision, for the fiercely loyal Lyon gathered together a rag-tag group of citizens, "political marching clubs" and some regular army soldiers, combined them into a "Home Guard" and went on the offensive. On May 9, Lyon, dressed in "female garb," toured the Rebel camp in a barouche undetected, gathering intelligence.[36] The following day Lyon's approximately 7,000-man "army," consisting largely of German immigrants, surrounded Frost's militia group of about 700 men, whereupon the latter immediately—and wisely and quietly—surrendered.

While Lyon and his victorious troops were marching their prisoners through St. Louis, they encountered an angry and vocal pro-secession element that quickly took on the aspect of a mob. The loud demonstration drew out many observers including William T. Sherman, erstwhile lawyer, not yet in the army, on business in St. Louis with his son Willie.

As Sherman watched in horror, shouting turned to shoving and then shots were fired on the mob by Lyon's men. Sherman was among the many that fell to the ground when bullets whirred overhead.[37] An Englishwoman,

An illustration in *Harper's Weekly* of a mob attack on Union soldiers in St. Louis, Missouri, May 10, 1861. The Civil War had barely started and yet the state of Missouri was tearing itself apart. The mob attack in St. Louis was an example of the kind of violence that would plague the state throughout the war, as communities turned against one another over the issues of secession and slavery. The melee erupted as Confederate prisoners were being marched down Fifth Street. It started with angry words and ended in an orgy of gunfire and death. When the shooting stopped two dozen people were dead or badly wounded, including women and children.

a Southern sympathizer, was seen screaming: "The Black Dutch [meaning Germans] are killing them all. They are shooting women and children in cold blood!"[38] When it was over more than two dozen people, including some women and children, were dead or badly wounded in the "battle" of St. Louis.[39]

On May 11, St. Louis witnessed another wild eruption of violence and bloodshed. According to eyewitnesses, the German Home Guards were marching on Fifth Street from the arsenal when someone fired into their ranks. A soldier was hit causing his comrades to shoot indiscriminately into the crowd of spectators that had been hissing and booing. Many of the anti-Union spectators joined the shooting affray. "The shower of balls for a few minutes was terrible, and bullets [were] flying in every direction, entering the doors and window" of homes and businesses. When it was over, six people, including four soldiers, were dead and many others were wounded.[40]

Despite the bloody outcome of the two incidents, the Union had secured the arsenal and St. Louis remained safely in Lincoln's hands. Controlling the arsenal and St. Louis was a critical step in the process of keeping Missouri in the Union.

On July 3, 1861, the Lincoln administration created a new Western Department that included Missouri. To take charge of the Union's western forces, Lincoln chose John C. Frémont, a charismatic and hawk-eyed man who was already a much-admired public figure.[41] Frémont was an explorer who earned the title "Pathfinder" for his ground-breaking explorations of the Northwest and the far West where he worked with the army corps of topographical engineers. Frémont was involved in the conquest of California during the Mexican War and he was an original Republican.

To the South, Frémont, and others like him, were "Black Republicans," dangerous revolutionaries whose activities threatened the plantation culture by encouraging slave uprisings. The "Black Republicans" were cursed and condemned in the harshest terms. They were "'infidels, freelovers, interspersed by Bloomer women, fugitive slaves and amalgamationists.'"[42]

Frémont—proud to be a radical—had been his party's nominee for president in 1856, and in 1861 he had the backing of the politically potent St. Louis family headed by Francis P. Blair, Sr. Frémont was indeed a strident, anti-slavery Republican whose every desire was in favor of the emancipation of black people. While Lincoln wasn't ready to pull that lever, he considered the appointment of the magnetic and radical Frémont to be both militarily and politically popular and expedient.

Unfortunately, Frémont was not able to combine his intellectual qualities with military skills, for he had none of the latter. He lost no time angering the people of Missouri, and he once issued a proclamation stating that any armed person caught within his lines would be subject to a court-martial and immediate execution. During his short tenure, he worried, fumbled and bumbled while in command in the West, a poor choice by Lincoln, who gave him the rank of major general.[43]

In 1856, when Frémont ran for president, Lincoln was an enthusiastic supporter and campaigner, making more than 50 speeches for the pathfinder candidate. But with the war underway, Lincoln was about to find out that the man he once thought was presidential timber was not up to being an effective wartime general.

When Captain Daniel McCook arrived in Missouri, along with his band of Kansas volunteers, he quickly learned that the troubled state was a hotbed of violence and ripe for all-out war. The loss of Camp Jackson did nothing to dampen the spirits of the Confederates, although Governor Jackson and his staff were on the run, heading in the direction of southwest Missouri. Driven from the capital at Jefferson City, the governor never lost his faith in the South and continued his struggle to rally supporters and organize resistance.

While most Missouri boys of a pro–Rebel bent joined the Confederate army, others gravitated to guerrilla or bushwhacker gangs who killed as if they enjoyed killing. Daring and charismatic men like William Quantrill—who once taught school in Ohio—and William T. "Bloody Bill" Anderson led their gangs that included the notorious Frank and Jesse James on raids against Union troops and pro–Union civilians in a deadly reign of terror for the duration of the war. Commerce was shut down, money was worthless and the social order was cast to the wind.

The people of Missouri were made to suffer as the rudderless state without unity or identity became a killing field. Neighbor suspected or feared neighbor forcing an unhealthy isolation within a climate of fear. A man could spend one day peacefully at work plowing his field, and the next day find himself strung up in one of his own trees, should he say the wrong thing to the wrong band of men.

A man who described himself as a "Loyal Virginian" wrote a letter to the *New York Times* pleading for help against the "outrages of the jayhawkers in Johnson County." He complained that innocent people "are daily and nightly hung or shot by bands of men from Kansas wearing United States uniforms," including a young woman who was hanged for "refusing to reveal her Father's hiding place."[44] The well-intended plea was to no avail as hangings, shootings and beatings without number occurred throughout the luckless state during the course of the war.

Captain Daniel McCook's company of volunteers, a part of the 1st Kansas Infantry regiment, was mustered into the federal service at Leavenworth, Kansas, on June 3, 1861. Although they were full-fledged soldiers, with company flags made by local women, the 1st Kansas and the men of the 2nd Kansas Infantry lacked uniforms that were normally furnished by the community from whence they came. Many of the men were poorly armed, some with old "smoothbores."[45]

Nevertheless, both Kansas units and the 1st Iowa Infantry were present at the battle of Wilson's Creek in Missouri serving under Brigadier General Lyon. Some spirited skirmishing took place on the 8th and 9th of August and a full-scale battle broke out at dawn on August 10, 1861, in the wooded hills ten miles southwest of Springfield when Lyon attacked a numerically superior, yet poorly armed and untrained Confederate force led by General Benjamin McCulloch, a former Texas Ranger. McCulloch's troops were part of a desperate attempt by the Rebels to gain ground in Missouri.[46]

Lyon, a die-hard Unionist, with his old-line Yankee Puritan blood boiling, was bitterly angry at the South for leaving the Union that he loved, and he was aggressive and willing to take great risks. He was actually retreating from McCulloch's advance when he stopped near Wilson's Creek, about ten miles from Springfield, where the Rebels were encamped.

That night—knowing full well that he was outnumbered—Lyon decided to attack the next morning, hit hard, kill some secessionists and then safely resume his retreat. He was determined to keep southwest Missouri out of Rebel control. Lyon divided his small army, ordering German native General Franz Sigel—who strongly supported the assault—to hit McCulloch's rear at sunrise on the opposite side of Wilson's Creek. Sigel attacked as ordered but his assault sputtered to an inglorious halt when he mistakenly believed he was firing on Union soldiers. Disaster followed in the wake of Sigel's decision to cease fire and his men broke and ran away, leaving all the fighting to Lyon's forces.[47] Despite missing Sigel's support, Lyon's frontal attack was successful in driving back the Southerners on what was called "Bloody Ridge."

Then Lyon was shot and killed while leading a charge. Without his strong leadership, his troops faltered and retreated toward Springfield and didn't stop until they reached Rolla, southwest of St. Louis. The Confederates, while getting the best of Federals, were too used up to follow. Still their gain in territory was considerable.[48] The battle of Wilson's Creek became a rallying cry and bragging rights for the Confederates in the early stages of the Civil War when they were hungry for some success in Missouri. The War of the Rebellion had arrived in Missouri.

While the official record does not reveal the role of Daniel McCook in the battle, he was present. Both the 1st and 2nd Kansas volunteer regiments were in the thick of the fighting and taking casualties, so it could be said that McCook received his baptism by fire on that hot August day in 1861.

Major John A. Halderman commanded the 1st Kansas at Wilson's Creek.

His official report states that his regiment was deployed as skirmishers in front of a battalion of regular army infantry. Then, receiving orders from General Lyon, the 1st Kansas advanced to the fighting at a "double-quick." They soon found themselves "in the very face of the enemy," fighting a Rebel force "four times their number." And yet for five harrowing hours they bravely held their ground in the face of "murderous fire of artillery and infantry." When the shooting stopped, a regiment of about 800 men had been cut down to about 500. Major Halderman closed his breathless report commending the men and officers who "fought with a courage and heroism rarely, if ever, equaled."[49] The *New York Tribune* covered the battle at great length, and while Dan McCook was not in the headlines, it was reported that the Kansas and Iowa boys fought like tigers.[50]

Lieutenant Colonel Charles W. Blair, who directed both Kansas regiments in the fierce battle, commended "every officer and man … for their self-possession and courage." Blair noted that although he was forced to retire, his men did so in good order, holding up remarkably well under heavy fire.[51]

It was that kind of battle. Fighting was intense, up close and personal as volley by volley the bloodied ranks on both sides were depleted by musket and flintlock fire. It was early in the war, but it was the savage side of combat. It was a bizarre and horrific struggle. The combatants seemed to lose their sanity and were caught up in a frenzy of killing and death, as if nourished by the smell and sight of blood. The battle reached a fatal, almost unconscious stage when men understood that their deaths were imminent and acceptable. Author Shelby Foote likened it to "reciprocal murder."[52] The 1st Kansas regiment suffered 106 deaths at Wilson's Creek, which ranks fifth all-time on the list of dead men from a single battle.[53]

It was also called the hardest four hours of fighting ever experienced in the United States, and coming on the heels of the disastrous defeat at Bull Run, it was nothing for the Union to cheer about. And yet the country was inspired and eventually Congress passed a resolution commending the men and officers who, "under the command of the late General Lyon, sustained the honor of the flag, and achieved victory against overwhelming numbers." The president ordered the resolution to be read in front of every regiment in the Union army.[54]

Any soldier who survived the fierce battle was off to a good start, having been singled out by Congress and lauded for bravery. New soldier Daniel McCook could not have failed to be inspired by the valor of his fellow soldiers and by the loyalty and reckless courage of General Lyon and the example he set for his men. Lyon, more than any other, was known as the man who saved Missouri for the Union. Here was a man to emulate.

The dithering, eccentric General Frémont, on the other hand, was not.

With the department permeated by graft and corruption, he fell out of favor with the Blairs who wanted him out. It was said that "when the Blairs go in for a fight, they go in for a funeral."[55] While Lincoln was not in the mood to go to that extreme, he was only too happy to accommodate his friends, the tough-minded Francis P. Blair, Sr., and his family. Acting with firmness, he removed Frémont and named General David Hunter interim commander on October 24, 1861. Not long after, Lincoln handed the command to Major General Henry W. Halleck who restored order to the department, renamed the Department of Missouri.[56]

On November 9, 1861, Daniel McCook was given a captain's rank in Company H, 1st Kansas Infantry. Being a soldier seemed to suit him. His new role embodied some of the elements of a frontier lawyer except that it encouraged and permitted a broader form of aggression. He had seen enough in Missouri to understand just what was at stake for his country, his family and himself. He understood that when the need to accept sacrifice was imposed from without, a man of courage willingly stood tall in the face of danger. What could be more glorious and worthwhile than to be a part of a war that crushed an unlawful rebellion and preserved the Union? Friends long remembered that as he left for a new field of endeavor, an exuberant Captain McCook said: "here's for a Colonel's epaulets or a soldier's grave."[57] It was a declaration of his willingness to make the effort and, if necessary, the sacrifice.

McCook spent the rest of his war-shortened life serving the Union cause, in quest of military rank, recognition and victory. Who can say that were it not for the Civil War, Daniel McCook, Jr., would have become a successful lawyer, married, raised a family and then died without historical consequence? But like others throughout history who are lifted out of the quiet and ordinary by larger-than-life events, McCook was not fully in charge of his destiny. Because of the war he was destined for fame, honors and a place in history—but not as a Kansas soldier. He was an Ohioan, and like his brothers Charles, Robert and Alexander, he eventually became associated with an Ohio regiment: the 52nd Ohio Infantry, a military unit of his own creation that became known as "Dan McCook's Regiment."

8

On the Warpath: Shiloh, Perryville and Stones River

"Move forward the legions now encircling the Secession monster, and crush its power to the earth."—*Cincinnati Daily Times*, May 7, 1862

After tasting battle and "seeing the elephant" at Wilson's Creek, Captain Daniel McCook began a long and dangerous odyssey as a soldier, marching into the dark heart of a widening war, following orders, giving orders, all the while playing a critical role in the great struggle to defeat the rebellion. Having left the Kansas regiment, he was attached to the 2nd Division, Army of the Ohio, serving with his older brother, Brigadier General Alexander M. McCook, the division commander. Dan's next fight and contact with carnage and death was at the battle of Shiloh, an epic two-day fight on April 6 and 7, 1862, near Pittsburg Landing on the Tennessee River.

The battle took its name from a small, rough-hewn Methodist church that rural parishioners called Shiloh. It was named after an Israelite town in Ephraim. The name meant "place of peace."[1] The plain-looking church stood about five miles from the bank of the Tennessee River and has been compared to a "respectable Tennessee corncrib."[2] Be that as it may, the Union soldiers casually set up their tents around the crude but holy edifice, while unbeknownst to everyone boards from the church would soon be confiscated to craft coffins for the dead. The church, however, would prove far too small to accommodate the demand for body boxes.

Aside from Wilson's Creek, the warring armies had not fought a major battle since Bull Run in July of 1861, but the Union, under a lightly regarded Major General U. S. Grant, had captured Fort Henry and Fort Donelson in northwestern Tennessee in February of 1862, thus opening up the way to Nashville. For his efforts, Grant was given some media applause and notice from the Lincoln administration. Suddenly, he was the up and coming general.

Always an aggressor, Grant ordered his Army of the Tennessee, consisting of six divisions, to occupy the area around Pittsburg Landing, near the northern border of Mississippi. Major General W. T. Sherman, in command of the 5th Division, was in charge of establishing an encampment.

Many of the soldiers were new recruits, later described by a Shiloh veteran

General U. S. Grant in a reflective pose. He graduated from West Point in 1843 and went on to serve in the U.S. army, including a stint in the Mexican War where distinguished himself as a leader. But in 1854, he resigned his commission because of a drinking problem. As a civilian, Grant's life was nothing noteworthy, a sad status that ended when the Civil War began. With America at war with itself, Grant proved to be a natural soldier. He quickly worked his way up the ranks and as a brigadier general he captured two Confederate forts in rapid fashion. Lincoln was greatly impressed. But it was at the epic two-day battle of Shiloh, in Tennessee, April 1862, where a stubborn U. S. Grant turned defeat into victory, causing both North and South to take notice of his ability.

as having never "'fired a shot in anger.'" For days the men lazed and lounged, "devoured their rations and slept in peace." They received no orders to prepare for an attack, for no attack was expected. But, as it turned out, "insufficient scouting and carelessness at headquarters" nearly proved fatal for the Union army at Shiloh.[3] One writer coyly suggested that no trenches were dug because "West Pointers in the army never had been instructed in the use of shovels."[4]

The large gathering of Union troops attracted the attention of the Confederates under General Alfred Sidney Johnston. Having received intelligence that the Army of the Ohio under Major General Don Carlos Buell was on its way to Pittsburg Landing to join Grant, Johnston decided to strike Grant before Buell arrived. Moving up from Corinth, Mississippi, Johnston and General Pierre T. G. Beauregard concocted a plan to attack Grant by surprise and destroy his army. After that the Confederates would move north, deal with Buell, retake Kentucky and be in a position to threaten Union cities on the Ohio River.

General Johnston was a man held in esteem throughout the South and was highly regarded by Confederate president Jefferson Davis. Johnston had served with distinction in the Mexican War. He was living comfortably in California when the Civil War started as a respectable member of the pro-slavery Democratic Party, appropriately called the "Chivalry." True to the company he kept, Johnston chose the South and returned to Richmond. After trading civilian clothes for a uniform, he immersed himself in army life. He was expected to rack up victories, but after assuming control of the Confederate troops in the western theater, his fortunes turned sour following dramatic loses at Fort Henry and Fort Donelson. He was looking for redemption at Shiloh.

Johnston's second in command, the gallant and soldierly General Beauregard, had emerged as a hero in the mind of the Southerners for his performance at Fort Sumter. He was hated by Jefferson Davis and he returned the hate. But men in the ranks generally liked the egotistical, self-styled "Little Napoleon," known as the "Creole," because of his dark complexion. A trooper writing to his father expressed the views of many Rebel soldiers, saying, "we love that little black Frenchman."[5] The expectation was that Beauregard would assist Johnston in hammering the Union in a great battle for dominance in Tennessee and throughout the Mississippi River valley.

For thousands of Union troops leisurely and peacefully encamped near Shiloh Church, a battle seemed most unlikely. Spring was making its way to the large encampment that featured orchards in full bloom and a woodland "carpeted with violets."[6] Looking back on those almost halcyon days, a veteran recalled that the grand Union army was merely a large gathering of "loungers," most of whom were inexperienced greenies. Army life seemed quite good just then, the men enjoying their rations along with the "vended luxuries" from the sutlers' wagons sold to them at "a profit of 100 per cent." Day after day, a squadron of cavalry would ride out toward Corinth and return with an "all is well."

But it was all a delusion. The Union army was ripe for the picking for it had lapsed into a state of complacency. On April 3, just three days before the attack, a group of officers and men were allowed to take a "picnic excursion" south of their encampment on the road to Corinth. They encountered some Rebel cavalry and dismissed the threat as merely a few bushwhackers, not worth cancelling a picnic over. Later that day they heard the muffled sound of drums in the distance, unmistakably getting louder. This should have been taken as the rhythm of an army on the march, but it too was laughed off by the picnickers. Still, some suspicion was in the air, and after about an hour, the group trekked back to camp.[7]

That muffled drumbeat that the Yankee excursionists heard was the Rebel army led by Johnston on the move toward Pittsburg Landing. It was little more than an ill-clothed and poorly-fed mob, and yet, on the morning of April 6, 1862, several brigades rushed forward in wave after wave of men yelling and shooting, while their bands played "Dixie." General Sherman, who had pooh-poohed the idea of preparing for battle, caught a glimpse of the onrushing enemy soldiers through his field glasses. In the next instant his orderly was shot in the head, causing Sherman to cry out: "'My God, we are attacked.'"[8] The Rebels had, indeed, successfully pulled off a surprise attack against unprepared Union troops, driving them back toward the Tennessee River. Thousands of panic-stricken Bluecoats took refuge under the river bluffs and neither encouragement nor threats could make them get back into the fight.

General Johnston had boasted that he and other officers would soon be watering their horses in the Tennessee River. He had also promised his troops that he would lead them in battle. In keeping his promise he was shot and died of a leg wound, proving that in battle, confidence and aggression can quickly give way to suffering and death. Beauregard stepped up and managed to conduct the battle and win the first day's fight. Had he pursued the battle into the evening hours, he might have succeeded in driving Grant's men into the Tennessee River, or at least force them to surrender. But his men were exhausted and he called off the attack, satisfied with the day's work of blood.

That night Rebel troops bedded down in the camp abandoned by the Yankees. Many went to sleep in Union tents, believing that the next day's assignment would be a mop up operation. The *New York Times* reported that a thrifty Beauregard ordered his troops not to destroy the "camp equipage taken on Sunday" because he fully expected to complete the work of destroying the Union army on Monday.[9] Then the Rebels could take it all and move on.

Relief for Grant's army was on the way, however, as the Army of the Ohio under Major General Don Carlos Buell began arriving at the landing while exhausted troops on both sides slept. This tipped the balance in favor the Union, and on the 7th, the Rebels were mauled and driven back to Corinth. Beauregard led his bedraggled army on the Corinth road after leaving behind his dead. He was observed by a Rebel soldier as riding "leisurely back to the rear, as cool and unperturbed as if nothing had happened."[10]

Something awful did happen over two days in the spring of 1862. The mighty clash of arms at Shiloh produced heavy casualties on both sides in numbers that shocked both the North and South. It was correctly declared to be the bloodiest battle ever fought on the continent. Captain Daniel McCook was a member of General Alexander M. McCook's staff, and while the battle raged, he was kept busy delivering orders and messages from his commanding officer. He survived the perilous duty, the Union won an important victory, and Captain McCook was commended for his brave service. But the terrible battle was both troubling and inspiring for the young captain, and he wrote an article about it that was published in *Harper's New Monthly Magazine.*

In the article he states that on the evening of April 5, soldiers from the 2nd Division of Buell's Army of the Ohio arrived at Savannah, Grant's headquarters, and waited for steamboats to take them to Pittsburg Landing. Captain McCook had been ordered ahead to see to the embarkation of the troops on a of flotilla steamboats. He was careful to recall that all was confusion and chaos in Savannah. He could find no one to report to or to get instructions from, as officers ran to and fro, bands played, drummers pounded, soldiers told tales of valor and disaster, frantic wagons jammed the trails and in the background there was the sound of artillery. One of the most memorable features was the sight of wounded men being loaded aboard the steamboats, "calm, quiet, and uncomplaining."

The young captain was struck by the sight of 9,000 men standing alert and waiting to be loaded on steamboats. He was impressed that when it started to rain hard, the drenched men used their "India-rubber" blankets to cover their rifles and ammunition. Their readiness and obvious concern for the fight ahead seemed to bode well for the Union. And yet the night was long and beset with "rumors of defeat, of panic, of men rushing into the river, of the annihilation of our army" and the prospect of surrender.

Captain McCook and men from the 2nd Division had a pre-dawn breakfast on the *Tigress.* Then, as the sun rose, a band performed "a gem from Il Trovatore," thus providing haunting music to match the horrible sight that greeted the disembarking soldiers. Getting off the steamboat was more chaotic than getting on as "rations, forage, and ammunition were trampled in the mire by an excited, surging crowd." McCook recalled seeing and hearing "sutlers, camp-followers, and even women adding their voices to the Babel of sound."

Strangely, out of all this chaos and confusion came military order, as the men marched out toward the firing. On their way to the front, the men came face to face with the carnage of the first day of battle. As they passed by mangled bodies, "the misty morning gave a ghostly pallor to the faces of the dead." McCook deployed fine writing skill with his explicit description of the awful scene: "The disordered hair, dripping from the night's rain, the distorted and passion-marked faces, the stony, glaring eyes, the blue lips, the glistening teeth, the shriveled and contracted hands, the wild agony of pain and passion in the attitudes of the dead—all the horrid circumstances with which death surrounds the brave when torn from life in the whirlwind of battle, were seen as we marched over the field."[11] It was how many men would remember Shiloh.

Shiloh, forever associated with suffering and death, was a word that came out with a shudder. It was the kind of experience that defied description, although Daniel McCook described conditions as well as any other eyewitness and far better than a writer of a distant time. The ultimate living nightmare, the Shiloh experience doubtless produced scores of bad dreams, if one was able to sleep after participating in the military madness. It was grotesque and it was horror incarnate and it was the first battle of the Civil War that produced wreckage and carnage on a massive scale that shocked the nation. Thoughts that once were cheerful turned to thoughts of charnel. In addition to human casualties, horses by the hundreds were killed adding to the stench that lingered in the smoke that wafted over what had been a lovely land of quiet woods and small farms. Surviving soldiers, visiting civilians, journalists, doctors and grave diggers would long remember what they saw and felt and could not be faulted for believing that both the Union and Rebel armies, having fought with unprecedented ferocity, had been rendered insane for two days in April of 1862.

The 2nd Division was fully caught up in the madness. After having boarded the steamer in the middle of the night, and steaming up river to Pittsburg Landing, the division disembarked and "bivouacked in the pouring rain until morning." Up before daylight, they "entered the thickest of the desperate engagement," fighting until the Confederates were routed and in retreat. All this with nothing to eat but "the scant, uncooked rations in their haversacks."[12]

The battle of Shiloh represents a major turning point in the war, causing both sides to accept that there were many terrible battles yet to be fought.

America was facing a prolonged, indefinite war that would stretch into the future on a long timeline of sacrifice and suffering. Grant himself had cast aside any hope of a short war, noting that after Shiloh, he "gave up all idea of saving the Union except by complete conquest."[13]

When word of the battle reached Washington, D.C., Secretary of War Edwin M. Stanton issued an "order giving thanks" to the men and officers of the Union army. He also gave thanks to "the Lord of Hosts, for the recent manifestations of His power in the overthrow of rebels and traitors."[14] The message of thanks expressed the gratitude of the nation for the bravery, sacrifice and success of its army, and it underscored the strength and importance of religious faith in American life in a time of great crisis.

The Shiloh experience did not cause Daniel McCook, Jr., to wilt or grow weary of army life, for his heart was decidedly in favor of crushing the rebellion and advancing his military career. But he did fall sick and needed rest. After a protracted illness, McCook returned to the army and threw his energies into organizing the 52nd Ohio Volunteer Infantry regiment.

To help with recruitment, an advertisement was placed in an Ashtabula, Ohio newspaper, headlined with this notice: **"50 Men Wanted for the 52nd Regt."** To attract volunteers, the ad promised that "clothing and subsistence" would be provided, along with a $25 bounty and a month's pay in advance. Volunteers could expect to receive $13 to $24 per month. The ad proudly announced that the "appointment of Daniel McCook as Colonel of this regiment has done much to add to its popularity."[15]

A Cleveland newspaper ad went even further, offering as a recruiting inducement a $75 bounty and a month's pay in advance, and $100 payable at the time of discharge. Reminding young men that "the war is not ended yet," the notice boasted that the leader of the new regiment was Colonel McCook, "one of the Fighting McCooks." All those interested in becoming soldiers were invited to the "RECRUITING HEADQUARTERS," at the "Phoenix Saloon" located at the corner of Superior and Water streets in Cleveland.[16]

McCook took to the stump, giving rousing, passionate and patriotic speeches in an effort to gather recruits. He was not fussy about the quality of the men who would soon be soldiers, and 20 of them were recruited from the Ohio State Penitentiary after receiving their pardon in exchange for enlisting.[17]

Finally, the regiment was mustered in on August 22, 1862, at Camp Dennison, Ohio, with "one company too many." The *Cincinnati Daily Times* proudly declared that the 52nd was a "splendid body of men" and that Colonel McCook "will soon have them in fighting condition."[18] In a letter to Major General H. G. Wright, Ohio governor David Tod asked that Colonel McCook, whom he called a "well-tried" and experienced officer, to be assigned to "your most important" position.[19]

The 52nd Ohio became Dan McCook's obsession; it was his pet project as well as *his* military unit. He looked after it as if it were his child. And like a devoted and loving father, he sought to shape its destiny, infuse it with his energy, as if he wanted it to take on his personality. As commanding officer, he insisted on having complete control over the regiment, especially promotions and officer assignments. If he sensed that something was going on behind his back, the high-strung McCook would become very angry and use his influence and will to get his way.

A lieutenant colonel who served in the regiment recalled that McCook had "fanciful ideas" about the future of the 52nd Ohio. After the war ended, McCook wanted to locate or create a "prosperous colony and village" where ex-soldiers could settle with their families. He dreamed of going so far as to designate "the variety of trades, occupations and professions" that his men would engage in based on his "intimate knowledge of the officers and men."[20] He, of course, would remain the respected father figure and was confident that history would reflect the truth of it.

But first, of course, the war had to be won and the Union reunited. And having gone very quickly from captain to colonel, Dan McCook's first assignment as a commanding officer put him and his regiment in the enemy crosshairs. Within a short time after leaving Ohio for Kentucky, Dan McCook's regiment was fighting in what was to be called the Perryville campaign.

At the time the Perryville campaign was underway, the American press was taking note of the McCook family and its participation in the war to quell the rebellion. In addition to individual heroics at Bull Run, Shiloh and Mill Springs, it was the sheer number of McCooks serving in the Union army that captured the imagination of newspapers and their readers. But the cheering articles sprinkled with McCooks meant that names and units were often mixed up, presenting interesting but sometimes inaccurate reports. Still, the press and public were especially proud of the "fighting family" from Ohio. Collectively and individually, the McCooks were among the best known Union soldiers, all of them serving and leading with bravery and skill.

Less than two weeks after being mustered into service, Dan McCook's 52nd Ohio was tramping along the Lexington and Richmond Pike, moving toward the Kentucky River. Its first assignment was to cover the retreat of General William "Bull" Nelson.[21] His division had fought and lost a battle at Richmond, Kentucky, and the victor, General E. Kirby Smith, was in the hunt to finish them off. Although Nelson escaped, McCook's mission was not well-executed.

One night McCook's men went into camp and the next morning they were given a rude awakening from the big guns of General Smith. The young Ohioans quickly abandoned their camp after artillery shells chased them "over the hill out of range." That afternoon they began a retreat to Lexington. Upon reaching that point on September 1, they marched on the Nashville Pike, passing by their camp where they were forced to watch their "tents, knapsacks and equipage of all kinds burning up." With only their weapons, canteens and haversacks, they continued on their weary way toward Louisville, their ultimate destination.

They marched steadily and the next night found them at Frankfort where the men of the 52nd Ohio camped in the street and resumed their trek the next morning. It was thought that they would board a train for Louisville, but instead they marched past the depot. Later they encountered some Rebel cavalry and Colonel McCook ordered his regiment to form a battle line. Skirmishers were sent out and shots were exchanged, the first for the 52nd Ohio Infantry regiment.

McCook then showed some creativity as a commander. Among the regiment's arsenal were two 32-pound Parrott guns that had been found "spiked and deserted in the Courthouse yard at Lexington." McCook attached them to his artillery unit as an "improvised section of a battery." His artillery men "went through the motion of swabbing, ramming home, and then running the guns into position ... all as a bluff." It apparently worked for the Rebel cavalry "fell back in the direction of their support" after the Federal skirmishers fired shots in the direction of the enemy horse soldiers. McCook's regiment continued on its way until it reached the "rear of our column."[22] He was referring to the Army of the Ohio.

At Louisville, Colonel McCook was elevated to brigade commander of the 36th brigade. It was placed under the command of Brigadier General Philip H. Sheridan, a division commander in the 3rd Army Corps headed by Brigadier General Charles C. Gilbert. All three men were serving under Major General Don Carlos Buell in command of the Army of the Ohio. Buell was a career army officer with excellent West Point credentials. He was widely respected by other officers and was looked upon by President Lincoln as a competent leader. Dan McCook had served with Gilbert, then a captain, at the battle of Wilson's Creek, where the latter was badly wounded.

Before gathering at Louisville, Buell's scattered army had trudged as far south as northern Alabama when he learned that the Confederates under General Braxton Bragg were stealing a march northward with a view of retaking Kentucky and thereby threatening Ohio and Indiana. General Bragg was heartened by the belief that after they arrived in Kentucky, pro–Southern men would join his army in droves. Bragg—who was to become a nemesis of the McCooks—had replaced Beauregard as commander of the Army of the Mississippi.

Bragg's mission was more just than military strategy; it had strong political overtones. The mid-term elections of 1862 were in the offing, and should Bragg be successful in pulling off a major defeat of the Union forces, the result would likely be demoralizing and weaken support for Lincoln and the Republicans. Furthermore, a big win for the South might earn that much coveted support from England and France.[23]

In the early stages of the campaign, Bragg attempted to break off a big chunk of the Union by urging people in the states of Ohio, Indiana, Minnesota, Michigan and Wisconsin to enter a separate peace with the Confederacy. With this unusual tactic, Bragg was hoping that by splitting up the Union, the war could be brought to an end with a minimum of bloodshed.[24] His "proclamation" completely misjudged the unity of the Northern states. While there were "peace at any price" people in the Northwest, they were outnumbered by those who were determined to defeat the rebellion militarily.

A West Point graduate, Bragg was intelligent and thoroughly military, having served the Union well in the Mexican War, but he suffered from serious health problems, including severe migraine headaches. Possibly because of this, he was quarrelsome, harsh, demanding and, at times, cruel. Deserters were shot with regularity and a Rebel soldier said that Bragg hanged 16 men on "a single tree" in order to establish discipline.[25] Throughout the war, he struggled with health problems and would fall into bouts of confusion, anger and inaction. He was always disliked and often hated, and it was

Confederate general Braxton Bragg, over the course of the war, proved to be one of the most unpopular officers to serve on either side. A West Point graduate from North Carolina, planter Bragg joined the Confederate in cause 1861, unhesitatingly. At times sickly, and at times bogged down in depression, Bragg was unable to maintain good relationships with his subordinate officers. They hated him and often did their best to ruin his battle plans. Bragg seemed to view the average soldier with contempt and heartlessly used them up like so many sacrificial lambs. His invasion of Kentucky led to the battle of Perryville, where he won a tactical victory, but was forced to leave the state when young Kentuckians refused to cast their lot with the Confederacy.

said that "getting along with others did not come easy for him."[26] While he was a close friend of Jefferson Davis, Bragg would have been hard pressed to find any other friends from among the Confederate army hierarchy.

Despite his personality problems and frequent mysterious bouts of lethargy, Bragg was a fighter of whom Union generals, including Don Carlos Buell, took note. The acerbic Bragg met with General E. Kirby Smith in Chattanooga on July 31 and developed a plan to win back Kentucky with Louisville as the primary target. Smith liked the plan and went north to Kentucky to carry out his role. He had a relatively easy time taking Lexington and Frankfort, spreading fear and anger across the North.

The Smith mission culminated in a fierce battle "near the cemetery in front of the town of Richmond." On August 31, veteran Rebel forces easily handled a smaller contingent of Federals, mostly raw recruits from Indiana, Kentucky and Ohio.[27] Once again Kentucky was in play; Southern success seemed possible and it was nervous time in Washington, where Henry Halleck believed that Cincinnati was just then vulnerable.

Also alarmed by the potential for disaster, Buell cancelled his plan to attack Chattanooga and got moving in the opposite direction. He was known to be a cautious general, not one to move fast, hence he was often accused of having a case of "the slows." But he found himself in a race, running essentially parallel to Bragg. Lucky for the Union, Buell got to Louisville ahead of Bragg, arriving on September 25, 1862. He was in a position to protect Kentucky and cities on the other side of the Ohio River.

Although he failed to get to Louisville ahead of Buell, Bragg found a way to enjoy himself. At Frankfort, the capital city, the Confederates anointed Richard Hawes the "governor" of Kentucky. During his inauguration address, those assembled were rudely disturbed by artillery fire from the big guns of General Joshua W. Sill of Alexander M. McCook's corps.[28] This broke up the celebration and Bragg backpedaled toward Perryville and, thinking that he would soon have company, picked the place where he would fight Buell.

This would give Bragg an edge, but logistics for both sides was complicated by the prolonged intense heat. The hot and dry weather meant that marching on dusty dirt trails without sufficient water was especially taxing on the troops. The men were accustomed to hardship, little or poor food and dirty water, but Buell's march to Perryville was one that tested the fortitude and loyalty of the most dogged soldier, for water, in any form, was almost impossible to find.

It was expected that abundant water would be found at Doctor's Creek, a tributary of the Chaplin River near Perryville. It was imperative that the Union secure the creek. Fighting men must have water, the only true elixir. It is as essential to success in battle as well-armed, well-trained soldiers.

Brigadier General Philip H. Sheridan's 11th Division of Brigadier General Charles C. Gilbert's 3rd Army Corps was given the task of taking possession of Doctor's Creek. This mission was recalled years later by Corporal Samuel Grimshaw of the 52nd Ohio, 36th Brigade. In a letter to the editor of *The National Tribune*, Grimshaw said that Sheridan's division approached Doctor's Creek marching on the Springfield Road. On the night of October 7, they camped about a mile west of the creek. Grimshaw and a comrade went to the creek for water to make coffee.[29]

In the pre-dawn hours of the 8th, Sheridan ordered the 36th Brigade, commanded by Colonel Daniel McCook, Jr., with a battery of artillery, to cross the creek and secure it. It was soon discovered that in order to claim the creek, it was necessary to take and control the range of hills that fronted the Chaplin River. For this Sheridan brought up an additional brigade of infantry and another battery of artillery.

According to Sheridan's report, there was little resistance from the Rebels and soon the hills were under Union control and a much-needed water supply was at hand.[30] Colonel McCook's report, however, notes that while his "regiments were fresh from their homes they moved steadily up the hills, driving the enemy, who contested warmly every step."[31] It was McCook's first dangerous assignment as a brigade commander and though he was nervous he did not falter. That his rookie troops handled the moonlight excitement quite well was both a tribute to their training and bravery and to their commander. The entire maneuver took 15 minutes and ended with six dead and 27 wounded.[32]

Sheridan's men started digging in to establish a position, annoyed constantly by Rebel sharpshooters. He found it necessary to send a brigade to chase them away and in doing so discovered a large body of Confederates formed in battle line on the opposite side of the Chaplin River. Then, while standing on high ground, he spotted on his left the 1st Army Corps led by Major General Alexander M. McCook marching forward on the Mackville road toward the Confederate battle line, apparently unaware of the presence of the enemy.

General McCook, however, must have been aware of the enemy for he halted his division and sent out men to do reconnaissance. Not long after he gave that order, his entire division was under fire from a Rebel attack by Bragg's army. Having picked the place he wanted to fight, Bragg had the upper hand and hurled his soldiers at McCook. The brigade of Brigadier General Lovell Rousseau bore the brunt of the Rebels' onslaught. Taken by surprise General McCook quickly rallied his division in an effort to withstand the attack, but he needed reinforcements.

Colonel McCook, whose brigade spent much of the afternoon on the hills above the furious battle below, was forced to watch Rousseau's division under attack. In his testimony at the post-battle inquiry, Colonel McCook was upset that Gilbert pulled his (McCook's) brigade out of line at about 2 p.m. and ordered it back upon the hill from its position in the woods because his troops were "raw." Apparently McCook had no such misgivings as his brigade withstood two Rebel attacks. He wanted action and was not satisfied with simply watching the fight.

With a division and two batteries lying idle, McCook said he "begged General Sheridan to at least allow us to open on them with artillery." The request was denied by Sheridan acting through Gilbert. Colonel McCook was told that this action "might concentrate the fire of the enemy's artillery upon our troops." McCook's response was that the troops could have been moved out of harm's way simply by taking them down the slope.³³ Finally, after watching Rousseau's men "pulverized" by Rebel artillery, Sheridan authorized Dan McCook to open up on the enemy with artillery fire. It was too late, however, to make a difference in the outcome.

Colonel McCook later found out that at about 2:15 that afternoon, Rousseau had sent a dispatch stating that he was being attacked, and that the dispatch went through the signal office, meaning Gilbert, or someone on his staff, knew of the attack. Learning this made the high-strung McCook extremely angry, and his post-battle testimony reflected great anger. He testified that in a "burst of indignation ... coupled with a few oaths," he demanded of General Sheridan to know "why we were ordered out of those woods."³⁴ The larger question, of course, was why was a division lying idle

Brigadier General Philip H. Sheridan was a division commander in the Army of the Ohio when the Union forces clashed with the Rebel army commanded by General Braxton Bragg at the battle of Perryville. A West Pointer, Sheridan spent eight years of military service on the western frontier. During first year of the Civil War, Sheridan was chief quartermaster and commissary of the Army of Southwest Missouri, service that included Henry Halleck's tortoise-like Corinth campaign. Then in May of 1862, he was given a cavalry command and from that point on his military career as a daring and successful fighter took flight. Sheridan is credited by many historians as one of the "Big Three" generals, along with Grant and Sherman, who won the war for the North.

when it was obvious that those fighting needed help? It was pointless to obey an order "not to bring on an engagement" when a fierce battle was well underway.

The battle of Perryville raged on until darkness and exhaustion silenced the guns and weary soldiers on both sides paused to clear their heads and rest their bodies. Incredibly, the division of General McCook had fought the Rebels almost entirely on its own, while two other divisions were essentially idle. Buell claimed that he was not aware of the fierce fighting by McCook's division, a position he had to defend at an inquiry. It was revealed that a freak, atmospheric phenomena known as an "acoustic shadow" prevented the sounds of battle from being heard at Buell's headquarters.

Well aware of the fierce fighting, Dan McCook had desperately wanted to help his brother, but he also wanted to get into the fight because he saw an opportunity to attack the flank and rear of the enemy. He believed that there had been an inexcusably poor exercise of leadership at the battle on that hot October afternoon. And while he didn't name names, it was certain that the main target of his criticism was General Gilbert.

In a piece he authored for inclusion in the epic *Battles and Leaders in the Civil War*, Gilbert put forth his own version of the battle of Perryville. After writing about the march toward Perryville and finding water, Gilbert went into a brief discussion of the battle. But far from finding any fault in his conduct, he ended the article by saying that "the center [his corps] contributed about one-third of its effective force to the relief of the left wing [McCook's] and saved it from destruction."[35] In other words, instead of being the goat, he was the man who saved the day.

Typically, when a battle ended badly, a verbal fight commenced with aggrieved men engaged in angry finger-pointing and the making of charges and counter-charges. After Perryville, a blast of highly-charged questions were directed at Gilbert for failing to offer substantial assistance to McCook; at McCook who was criticized for being rash and careless; and at Buell, the commander, responsible for the Army of the Ohio, who found his official head on the chopping block.

At the well-publicized and highly-charged inquiry that followed the battle of Perryville, General Buell was put under intense questioning for his conduct, and, more particularly, for his failure to send help to General McCook. A fiery Colonel Daniel McCook was one of those who testified. The weight of evidence was decidedly against Buell, who, to his credit, did not make excuses, but rather defended his conduct. But the inquiry board was not convinced of his ability to lead and he was removed from command. Gilbert was also censured and demoted.

Many years later, a writer for *The National Tribune* made a half-hearted attempt to defend Buell. He noted that "Buell was unfortunate in the subordinates with whom he commanded." He said that General McCook, "with all his undoubted gallantry, loyalty and soldierly qualities ... lacked the mental breadth as well as the iron will and determination absolutely necessary for the command ... of a corps." Major General Thomas L. Crittenden, he said, was a good Kentucky lawyer but except for having "courage and loyalty" he had nothing else to qualify him for command. Then, having mildly cut down two generals, the writer aimed his sharpest ax at Gilbert, calling him a "narrow-minded martinet, slavishly devoted to precedent and regulations," and therefore "unable to rise above the letter of orders or rules."

The writer also believed that jealousy among the commanders was rampant and resulted in dangerous inefficiency. As an example, he insisted that Gilbert was "fearfully jealous of McCook." All these negative factors—lack of ability, lack of experience, poor judgment and jealousy—contributed to the disaster at Perryville.[36]

General McCook kept his command, but suffered a dent in his military reputation that never went away. Gilbert—having served with distinction and gallantry at Wilson's Creek and Shiloh—was relieved and never again held a field command position.[37] Buell's career spiraled downward as well, another highly-regarded general tossed in the military bone pile. Sadly, he was remembered by many of his men as a "heartless martinet," a commanding officer who "marched the very life out of us."[38]

And so it was that from the lowliest private to the highest general, Perryville was a life-changing event, one that planted the sad seed that blossomed into bad memories. But it wasn't all bad. For despite the losses, the Union army had succeeded in stopping the Rebel Kentucky campaign and made it possible for people along the Ohio River to rest easy again. Kentucky would remain a Union state.

After the Buell inquiry, the Army of the Ohio was handed to Major General William S. Rosecrans, a West Point officer whose military star was in its ascendency. His military skill and leadership were responsible for the Union victories in western Virginia, and he performed heroically while leading his divisions against a two-day Rebel attack at Corinth on October 3–4, 1862. At each assignment, he showed unusual creativity and tenacity that inspired his men and impressed the War Department.

It was a popular and confident Rosecrans that took command and led the Army of the Ohio out of Kentucky into Nashville, a suffering city invaded for a second time by Union troops. Once again angry residents in the distinctive Southern city were forced to watch as the hated Yankees took over and occupied churches, schools, hotels, homes and public buildings. Ignoring the anger of the locals, Rosecrans vigorously set about reorganizing the Army of the Ohio and instilling a sense of pride and willingness to fight in brave men who had for too long wore out their feet and hearts under the harsh rule of the unpopular Buell. In Rosecrans the soldiers found an affable and talkative man, highly intelligent, high-spirited and with a friendly attitude toward the rank and file. He was a devout and profound Catholic, and his personal priest traveled with him so that he would never have to miss mass. "Rosy," or "Old Rosy," as he was called, was well-liked and respected by the men, including Colonel Daniel McCook.

Rosecrans restructured his army of about 35,000 able bodied men into three "wings." The left wing was under the command of Major General Thomas J. Crittenden, the center headed by Major General George H. Thomas, and the right by Major General Alexander M. McCook. Colonel Daniel McCook, Jr., served under Thomas as a brigade commander. His youngest brother, Lieutenant John J. McCook, was assigned to the staff of Crittenden.

Bragg and his Army of Tennessee had retreated to Murfreesboro, about 35 miles southeast of Nashville. Fall gave way to winter and it appeared to observers in both the North and South that the opposing armies had decided not to fight for the rest of the year. As the holiday season approached, events were planned by both sides. It all changed rather suddenly when Rosecrans ordered his wing commanders to ready their men for the march. At the urging of the War Department, the Union army would attack Bragg at or near Murfreesboro over the holidays. There would be no merry Christmas for the soldiers, blue or gray.

Nevertheless, the Union boys marched off in high spirits. There was skirmishing all the way to Stones River near Murfreesboro where the lines of battle for both sides were formed. Rosecrans' plan was simple: while McCook held down the right, Crittenden, on the left, would attack the Rebel right. Thomas was assigned to the middle. Bragg had a similar plan: his left would attack the Union right.

Rosecrans knew that the enigmatic Bragg was moody and unpopular, but he also understood that the Rebel commander could be shrewd and able to pull off a surprise. Bragg did so on the morning of December 31, 1862, getting his men up early, and after liquor for breakfast, the Rebel rush against the Union right began. A Union soldier recalled that he had just taken his "meat and coffee from the fire, and was sitting down on a cold rock" to eat breakfast, when shots rang in the woods. Then the Union pickets raced into camp followed by a mass of running Rebels, "yelling and shooting like demons."[39]

Caught unaware—and unprepared—McCook's line was overwhelmed by running, screaming Rebels with guns blazing. The rout of Union right was complete as soldiers in McCook's regiments fled to the rear en masse.

General August Willich was taken prisoner. Fortunately, Rosecrans kept his cool as did General Thomas, General McCook, General Sheridan and others. In the midst of chaos and confusion, the Union troops rallied and prevented Bragg from getting a stunning victory.

Two days later, Bragg made an ill-advised attack on the well-protected Union left. His soldiers, led by General Breckinridge, were driven back after great slaughter. The battle of Stones River was over and Bragg retreated further to the south while Rosecrans and his men were lauded and applauded by the administration, the public and a corps of Northern newspapers anxious for some good news to print.

For Southern newspaper readers, the news went from celebratory to perfectly gloomy. It was first reported that Bragg had won a great victory and that the Union army was in retreat. A deliriously happy Jefferson Davis spoke to cheering crowds in Richmond about the glorious win by the Confederates. But when it was learned that Bragg was in sullen retreat, the Southern press was forced to put the breaks on and respond with anger and disappointment. Bragg was suddenly the goat, labeled "Boomerang Bragg," because he had charged in and then abruptly marched away from Stones River just like he did at Perryville.[40]

Colonel Daniel McCook and his brigade did not participate in the battle, but he could claim credit for saving the day, so to speak. His moment of danger came while he was away from the field of battle, in command of infantry and cavalry from Ohio, Michigan and Tennessee regiments. They were escorting a train of 95 ammunition and hospital wagons to the Union lines. As the train progressed to within seven miles of Nashville, it was attacked by Confederate cavalry under General Joe Wheeler. Colonel McCook led a counterattack that dispersed the enemy horse soldiers.

A Vermont newspaper reported that McCook won a smashing victory, "routing him [Wheeler] completely." The article also stated that "the rebel canteens were filled with whiskey and gunpowder."[41] McCook's official report was equally glamorous. He wrote that he "was completely surrounded by rebels—wounding at least one with my pistol." He was soon joined by Colonel Toler and the 60th Illinois who put the enemy on its heels and in a retreat mode, thus saving much-needed supplies for the Union.[42] Had the Confederates been able to take the train and its ammunition, the Stones River story might have had an entirely different ending. Colonel McCook and his men were greeted warmly by war-weary troops when his train arrived at the Stones River battle site.

Upon his arrival, Colonel McCook revealed that after breaking through the ambush, he came upon a suspicious-looking rider. Believing the stranger to be a Confederate, he nevertheless greeted the man in the spirit of friendship.

He told the rider, "I know you're a Union man by your looks and I want to tell you a secret. Do you see these troops? Their [sic] some of old Rosy's Mississippi veterans. There are 25,000 of them coming, and we're going to give old Bragg hell." Having sold the ruse well, McCook told the man not to breathe a word to anyone about the "reinforcements." The man promised he would not and rode off. Dan McCook revealed his trickery to Rosecrans, saying, "I reckon he's been at Bragg's headquarters more than three hours by this time."[43] The funny story was just the icing on the cake that Rosecrans needed at the moment, believing he had won an important victory.

The Union success at Stones River brought a rush of good wishes and praise from newspapers and from the Lincoln administration. The president sent a personal message of thanks to Rosecrans and his gallant soldiers. Secretary of War Edwin M. Stanton and Lincoln's general-in-chief, Major General Henry W. Halleck, chimed in as well. Still, the news coming out of Washington wasn't all good. A "gentleman direct from Washington" informed an Ohio newspaper that Stanton and Halleck—never on friendly terms—had more than just a little falling out.

The collision happened at a cabinet meeting. While those present were discussing the disastrous effects of the battle of Fredericksburg, Virginia, Stanton called Halleck a liar. This remark came after "Old Brains" suggested that secretary of war was to blame for the Union defeat and the slaughter of so many men. The aggressive Stanton was known to carry a dagger for protection.[44] But it was Halleck who made the first move. Hearing the word "liar," Halleck "immediately shot out his left fist at the frontispiece of Stanton, handing him one on the left eye." The burly secretary was sent sprawling on the floor, "frescoing the left side of his face" in an "artistic manner." Stanton was ready to strike back, but Lincoln, their boss and a brawler in his own right, intervened and threatened to thrash both parties "if they didn't behave themselves."[45]

The dust up between Stanton and Halleck, however undignified, could not sully the importance of the victory at Stones River. The triumph meant that the year 1863 was off to a good start. After the high-casualty battlefield losses of 1862, coupled with the political gains made by Democrats and Copperheads, Lincoln needed something to lift his spirits and those of the nation, and despite the disaster on the Union right, the result produced a feel-good moment in the North. Rosecrans and his brave soldiers came through for the president and the country. And as promised, Abraham Lincoln issued his Emancipation Proclamation to be effective January 1, 1863, freeing enslaved people in those seceded states in open rebellion against the federal government.

History recognizes Lincoln's decision to issue the proclamation as an act of great political and moral courage. But in the immediate aftermath of making the famous proclamation public, reaction was decidedly mixed. Abolitionists praised Lincoln because they had long believed that the concept of equality demanded that slavery must end. The Copperheads and pro-slavery people—for whom equality of the black race was not an issue—were outraged. Their hatred of Lincoln intensified.

There was some anger and dismay among the Union soldiers, but many in the army saw the move as one that would shift the balance in favor of the Union as taking away slaves from the South would weaken the Rebel war effort. Fewer slaves would be available to do the hard work of supporting the Confederate army whether it be digging trenches, burying the dead, driving teams, preparing food or simply serving an officer. In other words, as Lincoln insisted, it was a war measure, necessary to ramp up efforts to defeat the South. It was also needed to keep England and France from choosing to support the South.[46]

The proclamation was followed by the creation of all-black regiments to join in the fight. While the decision to allow black soldiers to shoulder guns against the Rebels was not universally well-liked, the astute citizen had to recognize the numerical advantage that it offered to the North. And Lincoln was counting on astute men to support him. He hated slavery but loved the Union, and sensing an opportunity to express both emotions, he used the power of the pen to augment the sword arm of the army.

In late 1861, a Cincinnati newspaper stated: "Slavery is the Pariah of the whole civilized world, except the South."[47] While the remark was simply a taunt when it was set in print, by 1863, after nearly two years of intense fighting and thousands of casualties, the "civilized" world was compelled to take note of what was happening in America. Knowledgeable people came to the conclusion that the Confederacy was the first and only attempt by men to create a nation for the purpose of preserving and perpetuating slavery. Nobody knew that better than Lincoln. His eloquent Emancipation Proclamation had not changed his goal of preserving the Union, but by granting freedom to most of the slaves, he signaled to the world his determination to make certain that slavery was doomed and that the Confederate experiment was destined to fail.

9
Morgan's Raid and the Death of Daniel McCook, Sr.

"It is with deep sorrow that I have to announce the death of Major Daniel McCook, paymaster to the U.S. Army, whose gallantry and devotion to the cause have been so conspicuous from the commencement of the rebellion."—Major General Ambrose E. Burnside, July 22, 1863

If there is a storybook element to the Civil War, it resides in the larger-than-life image of the Confederate cavalry raiders. The Rebel cavalry—brazen, bold and consistently successful—was, throughout the war, the one bright light for the South. Rebel raiders were heroes to adoring Southerners and condemned in the North as murdering bushwhackers and plundering thieves. While Richmond struggled to match the federal infantry in numbers and could barely feed and clothe its foot soldiers, the Rebel horse soldiers spent much of the war ranging far and wide, with great latitude and discretion, living off the land, like men of good fortune, born for life in the saddle.

Cavalry raids were utilized by both sides to gather intelligence, destroy or capture supply trains, tear up railroads, burn bridges and barns and spread terror in their wake. Some raids rank high in the annals of the Civil War, such as General James E. B. "Jeb" Stuart's celebrated circling of General George B. McClellan's Army of the Potomac. General Nathan Bedford Forrest was another Rebel raider, so consistently successful, that he came to be known as "that Devil Forrest." His wizardry bedeviled many a Union commander and caused some of fellow cavalry leaders to emulate him. Despite his occasional outburst of cruelty, Forrest was admired and idealized for possessing natural military skills. A living legend, he inspired many futile attempts by the Union to nab him.

The reckless General John Hunt Morgan was another Rebel raider of dash and daring. A Southern gentleman and cavalier of the first order, Morgan

9. Morgan's Raid and the Death of Daniel McCook, Sr.

John Hunt Morgan with his young wife, whom he married during the Christmas season of 1862. Morgan was a dashing and daring cavalry commander who conducted raids against the Union, destroying bridges, telegraph lines and railroads, robbing supply stations and in general wreaking havoc and giving Lincoln and his generals major heartburn. In the summer of 1863, he launched the boldest raiding enterprise of his career, crossing Kentucky, entering Indiana and thence to Ohio, spreading death, destruction and terrorism throughout the towns and countryside. While he expected hundreds of Southern sympathizers to join him, they did not, and the raiders were routed by Union forces and Morgan was captured. Tossed into prison in Columbus, Ohio, Morgan and some of his men managed to escape and rejoin the Southern army.

was born in Alabama and grew up in Kentucky, a member of a wealthy, slave holding family. He was a restless youth and got kicked out of Transylvania University after being challenged to a duel by another student. He enlisted in the army and served in the Mexican War. He became a successful businessman—including slave trading—but preferred a military style of life so he joined a Kentucky militia. In 1857, Morgan created a militia called the "Lexington Rifles," men who later joined the Confederate army.

The Rebel raider engaged in many disguises and ruses which he played to the hilt, as if daring the enemy to discover his true identity. There is the unconfirmed report that Morgan once penetrated the lines of General Alexander M. McCook disguised as a miller. He pretended to be an informer and Union supporter and had the audacity to tell General McCook how to go about trapping and capturing him (Morgan). Supposedly, McCook took the bait and sent out 150 men, and all of them were captured by Morgan.[1]

A *New York Times* correspondent presented Morgan as fearless man of "daring coolness" whose grandiose plan was to capture a Union general. He seemed to take pleasure in menacing General McCook. The reporter recalled that Morgan had appeared at Bacon Creek, Kentucky, and "burnt the railroad bridge under McCook's nose," then shot a picket and escaped. On another occasion in March of 1862, he crept up on McCook's camp on the Franklin pike.[2]

Morgan played a minor role in the battle of Shiloh and in July of 1862 he conducted a daring raid through Tennessee and Kentucky, wrecking railroads, bridges and telegraph lines, costing the federal government many thousands of dollars. It was a raid that stunned the North and elevated his stature in the South to that of a hero. Morgan was an inveterate gambler and when it paid off, it paid off big. The heady and daring prince of cavalry carried out a 1,000-mile raid in twenty-four days in the summer of 1862, taking with him 1200 prisoners and tons of supplies.[3] Adored by women, it was claimed that there was "a dash and romance about him and his band," and the buzz that was created attracted young pro–Southern men to John Hunt Morgan's banner.[4]

When the armies of General William S. Rosecrans and Bragg were slowly coming together for the bloody battle of Stones River, Morgan struck a federal garrison at Hartsville, Tennessee, in the early morning of December 7, 1862. By skillfully utilizing his cavalry of about 1400 men, Morgan surprised and routed the Yankees, capturing about 1800 men and a large amount of supplies. It was termed a disaster by Union. Colonel Edward M. McCook, who reported that his 104th Illinois and the 2nd Indiana Cavalry units "fought gallantly," while other regiments "fled disgracefully."[5] When the fight was over, Morgan marched his cold and downtrodden Yankee prisoners into Murfreesboro where he was cheered by the people and greeted warmly by Bragg and Jefferson Davis, who immediately promoted him to brigadier general.

On December 14, the gallant and heroic John Morgan Hunt was married to the 17-year-old Mattie Ready of Murfreesboro, thus dashing the hopes of other female admirers. The young girl had made it known that she wanted to be the bride of John Hunt Morgan, a man she only knew by reputation. Morgan met her and after a short courtship proposed. Pretty Mattie accepted with enthusiasm. Their wedding ceremony, performed by the Episcopal bishop General Leonidas Polk, and attended by much of the Confederate brass, set in motion a series parties that lasted until Christmas.[6]

Unfortunately, his marriage unleashed some negative press. Newspapers complained that Morgan's devotion to his new wife had caused his daring attitude to diminish. He had suffered a setback in field when on March 20, 1863, his cavalry was hammered by Federal infantry at Milton, Tennessee. This was followed by another rout two weeks later. Then it got worse. On April 19, a Union cavalry unit handed him another awful defeat, even capturing his wife, who was released after a few hours.[7]

In the summer of 1863, Morgan's cavalry was still attached to General Braxton Bragg's Army of Tennessee stationed at Tullahoma, Tennessee. While Bragg was stalling and trying to figure out his next move versus Major General William S. Rosecrans, he ordered Morgan to conduct a raid in Kentucky to do damage to the infrastructure, including the destruction of bridges, lines of communication, railroads and other items of value to the north. Morgan, anxious for more glory, public adulation and booty, and eager to atone for setbacks earlier in the year, wanted to do more than terrorize Kentucky. He wanted cross the Ohio River, ravage northern cities and soil and recruit Southern sympathizers in Indiana and Ohio, but Bragg would not agree to such an invasion.[8]

Morgan proceeded according to his plan despite orders to the contrary. Success, it seemed, went to his head and Morgan listened to the voice of his ego and reputation instead of that of his commanding general. To prove that marriage had not made him soft, he decided to run a slash and burn campaign through southern Indiana and Ohio, and then turn south and ride through West Virginia, the newest state in the Union, having been admitted on June 20, 1863. Advance units had scouted out the river crossings to prepare for a major invasion.[9]

As they approached the Ohio River, Morgan sent five companies in different directions to confuse Union pursuers.[10] It was logical strategy but it failed, for on July 4, the raiders fought a three hour battle with Union troops at Tebbs Bend on the Ohio River. Morgan's losses were significant in dead and wounded. And while he had lost the element of surprise, and alerted the Federals, he retained his determination to cross the Ohio River and attack.[11]

Morgan and his horsemen crossed the Ohio River on July 8 at Brandenberg, Indiana, a little city known to be dominated by "secesh" folks. After commandeering two steamers including the *Alice Dean*, "the pride of all the Cincinnati rivermen," and after kicking off frightened passengers, the raiders were ready to land on the opposite side of the Ohio River. They had little trouble dealing with the Indiana Home Guard, a mere 45 men and "one 6-pounder." After brushing them aside, Morgan and his men crossed into Indiana. A single gunboat sent down river from New Albany was equally useless against Confederate cannon fire. Everything was going Morgan's way.[12]

Morgan's cavalry included four brothers—one of whom, Thomas Morgan, was killed early in the raid—and a brother-in-law, Colonel Basil Duke, said to be the "head and brains" of the expedition.[13] Duke was the only member of the band who knew that Morgan had disobeyed Bragg's order to confine acts of destruction to Kentucky.

The bulk of the cavalry consisted of a large number of young, raw Kentuckians, about 3,000 in number, although early estimates had the invaders at about 5,000 men and horses. Whatever the number, all of them were enthralled with their commanding officer and the bloody adventure about to unfold before their eyes.

His men had reason to expect something bad and bloody, for Morgan had a reputation for brutality. Earlier in 1863, a "Union lady" in Shelbyville, Tennessee, listened while a Confederate officer told a grisly story about the raider general. He said a federal officer had captured two of Morgan's men who were deemed to be bushwhackers. They were summarily hanged, and when Morgan learned of their fate, he vowed to avenge them. Then, after capturing 17 Union soldiers, Morgan kept his promise, shooting six, hanging seven and killing four others with an axe, "as you would kill hogs."[14] It was an incident so cruel and sadistic that an honorable man would deny its truth to his dying day.

While many people doubted that Morgan was capable of such acts, it was believed by some that he invaded the North with a secret mission in mind.[15] However, the Rebels were acting anything but secretive. They were free and loose with their talk at Brandenberg, stating that their mission was to burn and destroy "everything in the line of march, irrespective of party or creed...." One of their objectives was the city of Indianapolis.[16]

While taking Indianapolis might have been too much of a challenge, Morgan had some delicious possibilities to contemplate because not everyone would oppose him. The area he would travel through was considered "Copperhead" country. Copperhead was the pejorative applied to northern "Peace

Democrats" who openly sympathized with the South. Although not necessarily anti–Union, they blatantly and vociferously criticized Lincoln, slammed the hated abolitionists and the "black Republicans," while speaking out against the war. They naively believed that if the North ordered a cease fire, the Southern states would rejoin the Union if all things were returned to *status quo*. But if peace could not be arranged, the Copperheads were willing to let the South go its own way, keep its slaves, and create a new nation.

Morgan thought the Copperhead element would flock to his standard and he counted on members of the Knights of the Golden Circle and Sons of Liberty to join him once he reached Indiana, a state known to have a sizeable population of Copperheads.[17] It was even reported that former Ohio congressman Clement L. Vallandigham, the best known and most vocal Copperhead, was the instigator of Morgan's invasion. According to the report, Vallandigham assured Jefferson Davis and members of his cabinet that the "North was ripe for a revolution" and just waiting for a Southern army to embrace. Just cross the river where men, fed up with Lincoln and the war, were ready to saddle up and join the cause.[18]

Vallandigham had strong ties to the McCooks. His father had been a preacher in the New Lisbon Ohio Presbyterian Church to which the McCook family belonged. The elder Vallandigham had baptized many of the McCook children and the two families were closely allied by way of friendship and politics. But the alliance could not survive the Bible-based, pro-slavery, beliefs of Clement L. Vallandigham who also supported secession and was stridently anti-war and anti-Lincoln. After the war started and Vallandigham showed his true colors, the McCooks rejected and denounced him as a hardened traitor.[19] It was another friendship killed by the hard hand of war.

While Vallandigham was very popular and influential among the Indiana Copperheads, they were apparently not ready to fight and die for him and his cause. For when Morgan's pillaging horse soldiers rode through Indiana, people either ran away in terror or joined in the effort to expel the raiders. In one violent encounter at Corydon, on July 9, eight of Morgan's men were killed before the Indiana men were driven off by a saber charge.[20]

While recruiting was a disappointment, Morgan did inspire fear and panic from the citizens of a state that had sent most of its young men to fight in the South. In fact, the general belief in the early going was that Morgan's raid was conducted to force the Union to pull troops out of Kentucky in order to protect Indiana. There was also concern that Morgan might hit Camp Morton, an Indiana prison, and free some 2,000 Rebel inmates.

Loyal Indianans were celebrating the twin Union victories in Gettysburg and Vicksburg when news arrived that their state had been invaded by Rebels. The celebration was cut short, and before long Indiana took action against the invasion. Its governor, Oliver P. Morton, a powerful advocate for the preservation of the Union, took charge. On July 8, 1863, Morton placed notices in local newspapers, hoping to recruit 100,000 volunteers whom he intended lead personally against the invaders. Soon more than 60,000 responded to the governor's call. Take that, you Copperheads.

The audacious Morgan—who learned about Lee's Gettysburg defeat while having lunch at a hotel in Corydon—was streaking and marauding through territory under the jurisdiction of Major General Ambrose E. Burnside and the Army of the Ohio. Burnside had his sights set on East Tennessee and the Union loyalists who were waiting for aid when he learned that Morgan was in his rear. This caused him to stop his progress toward Tennessee and send his cavalry in pursuit of the wily raider and his merry men. Once again, the East Tennessee loyalists would have to wait.

On July 13—while New York City was bleeding and burning over the draft riots—Morgan's raiders crossed the Whitewater River into Ohio at Harrison, a mere 20 miles from Cincinnati.[21] But Cincinnati was a well-protected city so Morgan wisely slipped in and out of the surrounding area during the night. Sounding the alarm, both Burnside and Ohio governor David Tod ordered the state militia to action and proclaimed marshal law. They were hampered in their effort to find and attack the raiders because one of Morgan's men was a telegrapher "who could tap into the wires at will" and send phony messages that confused the Union pursuers.[22]

This allowed Morgan to continue his mission of destruction, burning, wrecking, looting and stealing or extorting money. About a mile and a half from Camp Dennison, the Rebels removed a section of rails so that the next train coming along would be derailed. The tactic yielded the desired effect. The engine turned over, the fireman was killed and the engineer injured, but fortunately for the passengers and unarmed soldiers, the cars did not capsize. Morgan's men marched off with the captives who were later paroled.[23]

A Union army captain was certain that Morgan's success was due to the blessing and assistance of the "Vallandighammers," including the Knights of the Golden Circle. He wrote a letter to a Cincinnati newspaper saying that while he was in the vanguard of the Union pursuit of Morgan, pro–Confederate men, believing he was with the Rebels, gave him "the salutation of the K. G. C.s, the grand crowning sign and the battle sign." Another group of men told him that they wanted to kill "forty-seven Lincolnites," and that they knew where to find the "treasures of the abolitionists." The captain even named names, stating that four men—Dr. Goodhart, Mason J. Cloud, John Ashby and Warren Tibbs, all of whom were "Vallandighammers"—offered him assistance, thinking he was a Rebel. In both Ohio and Indiana, the Rebel friendly civilians "offered to assist me in any way they could." Morgan, he said, had "good guides."[24]

9. Morgan's Raid and the Death of Daniel McCook, Sr. 145

The raid was not without some humorous incidents. According to a report, Morgan and his men stopped at the residence of a sympathetic "old peace" Democrat in Hamilton County, Ohio. The two engaged in conversation and Morgan learned that the man had eight horses. Always in need of fresh horses, Morgan suggested that his host surrender four of the horses and he would be allowed to keep the other four. When asked how he could do so, Morgan said that his rear guard would be coming up the road in about ten hours, and when the Copperhead saw them approach, he was to offer a cheer for "Vallandigham and Jeff. Davis" and he could keep his four horses. Later, at the approach of some riders, "Mr. Butternut" stepped out and gave the appropriate greeting. Unfortunately the soldiers were those of Union general Hobson. Needless to say, the general took the horses.[25]

Things were going Morgan's way, but that was about to change as Union forces were finally closing in on the raiders. One of those who picked up his rifle and joined the pursuit was Major Daniel McCook, Sr. Stationed in Cincinnati, he was a paymaster for the army, living with his wife at a boarding house, when the excitement started. Major McCook was anxious to assist in the destruction of the Rebel force that had the gall to invade Ohio because he believed that the man responsible for killing his son, Brigadier General Robert L. McCook, the year before, was riding with Morgan. Whenever Rebel prisoners were brought into Cincinnati, the elder McCook, fully armed, would visit the prison hoping to find Robert's killer among them.[26]

Although a staunch Democrat, the elder McCook was stridently pro–Union and was among the earliest volunteers to shoulder a rifle in defense of the cause. He was in his 60s when the war started and was not given a combat role. Undaunted, he wanted to serve the Lincoln administration, so he joined with Kansas jayhawker James H. "Jim" Lane and others and formed a group called the Frontier Guard. Organizing at the Willard Hotel in Washington, they marched to the White House and became Lincoln's personal body guards, serving in that capacity until actual troops arrived.[27]

McCook stayed in Washington with his wife Martha and served as a volunteer nurse at the battle of Bull Run, where he witnessed the fatal shooting of his son, Private Charles M. McCook. The old man later served as an "amateur" soldier in a skirmish at Bolivar Heights, Virginia, on October 16, 1861.[28] He was "knocked down by a spent cannon ball," but not seriously hurt.[29] But the battle of Ball's Bluff resulted in a "costly federal defeat."[30]

Like his sons and nephews, the elder McCook was a fighter and a patriot, possessed of great personal courage. Despite his advanced years, he had the aggression of a youth, and a temper that was likely to erupt at any time. Just months before Morgan's raid, the Major was walking along Walnut Street in Cincinnati when he decided to buy a copy of the *Cincinnati Enquirer*, a

Democratic newspaper. Suddenly a man standing nearby suggested that the *Enquirer* should be "leveled to the earth—by mob violence." Hearing this McCook gave the man a verbal thrashing, "couched in the most severe language ... calling the man a coward, unworthy to of being a citizen of a country whose institutions rested upon free speech and a free press." The recipient of the tongue lashing responded by saying that he had a gun and intended to use it. Hearing this threat, the old major drew his pistol and "leveled his gun at the scoundrel." A shootout was avoided by others who rushed forward and separated the two men. McCook left but only after he got the name and address of the "mobocrat."[31]

The highly-charged incident was picked up by other newspapers that tried to use it for political purposes. Apparently an abolitionist newspaper used it in an attempt to prove that the McCooks were all anti–Vallandigham, to which the *Daily Ohio Statesman*, a fire-breathing Democratic newspaper, took offense. It quoted Major McCook as saying that "'he had known Vallandigham since he [V.] was a small child, and that if there ever was a patriot and a statesman, that man was Mr. Vallandigham.'" These remarks were allegedly made in Butler County while McCook was "in pursuit of Morgan, and in reply to some offensive remarks about Mr. Vallandigham."[32]

Vallandigham was just then in the public eye and mind, inciting all sorts of remarks. Always blistering in his attacks on Lincoln, in the spring of 1863, he made some highly-charged speeches that were truly inspiring to his Copperhead audiences, but had the opposite effect on his enemies. As a result, early in the morning of May 5, 1863, he was arrested by a force of 150 soldiers that General Burnside had sent to his home. They broke down the door, roughly and hurriedly drug the Copperhead outside and took him away to prison in Cincinnati. Vallandigham was charged with violating Burnside's General Order No. 38, making it unlawful to give treasonable speeches that expressed sympathy for the enemy. He was convicted by a military tribunal and sentenced to spend the rest of the war in federal prison.[33]

Lincoln was in a bind over how to handle the Vallandigham matter. He was reluctant to interfere with Burnside's actions because he knew the general was acting in good faith, but he was also concerned about negative political backlash over an attack on free speech. The president came up with a novel solution. He banished Vallandigham to the Confederacy. General Rosecrans was given the dubious honor of escorting the Copperhead to a Rebel contingent in Tennessee. Once inside the Confederate lines the former congressman insisted he was a loyal American and had no intention of joining the Confederacy. He did, however, try to broker a peace deal that would end the war and reunite the country. The plan pleased neither side and Vallandigham soon found himself in Canada.

Major McCook's remarks about Vallandigham, as quoted in the *Daily Ohio Statesman*, were made when the celebrity Copperhead was in Canada, leveling verbal blasts at Lincoln while campaigning for the office of the governor of Ohio. Despite the long affiliation between the two men and their families, it is doubtful that McCook supported Vallandigham's candidacy, for that summer he was preoccupied by a matter of greater importance. When he learned of the approach of Morgan, the elder McCook gathered together a group of men that he planned to lead against the invaders. But the military authorities would not permit McCook and his men to strike out on their own. Their horses were confiscated and the men scattered. Undaunted, the major volunteered to serve with Major Tom Cook, although he (McCook) would not be "subject to military discipline."

The elder McCook was absolutely certain that Frank B. Gurley, the man who shot his son Robert, was among the raiders, and he made it clear that the man universally known in the North as a murderer would be killed on sight. McCook gave notice to General Judah that "he did not care what orders he [Judah] gave, or how much restraint he placed upon him," Gurley would die. McCook declared that if Gurley was taken as a prisoner, he would still gun the enemy soldier down, no matter what the consequences to himself. It was said that "the old man's eyes sparkled at the thought of avenging his son's death."[34]

So it was with great pride and pleasure that Major McCook rode with Brigadier General Henry Hobson in pursuit of John Hunt Morgan and his band of men. Hobson commanded the Second Brigade of the Third Division, 23rd Army Corps under Brigadier General Henry M Judah. McCook was given the title of volunteer aid-de-camp to General Judah. He had volunteered despite his family's wishes that he respect his age and stay in Cincinnati.

Burnside had another general in the field against the dangerous foe: Brigadier General James M. Shackelford, commander of the First Brigade of the Second Division, 23rd Amy Corps. All this fire power meant Morgan was in big trouble, provided they could find him.

According to Burnside, that would not be a problem. On July 17, Burnside wrote to General Henry W. Halleck, saying "all my cavalry is after Morgan." He also had a brigade of infantry with some artillery on boats, patrolling the Ohio River to prevent Morgan from crossing and escaping into Ohio. A confident Burnside said that Morgan was essentially trapped on the Ohio side of the river, between the brigades of Hobson and Judah, and promised that when this little affair was over, he would "move into East Tennessee."[35]

Early in the morning of the 19th, near Buffington's Island, close to Portland, on the swollen Ohio River, while feeling their way through a thick fog, Judah's Union forces came in contact with Morgan's men, also lost in the fog.

With his men tired out from the lack of sleep, Morgan intended to cross at this point into West Virginia and make his escape.

The two armies came together unexpectedly when the fog cleared, at which time the shooting started. At first Morgan held the upper hand, his riflemen driving Judah's men back in a panic. Hearing the gunfire, the federal gunboat *Moose*, stationed on the southern end of Buffington's Island, moved into position and opened fire on the Rebel ranks, "throwing shell and shrapnel over the heads of our lads into the ranks of the enemy."[36] The timely support enabled Judah to get control of his brigade.

Then, after about 30 minutes of heavy fighting, Judah's accurate artillery barrages and a cavalry charge by the 5th Indiana Cavalry caused Morgan's line to break, sending the Rebels back in retreat and right into the waiting arms of Hobson's brigade. After taking more casualties from Hobson and the *Moose*, the bulk of the Rebel force, including Colonel Duke, surrendered thus ending the fight that became known as the battle of Buffington's Island.[37]

The amount and variety of plunder recovered was astounding to the conquering Yankees. In addition to guns of all sorts, the battlefield was strewn with "hats, boots, gloves, knives, forks, spoons, calico, ribbons, drinking cups, buggies, carriages, market wagons, circus wagons and an almost endless variety of articles useful and all more or less valuable." It was said that "an inventory of Morgan's plunder would tax the patience of an auctioneer's clerk."[38] It was consistent with the outrageous nature of the plan from the outset, for somehow the Rebels intended to get all this booty across the river.

The Rebel prisoners were dressed "in every possible manner peculiar to civilized man." Many wore "large slouch hats peculiar to the slave states" and their "pantaloons were stuck on their boots." The colorful appearance of the invaders along with the bold and reckless nature of their mission made a favorable impression on some of their captors. For others it was hang 'em high. Sometimes fortune favors the foolish and sometimes it does not. History usually looks at reckless cavaliers with a blend of admiration and disdain.

Having lost most of his men and arms and much of his motivation, Morgan and a fragment of his broken and scattered band of men were still on the loose, riding hard and pursued by Shackelford. Burnside's dispatch to Halleck conveyed the belief that Morgan had deserted the major part of his invading force, leaving them to their own devices. Finally, on the 26th, at Salineville, close to Smith's Ford on the Ohio River, not far from the Ohio-Pennsylvania line, John Hunt Morgan and the rest of his 364 very tired and disillusioned men surrendered to Shackelford.[39]

It was an overwhelming, humiliating defeat for Morgan and his battered raiders. Defeat and capture was not the kind of publicity he was seeking; it added nothing except shame to his reputation. But his legacy was destined

9. Morgan's Raid and the Death of Daniel McCook, Sr.

to be stained from the beginning. His troops were arrayed against a superior and determined force, fired up in the face of an invasion. Even the weather was against them. After his capture, Rebel Colonel Basil W. Duke, Morgan's brother-in-law, confessed that he was stunned at the appearance of Judah's force that seemed to have "dropped from the clouds."[40]

As a result of the rout of Morgan's vaunted raiders, a happy Burnside reported that about 150 Rebels were killed and close to 3,000 were taken prisoner, including Colonel Duke, General Morgan and his brother, Colonel R. C. Morgan. Additionally the invaders lost all their horses, small arms, artillery and other equipment. The North suffered the loss of millions of dollars of property.

The great, foolish, and very long adventure of more than 1,000 miles across two states was over and the North could gloat in triumph. While it put an awful scare into the North, forcing Indiana and Ohio to rebuild and clean up, it accomplished nothing for the South and instead, proved to be a waste of time, money and men—all of which Bragg could ill-afford to lose. And yet Morgan his brave raiders, were long remembered in the South, by both civilian and soldier, in song and story, for their wild escapade through Indiana and Ohio.

Union casualties were comparatively light, but among them was Major Daniel McCook, Sr. He was shot in the chest while on the skirmish line, fighting like a common soldier at Buffington's Island. The wound was at first reported as "very serious, but it is to be hoped that it may not prove so." The sad news was announced in the *Cincinnati Weekly Gazette* which called the elder McCook a "patriotic, loyal, sturdy old gentleman who clung to the service for his country's sake, and especially because he desired, above all things to assist in ridding it of an armed tyranny and despotism" and because of a desire to take revenge on those who "murdered" his son Robert.[41]

McCook's wound proved to be fatal and he died on July 21, 1863, the third "Fighting McCook" to be killed in action. Like his sons Robert and Charles, the elder McCook was given to taking great risks and he died, as he believed one day he would die, in battle, like his sons.[42] His death occurred two years to the date that Charles died after he was shot at Bull Run.

Burnside singled out Major McCook for special mention, noting that the gallant old soldier was shot while "reconnoitering the enemy's force at Buffington Island." General Judah also wrote of his appreciation for the services of Major McCook, a volunteer member of his staff and army paymaster who died of his wound. Martha McCook, now a widow, buried her husband beside her sons Charles and Robert at the family plot in Cincinnati.

General Burnside was among the many prominent men who attended the grand funeral that paid honor to Daniel McCook, Sr. The impressive ceremony featured five companies of infantry, members of the Free Masons, the Cincinnati City Council, and General Alexander M. McCook, Colonel Daniel McCook and Captain John McCook, sons of the deceased.[43]

Not long after McCook's funeral, Governor Tod addressed the people of Ohio, talking about the recent invasion. He noted that the casualty total was relatively light, but among dead and wounded were "a few gallant spirits," including Major Daniel McCook. Tod went on to say that the major was the "honored father of the heroic boys who bear his name and who have won so much glory and renown" in the war. The governor closed his remarks by saying that the fallen man's "memory will be cherished by all and the sincere sympathies of all true patriots will be given to his widow and children."[44]

Martha McCook had every reason to feel that the war had exacted a heavy toll on her family. And while it pained her, she doubtless understood the nature of the McCook men, their loyalty, martial spirit and desire to serve. They were strong because she was strong and it was the collective family strength and pride that would sustain her.

Meanwhile Morgan and his men suffered in prison camp. The general and some of his key officers were locked up at the penitentiary at Columbus, all prisoners of war. But the wily general was still blessed with some luck. He escaped with some of his men on November 29, 1863, amid rumors that Union guards were paid off.

While it was never proven that money was exchanged, the guards did at least unintentionally assist in the prison break. The prisoners learned that beneath the floor of their cell was an air chamber large enough to accommodate a man. They asked the guards to give them some boards so that they could make the floor of their cell drier and more comfortable. Then they proceeded to dig down with table knives to the air chamber and from there to the outside world. They left behind a playful note from "Castle Merion." The note revealed that they commenced digging on November 5, spending three hours a day at their task. Their ended their note with some flowery French: "La patience est arrière, mais son fruit est doux."

Angry Union officials, unable to appreciate the offering of mirth, posted a $1,000 reward for Morgan's capture, but they were forced to admit that "chances of his apprehension are slim."[45] Vowing that he would never be captured again, John Hunt Morgan rejoined the Southern army where he was still deemed useful despite his history of disobeying orders and the big black eye on his service record.

After that it was pretty much downhill for Morgan. He was killed near Greeneville, Tennessee, on September 4, 1864, by a raiding party of Union troops led by General Alvan C. Gillem. News of the coup was conveyed in a simple telegram: "I surprised, [sic] defeated and killed Morgan at Greenville

9. Morgan's Raid and the Death of Daniel McCook, Sr.

[sic] this morning." The celebrated raider was dead, along with several others. About 70 men were taken prisoner.[46]

Morgan was killed at the home of friends, the Williams family, who were Southern supporters. Although it was a safe house, staying in Greeneville was unsafe because not everyone there liked Morgan or the Confederacy. When the Union soldiers rode up early in the morning, Morgan, who was awakened by gunfire, rushed to get the stable and his horse. Suddenly, a woman from across the street pointed to him, while calling out his name. Morgan, sensing he was trapped, called out: "'Don't shoot; I surrender.'" His plea had no effect on the Yankee who fired and crowed: "'I've killed the damned horse thief!'"[47]

The man credited for killing John Hunt Morgan was Andrew J. Campbell, a former Rebel.[48] Morgan's comrade, General Basil Duke, took charge of the famed cavalry unit but he had a strong sense that something vital was missing. Duke was quoted as saying that, with the death of Morgan, "the glory and chivalry seemed gone from the struggle."[49]

Although the Confederate high command never fully warmed up to the undisciplined Morgan, his loss was widely regretted. He was given a stately funeral—and much more. He was exhumed and reburied twice and each time he was memorialized and lionized by military and civilian dignitaries. Lexington, Kentucky became Morgan's final resting place in 1868. His third and final "funeral" was attended by several Union men.

Since Morgan was betrayed for reward money, caught off-guard, and then shot dead in the garden of the house where he had been sleeping,[50] Southerners called the shooting a murder, just as the Union viewed the killing of Robert L. McCook by Frank B. Gurley. Both sides had their martyrs and heroes, and in the death of a hero, there was usually a villain lurking somewhere in the shadows of the tale. Then as now, Americans love their heroes but need villains, for without villains, heroes are irrelevant.

The villainous manner of Morgan's death and his daring exploits as a raider caused him to be relevant and revered by the Southern people. As time went on John Hunt Morgan became "America's Robin Hood." His reputation soared on the wings of a song entitled "The Murder of John Hunt Morgan." Some people believed that he had not been killed, but rather escaped and went west to Oklahoma where he lived out his life as Dr. Jack Hunt Cole.[51] Although it is doubtful that any serious historian believes that tale, to this day Morgan's life of daring and reckless courage, as an intrepid defender of the "Lost Cause," is celebrated and honored. Unlike countless thousands who were killed and eventually forgotten, he remains a prominent part of Southern history, folklore and legend.

10

The Chattanooga Campaign and the Battle of Chickamauga

"Tell General Granger when my brigade retreats, he can report Dan McCook among the killed."—Colonel Daniel McCook, Jr., September 20, 1863

Every campaign of the Civil War was memorable and unique, creating unforgettable memories of rough terrain, pain and suffering. But for high drama and a strange mixture of ecstatic highs and dismal lows, combined with an interesting mix of personalities, the Chattanooga campaign stands alone. For Colonel Daniel McCook, Jr., the adventure started on January 27, 1863, when he was placed in command of the 2nd Brigade, 4th Division, Army of the Ohio, in accordance with General Order No. 6. By order of Major General George H. Thomas, McCook's brigade was made up of the 85th, 86th, and 125th Illinois infantry regiments and the 52nd Ohio.[1]

In May of 1863, McCook was in Nashville, where he "reviewed" his brigade in what was described as a "magnificent appearance." A correspondent of the *Nashville Daily Union* watched the soldiers as they passed in review, company after company. He confessed that he was little acquainted with Colonel McCook, but "from what I have seen of him I should say he is a man of transcendent ability, both as a scholar and a soldier."[2]

It was a high compliment to the young Colonel McCook, just then playing an important role in the western Union army as it emerged from a long period of camp life at Murfreesboro, Tennessee. All knew that much fighting was on tap for 1863, and General Rosecrans and his commanders began the work of re-equipping and re-supplying the army. The name was changed to the Army of the Cumberland and the old wing concept was discarded in favor corps.

10. The Chattanooga Campaign and the Battle of Chickamauga

The war-watchers were keeping tabs on Rosecrans with the expectation that he would provide more victories. Although Rosecrans was focused on defeating the rebellion, and gave no hint as to political ambition, there were those on the homefront who were eyeing him for political reasons. Among them were some leading Republicans who, having lost faith in Lincoln's ability to lead the Union to ultimate victory, wanted to see Rosecrans in the White House as commander-in-chief. The general famously turned down the offer, throwing his goodwill and support to Lincoln, the right man in the right place. The unequivocal and emphatic support for Lincoln quieted down calls for Rosecrans to run for president in 1864.[3]

General Rosecrans' huge Army of the Cumberland was on the move in June of 1863, after several months spent planning and preparing for the march. After seemingly endless, angry dispatches from Halleck and Stanton demanding action, Rosecrans—who doggedly stuck to his own schedule—finally broke camp. The Union target in the "western theater" was Chattanooga, Tennessee, a Confederate stronghold and an important conquest for the Union. Chattanooga was a critical railroad and supply center for the Confederates and for several months there was talk about a big battle that would, one day, be fought there.

Eighteen sixty-three would prove to be a pivotal year for war-weary people on both sides of the conflict. As the year began, the Union and the Confederate leadership were under considerable pressure as they struggled to prop up the lagging support of their people, when after two years of war and a shocking body count, there was no end in sight. Neither side had the advantage; it was essentially a stalemate. Jefferson Davis was losing popularity in the South because of his high-handed tactics that ran afoul of the sacred doctrine of states' rights. In his attempts to unify the South, he aroused the anger of the people and the press, all of whom distrusted, or hated, his "big government" policy. The Lincoln administration had experienced political fallout in the mid-term elections of 1862, but despite the losses, he had much more executive power at his disposal than his rival. And he would need it because Copperhead fever was rising in Indiana, Illinois and Ohio, where legislatures were decidedly anti–Lincoln. As if Lincoln wasn't having enough trouble adopting a winning military strategy, there was talk in those three states about pulling out of the Union and forming a "Northwest Confederacy."

Recruiting for both sides was a serious problem too because of the lack of progress on the battlefields and the high number of casualties that cooled the ardor of young men who no longer saw any glamour in being a soldier. Patriotism was drying up among the young men, and finding army life unappealing, deserters and draft-dodgers, from the North and South, headed for the western plains. Conscription was unpopular in both sections causing argument and confrontation, but the anti-draft riots in New York City in the summer of 1863 left death and destruction on a scale that no one could have predicted. After the shooting, looting and burning stopped, the recruiting continued, adding more young men to the ranks—unless, of course, the recruit came from a rich family and could take advantage of a conspicuous exception.

John D. Rockefeller, J. Pierpont Morgan and Andrew Carnegie were all up-and-coming young entrepreneurs. Each man paid a substitute $300 to take his place in the ranks. The trio had made a large pile of money from the war, and they were unwilling to risk injury or death when it was so easy to pay a substitute what was, for them, a mere pittance. They, and others, did so without shame or qualms of conscience. It was truly, as someone said, "a rich man's war but a poor man's fight," an attitude that did not build *esprit de corps*.

Despite the turmoil and anguish, Lincoln and the Union were rewarded for hanging tough in the face of growing pessimism with huge victories at Gettysburg, Pennsylvania, and Vicksburg, Mississippi. The double wins on Independence Day were a source of great joy for Lincoln and his administration and caused a seismic shift in the mood and attitude of the general public. The Union armies under General U. S. Grant and General George Meade had come through after mighty efforts, and with the North (minus the Copperheads) cheering, all eyes shifted to the Army of the Cumberland. Would there be another great victory? Lee had been driven out of Pennsylvania and the Mississippi River was in the hands of the Union. Would Tennessee be next to fall under Union control?

Major General W. S. Rosecrans' Army of the Cumberland consisted of three corps, headed by Major Generals George H. Thomas, Alexander M. McCook and Thomas J. Crittenden. The corps, acting in concert, drove the Rebels under General Braxton Bragg away from central Tennessee in a brilliantly orchestrated series of maneuvers known as the Tullahoma campaign. Rosecrans kept the pressure on, driving the enemy further to the south. Finally, Bragg abandoned Chattanooga and the Union forces under Crittenden entered the town unmolested and took control.

After buttoning up Chattanooga with sufficient troops to hold it, an eager and confident Rosecrans divided his command into three lines of pursuit. Thinking he had Bragg on the run, a confident Rosecrans was a man on the hunt, believing that it was just a matter of time before he would have the Confederates cornered. What he didn't know, however, is that Bragg was not running. He had snapped out of a bout of mental torpor and was planning an attack. Far from having been outwitted, the wily Confederate commander welcomed reinforcements from General Robert E. Lee and was in a position

10. The Chattanooga Campaign and the Battle of Chickamauga

to destroy Rosecrans' army one corps at a time. When Rosecrans realized he had made a serious mistake, he scrambled to get all three corps back together and in a position to make a coordinated fight.

Rosecrans had a Reserve Corps under Major General Gordon Granger that included the infantry brigade headed by Colonel Daniel McCook. Daniel's cousin, Colonel Edward M. McCook, was in charge of a division in the cavalry corps commanded by Major General Robert B. Mitchell. Captain John J. McCook, Daniel's youngest brother, was General Crittenden's aide-de-camp.

While Rosecrans' huge army was making its way toward a confrontation with Bragg's Confederates, Colonel Daniel McCook, known to be rash, lost his temper during a confrontation with a junior officer. On September 1, 1863, while the 52nd Ohio was crossing the Elk River in Tennessee, some mules and wagons got stuck in the mud and the stubborn animals refused to move. Lieutenant John J. Troxell, quartermaster for the 52nd, and other men and officers were struggling with the mules "in a frenzy of lashing, kicking, cursing and swearing" when Colonel McCook arrived and weighed in on the situation. Suddenly a heated verbal exchange between McCook and Troxell became a "violent altercation" in the presence of the mired mules. Somehow the mules got moving again, and it should have ended there, but a few days later McCook demanded, and received, Troxell's resignation. He was immediately ordered out the regimental camp while McCook and the 52nd Ohio moved on.[4]

General Gordon Granger commanded a Reserve Corps in General William S. Rosecrans' Army of the Cumberland during the long and bloody Chattanooga campaign in the summer and fall of 1863. Colonel Daniel McCook, Jr., was a brigade commander in the Reserve Corps. While on the march, some of McCook's hungry troops took to foraging for food, a practice that Granger had forbidden. This so angered Granger that he ordered the foragers severely punished, setting off a near-mutiny by men and officers who saw in Granger a martinet willing to engage in excessively cruelty. But cooler heads prevailed, the matter ended and was forgotten after the Union forces fought the two-day battle of Chickamauga, in which both Granger and McCook directed their men with distinction.

On September 12, Granger's Reserve Corps was encamped at Bridgeport, Alabama, when orders were received to make haste for Rossville, Georgia, just south of Chattanooga. After two long, arduous days of marching through "suffocating dust," Granger's corps arrived at Rossville, where his troops were positioned so they could protect Rosecrans' in the event that he was forced to retreat. Granger was also ordered to be prepared to move out quickly, should he hear the sound of battle.[5]

Of course battle was what everyone expected, and while waiting for the shooting to start, Granger became mired in an untimely command crisis. He had ordered that no foraging be allowed and threatened to punish, severely, all violators. But his troops were terribly hungry and many scoured the countryside in search of food. When Granger learned that this order had been disobeyed, he lost his cool, revealing the cruel martinet that lurked in the dark recesses of his conscience. He summarily ordered the foragers to be hung by their thumbs near his tent. They were to be whipped.

It was an act of military tyranny that would be long remembered by the men of Granger's corps, for it set off a storm of protest from among both enlisted men and officers. An officer in Dan McCook's 52nd Ohio said that the soldiers had been driven to desperation for the lack of food, and that had Granger not relented, he would have been "killed then and there." And it was only after a battery was pointed at the headquarters tent that Granger ordered the men released and angrily "slunk away into his tent, cursing everybody."[6]

Fortunately, Granger managed to get his anger under control so he could conduct himself like a commanding general. And just in time too, for very soon after the foraging incident, the first shot of what was to be a great battle was fired. On September 18, 1863, a soldier from the 7th Pennsylvania Cavalry fired on a group of officers in gray. He missed but it was a start.

Next, on the Union left, Colonel Robert Minty, with his cavalry brigade, found himself in a hot skirmish against advancing Rebels at Reed's bridge on the Chickamauga Creek. Granger ordered Daniel McCook's brigade to give Minty a hand. Colonel McCook hurried forward as he was not one to waste an opportunity to fight, especially if it meant that he would have the chance to perform with valor on the field of battle. One of his regimental commanders proudly declared that Colonel McCook was "always ready when the time comes to meet the enemy."[7]

Colonel McCook was single-minded, gutsy and ambitious. He could also be impetuous and rash, and one imminent writer called him dangerous "to both himself and his troops." But among his fellow officers, being overly headstrong was not universally thought of as bad, and McCook was looked upon by many as a coming man whose star was in its ascendancy. As a colonel, he had reached the goal that he set for himself when he enlisted in the Union

10. The Chattanooga Campaign and the Battle of Chickamauga 157

army. He was more than ready for a promotion, being only a colonel while his brother Alexander, just three years older, already wore two stars and his brother Robert had died a brigadier.

When Daniel McCook reached Reed's bridge, he sensed the grand opportunity was within his grasp. He managed to capture a few men trailing at the end of General Bushrod Johnson's brigade, including some members of the regimental band. While the prisoners refused to talk, McCook was convinced that an isolated Rebel brigade was lurking nearby, just waiting to be bagged.

Johnson's brigade had crossed Reed's bridge late in the afternoon on the 18th, but McCook apparently had no knowledge of the crossing. Bringing in a brigade of prisoners would certainly attract the attention of his superiors and win a recommendation for a promotion. When Colonel John G. Mitchell, a brigade commander in Granger's corps, arrived at the intersection of Reed's bridge and Jay's Mill, McCook buttonholed him and implored his assistance in effecting the capture of the band of Rebels. He was excited and could talk of nothing else. Mitchell finally agreed to support McCook on his dangerous venture and the two agreed to execute their mission early the next morning.[8]

Meanwhile, on the Union right, at Crawfish Springs, Daniel's brother, the two-star general, was relaxed and ready for a fight too. Most of the Union cavalry was under McCook's control. He reported that his guns had been silent all day on the 18th, but that his men had their rations and ammunition. General McCook closed his dispatch to General James A. Garfield with "My men are confident. Let us in."[9] Late in the afternoon McCook received a simple, direct response from Rosecrans: "Move up."[10]

On the morning of the 19th, John G. Mitchell and Daniel McCook were up and in the saddle early. But Colonel McCook's subordinate officers, who lacked his enthusiasm, didn't have the men in line. Instead, they were casually eating breakfast. McCook got moving, sending one regiment to destroy Reed's bridge, thereby denying Southern soldiers an easy crossing of Chickamauga Creek.[11] A sharp skirmish erupted between McCook's men and a brigade of Rebel cavalry at Jay's Mill, but there was no bagging of a brigade.[12]

Then a dispatch came from Rosecrans ordering McCook and Mitchell to withdraw. The mission was considered too risky so the danger was defused. Colonel McCook obeyed the order of course, but was extremely disappointed at missing the opportunity to display the gallantry needed to get his longed for promotion.[13] The coveted silver star was still just out of reach and the McCook family would be forced to wait a little longer before it could boast about having another general.

McCook was truly disappointed that the mission was not completed to his satisfaction. But his contesting of Reed's bridge on the 18th disrupted Bragg's plan of battle. In order to launch an effective attack on Rosecrans, Bragg had ordered all of his army across the creek on the 17th for an attack that was supposed to be launched at sunrise on the 18th. But Union resistance combined with slowness on the part of Bragg's generals thwarted the grand strategy.[14]

Although Colonel McCook was mistaken in his belief that a single brigade had crossed Chickamauga Creek, his error, according to one Civil War writer, precipitated the start of the one of the greatest and bloodiest battles in the entire war. As the Union command was quick to learn, Bragg's forces had crossed during the night of the 18th, and the fighting started the next day with both sides out of position.[15]

It didn't take long before brigades from both sides were in position and the firing of muskets and artillery created a terrible sound that would ring in the memory of survivors until they died. The epic battle of Chickamauga was a disaster for both the Union army and Confederate armies. The awful, two-day bloodbath took place on September 19 and 20, 1863, with horrendous casualties on both sides. A decisive win could easily have gone to the Union because General Thomas, on the left flank of the battle, had successfully beaten back attacks both days. It was on the Union right, however, that calamity occurred. Major General Alexander M. McCook was in charge of the right but his corps had been greatly depleted by Rosecrans who sent two of McCook's divisions to support Thomas.

Then an ill-timed and badly-advised decision by Major General Thomas J. Wood to pull his division out of position on the Union right, in response to an order from Rosecrans, left a wide gap in the battle line. Taking advantage of situation, Rebel General James "Pete" Longstreet hurried his columns into the gap, shattering McCook's weakened lines and scattering the troops. The result was a complete route of both the Union right and center. General McCook tried desperately to rally what troops were left but it was useless, useless.

Amid the smoke, chaos and thunder of musket and artillery fire, Rosecrans made the decision to leave the battlefield and go to Chattanooga to clear his head and regroup. His army had been badly mauled and he had to gather together what remained of it in order to retain control over Chattanooga. A stunned Rosecrans was joined at Chattanooga by generals McCook and Thomas J. Crittenden.

It was General George H. Thomas that emerged as the hero, for, unlike Rosecrans, Crittenden and McCook, he did not leave the battleground. In fact, Thomas found that he was positioned on high ground on which to make a stand. He was joined by Granger who decided that despite orders to the contrary, he would see what he could do to help out. Granger ordered Daniel McCook to stay behind and cover the Ringgold Road on the Union left. His last words to Colonel McCook were "hold the road to the last extremity."

10. The Chattanooga Campaign and the Battle of Chickamauga   159

McCook replied, "When my brigade retreats, he [Granger] can report Dan McCook among the killed."[16] Granger later ordered McCook to forget about guarding the road and instead take a position on an open ridge northwest of the McDonald farm. Obeying the order, Dan McCook and his brigade were in the thick of the fighting.

Granger found Thomas where the latter had rallied the troops on a place called Horseshoe Ridge, high ground that the triumphant Rebels felt they could and must take to make their victory complete. Thomas, with the use of Granger's fresh troops, stubbornly and courageously directed the battle, holding off the Rebels. He was fighting with the divisions of generals Absalom Baird, John M. Brannan, Richard W. Johnson, John M. Palmer, Thomas J. Wood and Joseph J. Reynolds. General Philip Sheridan, whose division in McCook's corps had taken a terrible beating, returned and joined the fray with about 1,500 men who still had some fight in them. But it was the timely arrival of the Reserve Corps that kept Thomas from being overwhelmed.

It quickly became clear that the stand could not hold indefinitely. Ammunition was running low and Thomas, who would hereafter be called the "Rock of Chickamauga," felt that his men had done all they could and ordered a retreat to Chattanooga after nightfall. At about 10 o'clock on the night of the 20th, Daniel McCook's exhausted brigade trudged away from Horseshoe Ridge onto McFarland's Gap Road, the last Union unit to leave the battlefield. The anxious officer who wanted so much to start the fight was the last to retreat. He reported the loss of just two men.[17]

Granger and Thomas were praised by the public and press for heroic service, but other generals fared far worse. For when a battle is lost, someone has to be blamed, and because they left the field of battle, thereby essentially conceding defeat, generals McCook and Crittenden were relieved of command. While their families and friends steadfastly supported them, both men were hammered by the press and subjected to courts of inquiry concerning their conduct at Chickamauga. Even though they were cleared of all charges, they would spend the rest of the war doing work other than commanding corps, or even divisions, in battle.

Rosecrans fared no better, and, at the urging of Secretary of War Stanton, President Lincoln decided to relieve him of command. General U. S. Grant was sent to Chattanooga and it was he who placed General George H. Thomas—America's new hero—in charge of the Army of the Cumberland. Thomas found himself in command of an army under siege in Chattanooga, suffering from hunger and under the threat of attack by Bragg's army.

Following the disturbing departure of his brother from the Army of the Cumberland, Colonel Daniel McCook, Jr., re-focused his efforts toward making further contributions to the Union cause, like the good soldier he was. If he

Major General George H. Thomas was a skillful, patient and preserving commander, respected by his peers and well-liked by the troops. He was from Virginia, but his loyalty was to the Union rather than his home state. Because he chose the Union, his sisters severed their relationship with him, for as a traitor to the South, he was "dead to them." They never spoke to him again. By the summer of 1863, Thomas had two years of leading men in battle, but it was at the battle of Chickamauga, on day two, that he showed America what he was made of. After the Union right and center had been decimated, Thomas stayed in the field and rallied his men at a place called Horseshoe Ridge, high ground that offered protection from the Rebels. They fought bravely until they were low on ammunition and were forced to retreat. For this courageous stand, Thomas earned the title "Rock of Chickamauga."

10. The Chattanooga Campaign and the Battle of Chickamauga   161

felt any anger at the army for unseating his brother, he kept it to himself or within the family. There was still a war to fight and an enemy to defeat. His work, and that of his brothers and cousins, was not yet finished. And besides, he and his family probably believed that Alexander would be given another field command. After all, he had a reputation as a fighter; he earned and deserved the title "Fighting McCook."

Unlike the fallen Alexander, Dan kept his command. Under the great rearrangement of the Army of the Cumberland, with General George H. Thomas at its head, the 52nd Ohio Infantry regiment was still Dan McCook's regiment. The 52nd, along with three Illinois regiments, made up the 3rd Brigade, 2nd Division, 14th Army Corps. The 2nd Division was led by Brigadier General Jefferson C. Davis (no relation to the Confederate president), another survivor of the post–Chickamauga housecleaning.

From the time it came together in August of 1862, the 52nd Ohio had played significant roles in three major campaigns: Perryville, Stones River and Chickamauga. While the regiment had not been cast in the role of an aggressor and had yet to take heavy casualties, it followed orders, performed admirably, and would always be known as "Dan McCook's regiment."

For most of October of 1863, McCook's 3rd Brigade was situated on North Chickamauga Creek, watching, gathering intelligence and sending it back to headquarters in messages to General James A. Garfield, another general who retained his position in the aftermath of Chickamauga. The Federals had been under siege in Chattanooga following the defeat at Chickamauga. The mountain terrain and the presence of Bragg's army on Lookout Mountain and Missionary Ridge left the Union with a single, narrow trail out of the trap. But something was in the works and whatever it was it had to happen soon for Union morale was low.

Following the debacle at Chickamauga, the dispirited Union army—aching for revenge—was bottled up in Chattanooga in the autumn of 1863, long before the shoe-shine boy popped his "boogie-woogie rag." The city they set out to conquer had become a stockade that confined them. Aside from the surrounding mountain scenery, there was nothing about the town that impressed its occupiers. Nestled in a deep valley on the south bank of the Tennessee River, Chattanooga was described as a dirty, rundown, nondescript place that the civilian population had largely deserted.

Those poor souls who did not leave lived in conditions so squalid that a Yankee soldier compared their plight to people living in "the worst tenement house in New York City."[18] A railroad town without a working train, Chattanooga, once a thriving trade center, was isolated and cut off from both North and South. The city bore the appearance of gloom and doom, as if it had been sentenced to a slow death.

Desperate soldiers did the best they could to keep themselves alive while their horses and mules starved due to the lack of forage. Homes and churches were confiscated and used for storage, arsenals, hospitals or other purposes. Trees were felled and the city was ransacked for material that was used to fortify it in the event of an attack. As the scrounging Union troops busied themselves, observing Rebels called them "beavers in blue."[19]

Amid the anxiety and deprivation, there were some cheery and timely diversions. The wife of an officer recalled that she had access to a "wheezy piano" that was brought to her quarters from "a deserted house." While she played, others gathered around and sang patriotic songs such as "We'll Rally Round the Flag." Writing about it years later, she suggested that the rousing renditions of the songs were like a signal to the outside world that hungry men and women were struggling in Chattanooga, but they had not given up for they had the will to carry on.[20]

Thomas had vowed to hold out until starvation took effect. The situation

Chattanooga, Tennessee, was a small but important railroad town at the foot of a mountain, thus it was coveted by both North and South. In this photograph, taken in 1864, Lookout Mountain looms in the background. It was on this mountain that the so-called "Battle Above the Clouds" was fought in November of 1863, getting its name from foggy, misty conditions that Union troops were faced with when they made a showy assault on Lookout, driving off the out-numbered Confederates. The spectacular but overrated victory by General Joe "Fighting Joe" Hooker's XX Corps, Army of the Cumberland, was the cause of celebration throughout the North.

10. The Chattanooga Campaign and the Battle of Chickamauga 163

was so dire that U. S. Grant took immediate steps to get food and supplies into Chattanooga. According to Grant's *Memoirs and Selected Letters*, all supplies coming in to Chattanooga came from Nashville. But because Bragg controlled the railroad coming from Bridgeport, Alabama, along with the best wagon roads leading in and out of Chattanooga from the north and south, provisions had to be carried over a rough, hazardous, mountainous trail for a distance of about 60 miles. Grant was familiar with this trail for he had traveled it himself, a trip made even more painful because he was suffering from an injury that resulted from a fall from a horse.

On October 24, after talking with Thomas and General W. F. "Baldy" Smith, an engineer, Grant set in motion a plan that required coordination, stealth and daring. Troops from the Army of the Potomac, under the command of General Joe Hooker, stationed at Bridgeport, were selected to carry out part of the mission. They had been sent by Halleck, prior to Grant's arrival, to reinforce Rosecrans. Another 1,800 troops from Chattanooga, under the command of General William Hazen, were ordered to float, at night, on the Tennessee River on pontoons boats toward Brown's Ferry. At the same time General "Baldy" Smith marched with more soldiers toward Brown's Ferry overland on the north bank of the river.[21]

On the 26th, Hooker marched out of Bridgeport, going east to converge with the other Union troops at Brown's Ferry. Hazen's men succeeded in disembarking at Brown's Ferry and thereafter surprised and captured the Rebel pickets. Smith's men crossed the river on a pontoon bridge, and Hooker moved in to occupy much of the Lookout Mountain valley, with his 154th New York Infantry regiment leading the charge.[22] The combined forces fortified their position and formed a connection with the rest of the Union army. The net effect of the mission was to gain control of the Tennessee River from Lookout valley to Bridgeport, thus ending the tortuous 60-mile march through the mountains. The threat of starvation was lifted and soon a well-fed, newly-clothed army was ready for further action.[23]

As was General Grant. He had a rejuvenated army and he was anxious to use it. And to further his plans for driving Bragg off his perch, Grant summoned Major General W. T. Sherman and his Army of the Tennessee. Sherman had become Grant's friend and most trusted ally. As such, he was destined to play a key role in future events.

To force a Rebel retreat, Grant and his generals came up with a plan and Dan McCook was given a major role. The plan was to move a portion of the Union forces at night across the Tennessee River on a pontoon bridge and attack Bragg's right flank on Missionary Ridge. Sherman's Army of the Tennessee was chosen to do the flanking. His friend and former law partner, Daniel McCook, was given the daunting task of moving of troops to the place where they would cross the river. The troops would be transported in small boats on the Chickamauga Creek to the pontoon bridge, moving quietly under the cover of darkness.

Colonel McCook's brigade went about "selecting the roads, clearing the creek, furnishing the crews for the boats and keeping the citizens under guard." He had to accomplish all this without attracting the attention of the enemy. As if relishing the opportunity to both impress high command and accomplish an important mission, Dan McCook went to work with energy and zeal. By Friday, November 20, 116 boats were under guard, well-hidden and ready for the troop movement.

Lieutenant Colonel Allen L. Fahnestock in McCook's 86th Illinois kept a diary on the clandestine maneuver. November 20, he noted, was "clear and warm." Each man was given 100 cartridges with the expectation that they would move out on a "moment's notice." The next morning, a Saturday, volunteers with experience in rowing a boat were called for and many men stepped up. Next, he noted in his diary on the 22nd that the men "remained in camp," but were ready to "float down the Tennessee River."[24]

Everything was going as planned when McCook, in a dispatch to headquarters, said that one of his pickets was greeted by a Rebel picket from across the river. The Confederate soldier asked when the pontoon boats would be ready. He then said, "you Yankees think you will take us by surprise." McCook took this mean that the mission was no longer a secret and that the troops could expect a rough crossing. McCook was not surprised, however, because before he was fully apprised of the grand scenario, a civilian appeared at his camp and revealed the plans in detail to a captain.[25]

Despite this unfortunate turn of events, McCook went ahead according to orders. To prevent the Rebels from establishing their artillery at the opposite side of the river, he sent the 110th Illinois across to get into position at the point where Sherman's troops intended to land. He ordered the regimental commander of the 110th to "'silence their [the enemy's] guns at all hazards'" should the Rebels fire on the flotilla.[26]

McCook's official report reveals the importance of his role in the mission. Success depended upon good timing, hard work, discipline and more than a little luck. In order to transport the pontoons "under the cover of the woods and out of rebel sight," it was necessary to build a road three miles long to North Chickamauga Creek. Next McCook arrested all the civilians in the area on the pretext that he had been "bushwhacked" and therefore no one could be trusted.[27]

Everything was ready on schedule. Sherman's divisions were hidden in the trees eating their evening meal while McCook's pontoon boats were inspected and deemed ready for the mission. At midnight on November 23,

10. The Chattanooga Campaign and the Battle of Chickamauga 165

the boats with "Sherman's Boys" on board were launched and sent floating on the creek to the point of crossing. Each boat held 25 to 30 men. The current was swift and it was so dark that one boat was almost invisible to the next. An officer writing home to his wife called it a "lively and exciting time."[28] And yet despite the darkness and danger, all the boats landed quietly and safely on the left bank of the Tennessee River and the troops immediately began crossing on the shaky pontoon bridge that consisted of a string of boats nearly 1,400 feet long.

The plan was to utilize two "flying ferrys" but due to high, rough water, only one was available. This was the cause of further delays that tested Grant's patience and prevented Sherman from getting into position in time for a coordinated attack. Finally, according to McCook's report, the "landing was completed without opposition or even knowledge of the enemy." The risky mission was a success. By daylight 8,000 troops had crossed the river. They were lined up and ready for battle, waiting for a clear-headed General Sherman—still free from his old demons—to give the order.[29]

Grant's forces were now in a position to squeeze Bragg and force him off his high perch. With Sherman on the Rebel right, Hooker on the left and Thomas pounding away at the center, the Union forces took Lookout Mountain and Missionary Ridge in spectacular fashion that thrilled the North, restored troop morale and added to the fame of Grant, Sherman, Thomas and Hooker. Bragg was handed a devastating defeat and his troops and wagons were soon on their way into northern Georgia.

While Georgia was the logical direction for the Union army in its seeming endless pursuit of Bragg, Sherman, with six divisions, was diverted to Knoxville soon after the battles for Chattanooga. The goal: relieve General Ambrose Burnside who was believed to be in danger of an attack by Longstreet, with vastly superior numbers. Longstreet had taken his army corps off Lookout Mountain in early November to get away from Bragg and to link up with a portion of Robert E. Lee's army for the purpose of driving Burnside out of East Tennessee.

Burnside had been in Knoxville since early September, having scored a bloodless victory that was whooped up in many newspapers. Among them, the *Cincinnati Weekly Gazette* praised the Union effort, calling it "skillfully planned and energetically executed." In an excited report, the *Gazette* declared that the Union was, at long last, in "full possession of East Tennessee." Calling the march an "ovation" the reporter noted with pride that "thousands of people of every age, sex, color and condition lined the road" as Burnside and his men entered the city. "Shouts and cheers and tears intermingled in the martial music, and joy reigned supreme."[30] But because of the threat posed by Longstreet, joy turned to worry, and another timely rescue was needed.

While Sherman recalled that the order to move out was given "unexpectedly and without due preparation,"[31] the move was precipitated, in part, at least, by Major General Henry W. Halleck's dispatch to Grant dated November 14, 1863. Halleck asked: "Cannot Thomas move on Longstreet's rear and force him to fall back?" The general-in-chief reasoned that should Burnside retreat, East Tennessee would be abandoned to the Rebels, which would be a "terrible misfortune, and must be averted if possible."[32]

Grant—who had been anxious to send help to Burnside—agreed, and soon after driving the Confederates away from Chattanooga, he ordered General Gordon Granger and his Fourth Corps on their way to Knoxville. But Granger drug his feet much to the dismay of Grant, who then ordered his dependable friend Sherman to take charge of the expedition. The energetic and buoyant Sherman, at the head of Major General Oliver Howard's corps and General Jefferson C. Davis' division, was soon on the march. The Knoxville mission took on the urgency of a forced march. Burnside, known as "Burn" to his friends, was thought to be in a tight spot, and help was on the way.

Beginning on November 29, Colonel Daniel McCook, whose brigade took part in the Knoxville relief effort, recalled marching for "ten days, without shoes, blankets, or overcoats, and almost without regular rations."[33] Another regimental commander, Colonel Oscar F. Harmon, commended his tattered troops for enduring the harsh, cold conditions, saying, "I doubt if any army in the history of our country suffered more or as heroically."[34] That McCook reported only two killed and five wounded indicates that little fighting was done along the way.

When the rumpled, foot-sore and hungry troops marched through the fertile valley of East Tennessee, the long-suffering pro–Union men emerged from hiding to hail Sherman's army. Loyalty was at long last rewarded and Lincoln's fondest wish had come true. Although conditions were cold and miserable, from town to town the Yankees were greeted with cheering and music.

In his memoir, Anson G. McCook described the East Tennessee loyalists as the "most patient and uncomplaining people I ever knew."[35] They had suffered mightily under Confederate domination after Tennessee seceded and their dogged determination to stay with the Union led to continual retribution by their occupiers. To punish them, the Confederates captured and hanged many Union men, the news of which brought Lincoln to despair.[36]

Now, with the approach of Sherman's soldiers, serious help was in the offing, but there would be no battle. As Sherman drew near, Longstreet pulled away from Knoxville and trailed off toward Virginia. The Southern command believed that should the Union successfully drive Bragg off Lookout Mountain,

10. The Chattanooga Campaign and the Battle of Chickamauga

Longstreet would be forced to leave Knoxville, since his "rear would be so seriously exposed" to attack.[37] Since Bragg had, in fact, been pushed off Lookout Mountain, and with Sherman's army moving on Knoxville, the usually cautious Longstreet made the prudent decision.

When Sherman entered the city, he was astonished to find the amiable Burnside comfortably ensconced in a mansion with a table laden with good food. In his *Memoirs*, Sherman recalled that had he known Burnside and his troops were not starving, he would not have driven his men so hard. Having accomplished his purpose, however, Sherman set his ragged and mostly shoeless soldiers on a course, à la Valley Forge, back to Chattanooga.[38]

From Chattanooga Sherman wrote to General Davis with special pride, commending the "soldiers and patriots" who marched "through cold and mud without a murmur, trusting to accidents for shelter and subsistence." He characterized the miserable campaign as "short but most useful" and singled out for special commendation Davis' brigade commanders, including Colonel Daniel McCook, his law partner in the pre-war days at Leavenworth, Kansas.[39] Sherman would need that kind of dedication and loyalty, for he was about to march his army where no Union army had gone before: into the heart of Georgia. Tennessee would never again be seriously threatened by the Confederacy, Lincoln was pleased, and it was time to take the war further south.

Some kind words were probably just the tonic McCook needed after the miserable march. He was so sick and run-down that he went to an army doctor and then applied for a leave of absence. The examining surgeon certified that having conducted a careful examination of Colonel McCook, he found "that the lower one third of his right lung is hepatised, apparently from a previous pneumonia." The surgeon recommended that in order to prevent possible permanent disability, McCook be given "freedom from exposure to the vicissitudes of camp life." It was approved by General Jefferson C. Davis and McCook went to Washington and then to Steubenville, Ohio, for much-needed rest and family time.[40]

11
A Dead Stop at Kennesaw Mountain

> "This noted eminence [Kennesaw Mountain] is a second Lookout [Mountain] among its fellows, and forms a complete barrier to our approach to Marietta."—*New York Times*, July 8, 1864

With the resounding rout of Bragg's army at Lookout Mountain and Missionary Ridge, the Union's prospects were once again on the rise. Free from hunger and siege at Chattanooga, the Army of the Cumberland regained its pride and fighting spirit. Once again General George H. Thomas had done well, even if he did have to accept the uncomfortable fact that General Grant and the armies of Sherman and Hooker helped him out of a tight spot. Whatever feelings of jealousy or discomfort Thomas may have harbored, he kept them to himself, and like the good and loyal soldier that he was, the Virginia native was pleased to be a part of the big victory and looked forward to the next phase of the war.

Thomas and his colleagues would soon be pursuing the Rebels again, but they would not have to tangle with General Braxton Bragg. Their wily old foe and nemesis was removed from command. After Chattanooga was lost, Bragg knew that he too was finished and asked to be relieved. Jefferson Davis granted his old friend's request and placed Major General Joseph E. Johnston at the head of the Confederate Army of Tennessee. Bragg packed up and went to Richmond to assist Davis with the military operations of the armies of the Confederacy.

After the Chattanooga debacle, Bragg's usefulness and popularity were at an all-time low. He never seemed to be able to connect with and earn the respect of his soldiers and was always at odds with his subordinate field commanders. Developing and maintaining good relationships with others was not his strong suit. The caustic and gloomy Bragg was called "the most unpopular General in the South" following his removal from command.[1]

11. A Dead Stop at Kennesaw Mountain

A career army officer, Joseph E. "Joe" Johnston, a Virginia native, graduated from West Point in 1829 and after a stint as an Indian fighter, served with distinction in the Mexican War. He rose to the rank of brigadier general in the U.S. Army and owned the dubious distinction of being the highest-ranking officer to resign and join the Confederacy. Johnston suffered a disabling injury in 1862, but he recovered fully and re-entered the war with a confident attitude. He was well-respected in the South and well-liked by his soldiers.

General Johnston would prove to be an elusive opponent for the Union pursuers. He adopted a thoughtful, more defensive posture than did Bragg. Johnston would fight defensively when forced into battle, but his emphasis was on preserving his army while watching for an opportunity to strike Sherman, whom he respected. Also, protecting Atlanta was forefront in his mind. Despite being hated by Davis, Johnston was the best option for the Confederacy as the war entered its third year.

To engage Johnston's army the Union brass first had to find it. So, in February 1864, General Thomas decided to conduct a reconnaissance of the Rebel positions that were located near Dalton, in northwest Georgia, approximately 30 miles south of Chattanooga. Colonel Daniel McCook had returned from leave and reported for duty in the Army of the Cumberland just in time to participate in the search. McCook's brigade moved out toward Dalton, embarking on a tense operation.

McCook's report reflected with pride the brave, well-ordered work of his brigade. He noted that his brigade joined Davis' division on February 23 and by the next day had advanced as far as "Buzzard Roost Gap, where the enemy were [sic] found in full force." On the morning of the 25th his skirmish line advanced steadily despite facing the sun and haze. By mid-afternoon, his men faced heavy enemy fire and he ordered the reserves of the 85th and 86th Illinois to join the skirmish line. They held their position until dark when relief came. McCook praised his artillery, although not for what it did to the enemy, but rather for something self-inflicted. In a convoluted and strangely written line, he said that it "so admirably served that it managed to kill one man at least, who belonged to the eighty-fifth Illinois." On the whole, however, casualties were light and McCook reported a loss of four killed and 18 wounded. He concluded that "every man and officer did his duty."[2]

It was the modest beginning of a long, historic and tortuous march through Georgia, one that would climax in the capture of Atlanta and Savannah, cut north through the Carolinas, and ultimately result in the final defeat of the Confederacy. Lincoln placed the strategy for victory in the hands of the man who had proven to be the most effective general in the Union arsenal, namely, General U. S. Grant.

Grant had become the most popular general in the North, and on March 10, 1864, he was appointed to the rank of lieutenant general, making him the highest-ranking officer in the Union army. At General Henry W. Halleck's request, Lincoln gave Grant command over all the nation's armies. Thus for the first time Grant outranked Halleck. Almost immediately, however, Lincoln gave Halleck a new title: chief of staff of the army. Although he was no longer general-in-chief, Halleck's role remained essentially the same. He would continue to be a Washington, D.C., insider immersed in politics, planning, power struggles and intrigue, while Grant stayed in the field; both men were fully settled into the roles that best suited them.[3]

Grant went to Washington to meet Lincoln and receive his new rank and honors. Then he was reunited with Sherman in Cincinnati, where the two generals developed a strategy for cutting a wide swath through Georgia and from there through the Carolinas. If it went as planned, the result would be the final defeat of the South. Part of the plan was to make Sherman the commanding officer of the Military Division of the Mississippi, giving him control over three large armies to use in the upcoming campaign: Thomas' Army of the Cumberland, the largest, Major General John Schofield and the Army of the Ohio, and Major General James McPherson, who took Sherman's place at the head of the Army of the Tennessee.

The Division of the Mississippi featured some of the most prominent and experienced Union generals. "Fighting" Joe Hooker commanded the 20th Corps, and John A. Logan had the 15th Corps, including his "Dirty First," the 31st Illinois Infantry regiment. Other key generals were Jacob D. Cox, John M. Palmer, Henry M. Judah, Oliver O. Howard, John M. Schofield and Grenville M. Dodge. With 110,000 effectives and loaded with military talent, the "grand army" was easily the largest army the Union had fielded in the west.

The "Fighting McCooks," brothers and cousins, were well-represented in the Army of the Cumberland, commanded by General Thomas. Colonel Edwin S. McCook was in charge of the 31st Illinois Infantry. Colonel Edward M. McCook commanded a cavalry brigade and was commended by General Thomas "for efficiency and gallantry during the operations of this army." Colonel Daniel McCook, Jr., commander of the 3rd Brigade, 2nd Division, was also complimented by Thomas for having duly handled his responsibilities as a brigade commander for more than a year.[4] And finally, there was Colonel Anson G. McCook, with his 2nd Ohio Infantry, his reputation enhanced by sterling service at Lookout Mountain and Missionary Ridge.

Prior to being removed from command, General Rosecrans recommended that Colonel Daniel McCook be promoted to brigadier general.[5] Dan, of course, had to be pleased with the recommendation, and could not be faulted for thinking that one or two more examples of leadership under fire might bring the rank he had long sought. Personal ambition combined with loyalty and *esprit de corps* had brought him through almost three years of war and now, in the spring of 1864, he was an integral part of what many believed to be the greatest army ever assembled on the American continent.

Another personal honor was bestowed on Dan McCook on April 23, 1864, when the Union army was gearing up for the Georgia campaign. In solemn ceremony, while in camp, "the third degree of Masonry" was conferred upon the young officer.[6]

An important addition to McCook's brigade came in the person of Dr. Mary Walker, volunteer surgeon from Oswego, New York. The "very pretty young lady" was ordered to report to McCook in May of 1864.[7] Female doctors were extremely rare in those days and it was even more unusual that a woman—who dressed like a man—would be allowed serve as a surgeon in wartime. General George H. Thomas, however, overlooked the objections and "handpicked" her to work as a "civilian contract surgeon" for the 52nd Ohio to replace a doctor who had died.[8] McCook was glad to have her services, although many of his subordinates were less than favorable in their feelings toward this brave woman.

Dr. Walker served in another capacity, treating local, non-military people, a worthy and selfless activity, but it took her too close to a Rebel camp. She was captured, charged with being a spy, and spent several months in the notorious Richmond's Castle Thunder, a filthy, rat infested prison. The Confederates didn't know what to make of her. They were entirely confounded over the little lady doctor, something only a "depraved Yankee nation could produce." The spy charge didn't stick so she was exchanged for a Confederate officer.[9]

After the war ended, the diminutive Dr. Walker witnessed the execution of the four Lincoln assassination conspirators, the only woman to do so. She was awarded a Medal of Honor in 1866 for her bravery and services to the Union. Because she was a woman and was determined to practice her chosen profession, she was subjected to ridicule and abuse, both during and after the war. Yet through it all, Dr. Walker remained strong and unyielding. She died at age 86 in Washington, D.C., after a fall on the Capitol steps.[10]

General U. S. Grant made no fuss over Mary Walker, the lady doctor, nor was he likely to be bothered by other minor diversions. Always looking at the big picture, he was preparing to go to Virginia and take on General Robert E. Lee, determined to succeed where no one had succeeded before. Before leaving Cincinnati, Grant ordered Sherman to take the three armies and pursue Joe Johnston and his Rebel army. Sherman was to act on his own accord and good judgment, but at the same time keep Johnston busy and moving, pressing the issue at every opportunity. Allow the enemy no rest. If he had the chance to destroy Johnston, Sherman was to drive in the sword; if not, then wear him down and make it a war of attrition. Grant stressed that Sherman was to inflict "all the damage you can against their war resources."[11]

If all worked out as planned Johnston would have no chance to go to Lee's assistance. Grant wanted no replay of the first battle of Bull Run when Johnston's escape from Union general Robert Patterson and subsequent arrival at Manassas resulted in a Rebel victory.

Sherman took on the challenge with eager confidence and with a view of performing in a manner that would not only bring prestige to himself, but also bolster the fortunes of his friend U. S. Grant. On May 5, 1864, after sufficient time to make plans, Sherman's march began. It would now be a harder, meaner fight, an unrelenting struggle to the finish; both civilian and soldier would feel the cruel lash of war. During the course of the next several months, a persistent and mentally sharp Sherman and his equally determined officers and men would break the back of the South and crush its proud heart. Along the way, honors and lasting memories were made by men who participated in the campaign that yielded a terrible harvest of conquest, death and destruction. The coffin makers, embalmers and gravediggers were kept busy as each major battle usually meant the creation of a new graveyard.

The manufacturers of artificial limbs were also hard at work. To meet the rising demand by limbless soldiers, B. Frank Palmer, "Surgeon and Artist," was advertising and selling the "Palmer Arm" and "Palmer Leg." Claiming he had the backing of the surgeon general of the U.S. Army, Palmer—with offices in New York, Philadelphia and Boston—urged discharged and disabled men to write for particulars. He promised to "give full information."[12] So great was the need for artificial limbs that the federal government placed an ad in the *New York Times,* asking that all inventors of arms and legs "bring their specimens to be evaluated by the Board of Medical Officers for the Acting Surgeon General."[13]

An aggressive, impatient man like Sherman was likely to create customers for the enterprising Palmer and his competitors. Sherman's opponent, the thoughtful and cautious Joe Johnston, could be counted on to produce customers as well. Johnston had a well-earned reputation for drawing back, seeming to retreat, all the while luring the enemy into a trap. Sherman understood this, of course, and planned a series of flanking moves, attacking from the oblique, to keep Johnston turning and off course and off balance, all the while pushing deeper into Georgia. It was a tough assignment, for while the Rebels would be outnumbered, Johnston would not be a pushover.

Once the Union mega-army got moving, Sherman was anxious to know the position of the main body of Johnston's army, and, of course, Johnston

11. A Dead Stop at Kennesaw Mountain

was interested in knowing the location of his enemy. Johnston made the first move, sending General Joseph Wheeler's cavalry on a reconnaissance. He collided with Brigadier General Edward M. McCook's horse soldiers who were positioned on the left of Schofield's Army of the Ohio near Rocky Face Ridge. Wheeler bested McCook in the fighting that followed, but it would not be the last time the two cavalry generals would clash.

Another major clash of arms occurred at Resaca, about 15 miles south of Dalton that featured artillery bombardment along with skirmishing as both sides fought behind earthworks. After two days of intense fighting, Johnston was forced to leave Resaca, having lost about 3,000 men wounded and dead. Sherman's casualties amounted to about 4,000. But in the numbers game, Sherman was still dominant.[14]

On June 1, 1864, Sherman, having succeeded in pushing Johnston closer and closer to Atlanta, wired Halleck, saying that he expected to engage the enemy at Kennesaw Mountain, near Marietta, Georgia. But he quickly added, "but I will not run head on his fortifications."[15] He would not be rash and waste his men.

While Sherman was confident and clear headed, he faced challenges every day. The June weather in northern Georgia was especially troublesome. Heavy rains made roads muddy if not impassable, and crossing streams was difficult. Through it all the two armies were "constantly in a state of action; heavy skirmishes reaching almost the importance of battles."[16] Still Sherman pressed on.

A correspondent traveling with the Union army, writing for the *New York Times* under the *nom de plume* "Nickajack," described an army in high spirits. Having traveled 100 miles, all the while driving the Rebels back toward Atlanta, the mammoth army found itself "deep in the mazes of a magnificent forest," where soldiers camped among "lizards, snakes and other indigenous reptiles." The abundance of peach trees was a plus. But the heat was intense and unbearable, and while no one seemed to dwell on that form of discomfort, Nickajack warned his readers that as the troops "approach Atlanta obstacles accumulate." Stopping to rest near Marietta, the correspondent predicted that "our progress forward henceforth will doubtless be more eventful." It was a casual remark but it was loaded with terrible truth.[17]

Although General Sherman was being thoroughly tested by his able opponent, General Johnston, the Union commander managed to stay on top by staying aggressive. On June 10, the Rebels burned a railroad bridge that Sherman needed to transport supplies for his large army. Undismayed, the very next day, a train brought Union bridge builders and timber, and the bridge was promptly repaired.[18] The sound of the train whistle was a signal to Johnston's army that the bridge was as good as new.

Not long after the bridge incident, Sherman was able to knock out one stout leg of Johnston's support by the chance killing of General Leonidas Polk. On June 14, Polk, Johnston and General William J. Hardee decided to have a look at the Union lines from atop Pine Mountain. The trio was about 600 feet away from where General Howard had his guns set up. Sherman rode up and, looking toward the three generals, said, "how saucy they are." Not knowing who they were, he ordered one of the batteries to open fire. With the first blast, Johnston and Hardee hurried to take cover. The portly Polk, however, was apparently unmoved and walked slowly to the edge of the hill for a better look. It was his last look, for the next round struck him in the chest. The controversial "Fighting Bishop," since 1861 a leader in many western campaigns, was dead, his faith insufficient armor against the weapons of war. Later, when Sherman learned that he killed the bishop, he allowed the Confederates to pick up Polk's body under a flag of truce.[19]

Sherman did not celebrate Polk's death, noting only in his report that "'we killed Bishop Polk yesterday, and have made good progress today.'"[20] As always, his focus was on the bigger picture. With skillful use of his cavalry and constant troop movements, Sherman had Johnston entrenched in a line on triangle of mountains consisting of Lost Mountain, Pine Mountain and Kennesaw Mountain, with the latter being the southernmost of the three. But Johnston apparently decided his troops were too spread out so he withdrew from Lost and Pine Mountain and by the 20th he had gathered all his forces on Kennesaw.[21]

Johnston's withdrawal was accomplished with such great stealth and secrecy that it was at first believed that he was in retreat.[22] Instead he had concentrated his army in a fortified line of troops seven miles long across the rough terrain. This new Kennesaw position was "the ninth fortified Confederate position of the campaign." The earthworks they constructed are still "well preserved."[23]

Kennesaw Mountain was a large land mass, about two miles long, detached from the other mountains. It bore the appearance of a having been thrust upward and out of the surrounding earth. The Georgia State Railroad ran along the base of the mountain to Marietta, a town only about three or four miles to the south. Although only a small mountain when compared to the Rocky Mountains in the far west, it was a large, perplexing obstacle between Sherman's men and Atlanta.

The *New York Times* correspondent called the great land mass "Kenesaw" Mountain. In his article, he wrote that it was commonly believed that the ridge, running southeast to the northwest, was named after a Cherokee Indian chief named Kenesaw, who was killed, accidently, on the mountain.[24]

Sherman was familiar with the area, having explored it in 1840 when,

11. A Dead Stop at Kennesaw Mountain

Major General William Tecumseh Sherman, a West Point Academy alumnus, was an intelligent combination of enigmatic defeatist and hard-headed realist. Plagued by business failures and faced with a life of mediocrity, Sherman's fortunes, like those of his friend U. S. Grant, were sent soaring to great heights of achievement and success by his performance in the Civil War. Early on his erratic nature caused journalists to declare that Sherman was insane, but he fought through the mental fog and by the time the battle of Shiloh was over the demons were gone—realist had triumphed. Sherman had a caustic way about him, and yet he was liked and respected by the troops. His tactics were for the most part thoughtful, and yet his decision to assault well-entrenched Confederates on Kennesaw Mountain in Georgia was a disaster that resulted in the needless slaughter of many good men, including his friend and former law partner Colonel Daniel McCook.

as a young officer, he climbed up Kennesaw Mountain.²⁵ That mountain, that great obstacle between the Union army and Atlanta, had three peaks, namely Big Kennesaw, about 700 feet, Little Kennesaw, 400 feet, and Pigeon Hill, 200 feet above the surrounding plain. It was to this ridge that Johnston brought his army on the night of June 19 during a rainstorm. Sherman set his engineers to work establishing defensive entrenchments in a north to south line.²⁶

Meanwhile Sherman was growing impatient; time was not on his side. He had yet to deliver a telling blow against Johnston and looked back on missed opportunities, including the time that McPherson failed to strike at Resaca where the enemy was turned and vulnerable. Because McPherson had been overly cautious, Sherman was forced into a two-day battle at Resaca. Still he was satisfied with McPherson and Schofield too. But he grumbled about the lack of effort from other generals and suggested that the entire Army of the Cumberland, from Thomas on down, was lazy. In a message to Grant, Sherman said the "whole Army of the Cumberland is so habituated to be on the defensive.... I cannot get it out of their heads."²⁷ It frustrated him that the troops had become timid, too quick to stop and dig in, so something had to be done to inspire them and make them press hard. At the foot of Kennesaw Mountain, looking up toward Johnston's breastworks, Sherman sensed the opportunity to strike a daring and deadly blow was at hand.

Despite his promise to himself that he would launch no frontal attacks at an entrenched enemy, Sherman decided to do just that. A bold, unexpected assault would catch the enemy off guard. Sherman's impatience and desire to strike a blow was evident in a letter to his wife, in which he wrote, "we are now all ready and I *must* attack direct or turn the position." He admitted that either choice would result in losses, but circumstances dictated that he try one or the other.²⁸ He could not risk becoming stalled or stuck on what was to be a brisk-paced mission.

Sherman was essentially stopped in his tracks, blocked by a small mountain and an army of well-protected enemy soldiers determined to keep the Union in check. Day and night, Rebel artillery randomly blasted away at Union targets. There were other problems: June 21 marked the 19th straight day of rain. Along with the incessant Georgia rain, the rough, rocky and wooded terrain presented serious obstacles. On June 23, Sherman sent a telling message to Halleck: "the whole country is one vast fort, and Johnston must have fully fifty miles of connected trenches with abatis and finished batteries."²⁹

In point of fact, Johnston's entrenchments and breastworks were "characteristically formidable." The state of the art defenses consisted of an "intricate network of young trees that had been standing in a thicket but were now hacked on one side, bent forward and held in place by heavy stakes driven crosswise into the ground, while all the limbs were trimmed to sharp points." Assuming they could get past the trees, the Union assaulters would encounter earth and log impediments, built high and designed so that only "the defenders eyes could be seen."[30]

Johnston's defenses were formed in a large half-circle that stretched out about six miles, fronting his railroad, the nearby town of Marietta and the roads leading in and out of that place. His center faced the west. He had constructed "well-planned forts" at strategic points, each connected to the other and each well-stocked with artillery. Sixty thousand veteran Rebels manned the breastworks and entrenchments.[31]

It presented a daunting, deadly challenge against virtually impregnable defenses, but Sherman knew he had to make an assault or a maneuver out of the area. Feeling the sting of criticism from the press and public for being slow and overly cautious, he gave in to his innate, aggressive tendencies. Besides, the Confederates would not expect him to attack their entrenchments so he had the element of surprise to work with. Atlanta, his ultimate target, lay waiting to be taken. Sherman had often been heard to say that he could "corkscrew the rebel hounds out of Atlanta whenever he saw fit."[32] But what he was about to do, however, more closely resembled the use of a sledge-hammer, not a cork-screw.

Historians and Civil War buffs have long been puzzled by Sherman's Kennesaw strategy. He was a thinker, not

Confederate general Joseph E. Johnston in civilian garb. He was from Virginia and a classmate of Robert E. Lee at West Point. During both the Seminole and Mexican wars he served with great distinction while suffering serious wounds. At the outset of the Civil War, he resigned his commission and joined the Confederacy. His ability to move his army to Manassas Gap in July of 1861 turned the tide of battle of Bull Run toward the Confederacy. Johnston's composure and thoughtful decision making were assets he put to work trying to outwit and out maneuver General W. T. Sherman, as the two great armies moved through Georgia in 1864, fighting battles along the way. But Sherman had greater amounts of men and munitions, and Johnston was unable to stop the Union juggernaut. He was relieved of duty by President Jefferson Davis, but he met his old opponent once again when, on April 26, 1865, Johnston surrendered his army to General Sherman.

the type of commander who carelessly and needlessly used up his men. Why on earth, then, would he make such a risky frontal assault, a maneuver that was contrary to his own prior statement? One of his generals thought he had the answer. John A. Logan observed that Sherman had been reading newspaper accounts of Grant's assaults on Lee that both captivated and shocked the nation. The bold moves with staggeringly high casualties were attracting all the attention; Grant was getting noticed and Sherman was being ignored. It was time to put his army back into the national spotlight and a bold, frontal attack would do just that.[33]

Sherman's *Memoirs* states that he consulted with Thomas, McPherson and Schofield, and all agreed that it was not prudent to stretch the Union line any further, and "therefore there was no alternative but to attack 'fortified lines,' a thing fully avoided up to that time." Having been backed by his leading generals, Sherman reasoned that the logical place to strike was at the center of the Rebel line, where a strong thrust would breach it. June 27 was the day chosen for making that strong thrust—the same day that President Lincoln accepted his party's nomination for re-election as president.[34]

The timing was merely coincidental, but the bold, risky battle strategy was in step with the pace of national politics. A profound and radical movement had emerged that reflected the urgency of the Lincoln administration and the mood of the nation. The Republican Party changed its name to the Union Party to reflect Lincoln's steadfast belief that the war was being fought to restore the Union. It was another flag of defiance and determination to wave at the South. Whenever Lincoln held a trump card, he knew how to play it.

Another broadside came in the form of a proposed Constitutional amendment that would eradicate slavery, which many people recognized as having caused the war. Moving beyond the Emancipation Proclamation, the Union Party national convention that met in Baltimore unanimously adopted the slavery killing amendment to "terminate and forever prohibit the existence of slavery within the limits of the jurisdiction of the United States."[35] The convention also nominated Lincoln as president, much to the displeasure of the South.

Henry J. Raymond of the *New York Times*, in a carefully crafted editorial, laid out the history of events leading up to the adoption of the groundbreaking "slavery exterminating amendment." He noted that, while the war continued to grind on, the public sentiment had gravitated toward freedom for the slaves, and at this juncture in history, the anti-slavery current was traveling at a fast pace, making it a "moral necessity" to act. As if he understood that newspapers are a rough-draft of history, Raymond declared boldly, and with great eloquence, "The rebellion sprang so directly from slavery, and was so closely connected with slavery in all of its objects and policies, that it was not possible to make war against the rebellion with a whole heart and yet remain well affected toward slavery." Raymond believed the North was ready for Congress to approve a Constitutional amendment abolishing slavery, thus dealing a "final extirpation of Slavery, through the whole length and breadth of the land." He concluded that it was not the president, the press, or "debate in Congress" that dictated the flow of events, but rather the "logic of the war itself, silent yet irresistible."[36]

Lincoln could not have said it better, and he most certainly knew that men like Raymond, who wrote about the war, had many more chapters to write. And at a date approximately a year past the historic battle of Gettysburg, two great armies were facing one another, ready to unleash death and desolation on a Georgia mountain side.

Edwin D. Levings, a soldier with the 12th Wisconsin Infantry regiment, conveyed the fear and forebodings felt by many men when, on the 26th of June, he wrote a letter to his parents from his camp. He described the position of the armies, the blasts from muskets and artillery, and then he advised his parents that "we are in more danger here than we were at Vicksburg."[37] To state it another way, no one but an experienced soldier had the ability to sense the danger and come to grips with the understanding that many of them would soon be dead. Kennesaw Mountain beckoned like an oracle of death.

12

A Soldier's Death

"How can a man die better than facing fearful odds...?"
—Colonel Daniel McCook, Jr., June 27, 1864

To the astute General George H. Thomas, commander of the Army of the Cumberland—who undoubtedly also sensed the great danger—went the honor of directing the riskiest assault: on the Rebel center. While this frontal assault was being conducted, Schofield and Hooker would keep General John B. Hood occupied on the southern end of Sherman's line and McPherson would demonstrate to the north and northeast of Big Kennesaw before making a secondary attack. Sherman's plan, if successful, would prevent Johnston from reinforcing his center, leaving it vulnerable to Thomas' chosen assault team. If the assault was successful, the Rebel army would be split into two sections, leaving both vulnerable to the onrushing Union forces.

It seems that the more Sherman thought about the plan the better he liked it. He was quoted as saying: "an army to be efficient must not settle down to a single mode of offense, but must be prepared to execute any plan which promises success." He went on to say that "I wanted, therefore, for the moral effect, to make a successful assault against the enemy behind his breastworks." Since everyone, including his own commanders, expected him to flank, the bold strategy contained the element of surprise.[1]

It was up to Thomas to plan the details of his role in the attack and select the attacking units. He chose two divisions: those of General Jefferson C. Davis, from the 14th Corps, and General John Newton, from the 4th Corps. To spearhead the two-prong attack, Davis chose the brigade of Colonel Daniel McCook. The other prong would be projected forth by Colonel Charles Harker of Newton's division. Both McCook and Harker were highly regarded for their ability and gallantry and were considered up-and-coming men and future generals. They would be joined in the assault by three brigades from Logan's 15th Corps attacking to the north at Pigeon Hill.

Writing about it many years later, a Union general noted that "no finer body of troops could have been selected for this hazardous and heroic enterprise."[2]

The principal strike force consisted of 14,500 men with more troops in reserve.[3] A *New York Times* correspondent recalled that the Union attack line occupied a variety of terrain and conditions, including swamps, thick woods and hills. He said the advance would be "an acclivity from the word go."[4]

McCook's 3rd Brigade consisted of his original 52nd Ohio Infantry regiment, along with the 85th, 86th, and 125th Illinois Infantry regiments and the 22nd Indiana Infantry regiment. McCook and Harker were facing two of Johnston's best commanders: generals Benjamin Franklin Cheatham and Patrick Cleburne. Both were battle-tested veterans who could lead and inspire their men. They were faced with the daunting task of repulsing a mass attack, but their soldiers had the advantage of high ground and were well-covered by earthworks, trenches and timber breaks. The topography was heavily wooded so details of the Rebel position could not be seen at all from below. McCook met with his regimental commanders and told them that they were about to charge into enemy fortifications, about which they knew almost nothing.

Some of Colonel McCook's subordinate officers expressed grave doubts about the success of the mission. Upon learning of the mission, Lieutenant Colonel Allen L. Fahnestock admitted to other officers that he would prefer to surrender rather than send his regiment, the 86th Illinois, out to be wastefully shot up. Another, James Lewis Burkhalter, was so depressed over the matter that he refused to inform his troops as to the danger, despite orders to do so.[5]

McCook's brigade was up before dawn and facing Cheatham's division located well above Union camp on a prominence that would thereafter be known as "Cheatham Hill." McCook selected the 85th Illinois to move out first as skirmishers followed by the 125th Illinois would be the first regiment to cross the enemy line. The 86th Illinois was next in line, followed by the 22nd Indiana and the 52nd Ohio. To the north, Harker prepared his brigade for its role in the coordinated assault.[6]

General Davis understood full well the dangerous nature of his assignment, but he considered it "distinguished duty" and felt honored that he and his men were selected. Like McCook, Davis was reckless and bold, and like McCook, he saw potential glory, should the assault succeed. Still, in a last word with McCook as both knelt beside a tree, Davis advised, "Don't be rash, Colonel, don't be rash."[7]

McCook's men waited in anxious silence, lined up behind their earthworks. His attacking force consisted of about 1,800 men, arranged in a wide front with a shorter and broader column. Many of them tore up letters received from home, a gesture that matched the gloomy, fatalistic feeling shared by all. A veteran from the 52nd Ohio was heard to say, "Aye! God, Jim, that hill's going to be worse'n Pea Ridge. We'll ketch hell over'n them woods." While he spoke federal artillery pounded away, shaking the ground, in anticipation of the charge. Sharpshooters from above were targeting the nervous Union soldiers, waiting for the signal. On the whole the Union troops displayed too much fear and anxiety; they were not mentally prepared for what they were about to face.

To his credit, McCook tried to prepare them for what he must have believed to be a near impossible mission. He walked in front of his brigade, along the line, facing his men, in a moment of high drama. It has been written that he was disliked by the Illinois regiments, and in fact was held "in utter contempt," by a captain of the 86th, who proclaimed that if given the chance, McCook would be shot during battle by one of his own men.[8] If true, it would be interesting to fathom the thoughts of the Illinois soldiers standing in the silent ranks on that June 27.

While waiting for the signal to move out, McCook broke the silence. He spoke to his men in a loud, shrill but calm voice, reciting a verse from a pagan poem, translated from ancient Latin by Thomas Babington Macaulay:

> Then out spake bold Horatius
> The Captain of the Gate,
> To every man upon this earth
> Death cometh soon or late.
> And how can a man die better
> Than facing fearful odds
> For the Ashes of his fathers
> And the temples of his Gods?[9]

A member of the 52nd Ohio called it "McCook's death song," recalling it was spontaneous, moving and appropriate.[10] The bold words were meant to inspire his men and probably were needed to raise his level of courage as well. McCook knew full well the gravity of the mission and understood that many of his men—and possibly he himself—would die on this day. But he was a leader and he was ready to lead. He was also a good soldier who followed orders and understood that in order to achieve a worthy objective men must sometimes have to be sacrificed.

Dan McCook knew that a good leader led by example, and that in order to inspire ordinary men to acts of uncommon valor, the leader had to equal or exceed the bravery of his soldiers. So he prepared himself and his men to be sacrificed in the line of duty, something only a dedicated soldier could understand. He would not stay behind and watch; he would lead the charge. He would fight shoulder to shoulder with his men as they charged for a distance of approximately 581 yards knowing that he would probably be shot.[11]

McCook's friend Harker had similar forebodings when he received his charging orders, saying, "I shall be killed."[12]

While the Union soldiers readied themselves for the terrible assault, Confederate general Samuel G. French and others were looking down at the Federals aligned in battle formation. He later recalled that "we sat there perhaps for an hour enjoying a bird's eye view of one of the most magnificent sights ever allotted to man."[13] French saw in the massing of troops a brave and gallant expression of military might. But another man—schooled a different way—might have looked upon the scene with the thought that there would soon be a population explosion in heaven.

Before the battle started, the Confederates felt assured of success, having the tactical advantage. Years later, a Union general conceded that point when he wrote that Johnston "did well to mount Kenesaw [sic] crest," for he had had "better advantages over Sherman than Meade had over Lee" at Gettysburg.[14]

Although Sherman had ordered the attack to begin "precisely" at 8 a.m., the signal to charge was finally given "a little before 9 o'clock."[15] Then the boys in blue began their difficult ascent in a line approximately ten miles long, with artillery fire raging in both directions, decorating the sky. On the north end, three brigades of Logan's Corps struggled over rough, rocky, well-wooded terrain to reach their objective. On the hottest day of the month of June 1864, Black Jack Logan, his long, wild black hair flowing like a dark flame, rode the length of his lines, urging his men into the teeth of murderous fire. After beating back a Rebel skirmish line with bayonets and hand-to-hand fighting, Logan's brigades were overcome by musket and cannon fire, his men were bending and dropping like broken matchsticks, and he was forced to withdraw the survivors. A Rebel soldier from Missouri later told his sister that "we mowed them down like hay."[16]

Meanwhile, to the south, Davis' division threw itself into the fight with a terrible ferocity. It was said that Dan McCook's brigade had heretofore managed to avoid the head-on fighting that decimates regiments and sends hundreds of men to early graves. Kennesaw Mountain changed all that in a matter of minutes. If there was such a thing as luck in time of war, it just ran out for McCook's brigade.

The Union target was a salient that was deemed the weakest point on the Confederate line. McCook's orders were to hit it directly, while Harker was to strike it to the north of the salient. This area was chosen as the point of attack because from below it appeared to be unprotected.

It wasn't unprotected. Taking heavy casualties as they surged forward, Harker's brigade managed to reach the ridge, stopping short of the Rebel line. Seeing this and believing his death was imminent, Harker, with hat in hand, waved to his men to rise up and charge. Obeying his order his ranks were

This photograph shows a panoramic view of Kennesaw Mountain in Georgia. The battered trees are stark evidence of the terrible battle fought there on June 27, 1864. Well-entrenched Confederate soldiers poured volley after volley of hot lead into on rushing ranks of Union soldiers as they surged upward through rough, rocky, wooded terrain during an extremely hot summer day in Georgia, forever remembered by survivors as "bloody Monday." The loud, thunderous sounds of battle could be heard as far away as Atlanta. The battle raged for about an hour and a half, and after the guns fell silent and losses were tallied, the number of Union troops dead, wounded and missing totaled 3,000.

decimated by Rebel fire. Harker was shot and killed, as was his white horse, after which the gallant effort of his brigade collapsed into writhing and bleeding chaos. Another phase of the grand assault ended in carnage.

With the command "Attention battalions; charge bayonets!" Dan McCook's brigade joined the carnival of madness, as did the brigade of Colonel John G. Mitchell on his right. The skirmishers led the way followed by four regiments whose battle flags were fluttering in the sweaty summer heat. Seeing this, Rebel shooters aimed at the flag bearers. The flag of the 52nd Ohio was dropped four times only to be picked again out of the hands of a fallen soldier and held high in defiance of the hail of gunfire from the enemy.

Running uphill over rocks and through the trees and brush, McCook's lead unit, the 125th Illinois, was the first reach the crest, whereupon many were slaughtered by Cheatham's men yelling "Chickamauga" and "Come on" at the charging Yankees. The 86th Illinois was treated just as rough, losing 98 men in the close range barrage of gunfire. The enemy was well-concealed, firing in rows behind works "fringed with pikes," and "sharpened pins driven into logs ... pointed toward the attackers."[17] In addition to sheets of cannon fire that tore away arms and legs, the Rebels lit and tossed hand grenades and rocks at the onrushing Yankees. A soldier who experienced the nightmare and lived to write about it said: "Oh! How the fire of hell beat in our faces!"[18]

A correspondent to the *Cincinnati Daily Times* described the battle in these terms: "wild bullets and shot and shell were whistling and screaming through the air, tearing through the tree tops and crashing among the undergrowth; at the same time a sea of fire seemed to be surging around Kenesesaw [sic] Mountain, while the very earth and hills trembled as though all things were tumbling back into chaos."[19] The terrible sounds of battle could be heard in Atlanta, 22 miles away.

Another Cincinnati correspondent compared "the advance of Colonel Daniel McCook's brigade to nothing less strong and energetic than the rush of a tornado." It was a "magnificent spectacle," an unstoppable force "rolling onward and sweeping away all obstacles to its progress." The breathless reporter said that McCook "jumped across the ditch," mounted the "summit of the works, and defiantly waived his sword" while all around him men were going down.[20] Another observer declared that the "persistency of McCook's men at Kenesaw [sic] has no parallel."[21]

Those who were not shot were overcome by the thunderous noise, intense heat and exhaustion, and many collapsed. As the last unit in the chain, the 52nd Ohio, joined in the macabre dance of death, they were met by wounded men struggling to get back downhill. All hell had broke lose in Georgia on a "bloody Monday." The thunder of artillery and the cracking of muskets mingled with shouts of officers and cries of the wounded and dying. All logic, order and purpose seemed lost in a fiery whirlwind of gunfire and death. Crowded in a space of about a thousand square feet, it took only half an hour for 900 men in two brigades to fall, shot down by almost point blank enemy fire.[22]

Colonel McCook was in that number. He was at the head of the 125th Illinois, on foot, having actually reached the Rebel fortifications at a point that would thereafter be known as the "Dead Angle." He yelled, "Come on boys, the day is won." Then, at the next moment, the sacrificial soldier learned what it felt like to be shot and he didn't utter a question or complaint.

At first it appeared as if the defenders were prepared to capture McCook, for he had climbed up the breastworks and stood facing the Rebels.[23] A soldier from the 86th Illinois recalled hearing McCook shout, "bring up those colors!" Next McCook was seen to grab and hold the colors high in his left hand, and with his sword in his right hand, fighting with Rebels, also with swords in hand. The soldier, Private Samuel Canterbury of the 86th Illinois, yelled, "Colonel Dan, for God's sake get down they will shoot you!" McCook, full of fire, turned to the soldier and shouted back, "God damn you, mind your own business!"[24] McCook was thoroughly caught up in the mad ritual and inevitably became its victim.

It was then that McCook was shot at point-blank range, struck by a bullet that entered his body about four inches below the collarbone, tearing into his lungs. He said that an instant before being shot, he had placed his "left hand on the head log and turned to Capt. Fellows and called to him to tell Col. Harmon to bring up the right wing double quick."[25] Canterbury grabbed McCook's jacket as he was hit, pulling him away from the Confederates, or he might have fallen into their ranks.

According to a Confederate soldier who spoke to a Yankee during a burial truce, McCook, with his sword in his right hand and his hat in his left, shouted out defiantly, "'Surrender you damn traitors,'" after which he was shot. This was confirmed by members of the 86th Illinois. Although badly wounded, McCook did not order a retreat but rather told his men, "Stick it to them boys, I am wounded."[26]

Like the universal soldier who knew it was coming, Daniel McCook. Jr., embraced the bullet that invaded his body. He accepted it because he was a soldier who understood that in battle good men must die. He accepted it for the Union and the great cause, for the love of his mother and dead father, and for his two brothers who had died from battle wounds. He accepted it for a resting place next to his brothers in a Cincinnati cemetery, beneath a majestic Civil War monument, where future generations would gaze in awe and wonder. The brave Daniel McCook, Jr., a cool, capable officer, "whose tendency to rashness was tempered by good judgment,"[27] accepted it thus adding luster to the lore of the "Fighting McCooks" of Ohio.

Seeing McCook on the ground, Colonel Oscar F. Harmon, in command of the 125th, took charge, and was yelling to encourage his men when he too was shot dead, falling beside McCook. After Harmon fell, the next officer in line to lead the brigade, Colonel Shane, was killed. Having three brigade commanders killed in succession was a tragic and unusual feature of the battle, a turn of events that probably never occurred before, nor after, during the Civil War.

McCook was carried off the field by four enlisted men, under fire but protected by the rear regiments. One of the four, Corporal James T. Seay of the 85th Illinois, had mercy killing on his mind when he pointed his revolver at McCook's head. The colonel said, "soldier, throw that gun down," and, of course, Seay did as ordered. McCook was then taken to the tent of the brigade surgeon, Dr. Masena M. Hooton, who examined the wound and did what little he could do for his patient, sensing the wound was fatal. The bullet broke two ribs and then it fragmented, part of it breaking the collar bone and another part exiting his body through his back. Although badly hurt and in pain, McCook managed to tell the doctor that he hoped he had not fought his last battle.[28] He also had words for those directing the operation: "'Tell General Thomas and General Palmer that we did all we could to break the rebel line, I was on their works when I fell and other were with me, but it was impossible.'"[29]

Dan's cousin Colonel Anson McCook was called to the tent. Seeing Anson, Dan said with pride that he came so close to success and that given another minute, his mission would have succeeded. Anson's thoughts were far less sanguine; he wrote in his field manual, "poor fellow, I fear the result of his wounds."[30]

Future U.S. president Colonel Benjamin Harrison was one of those who watched the spectacle. He was then the commander of the 70th Indiana Infantry regiment in the division of Brigadier General William T. Ward, Army

In this engraving, a twenty-eight-year-old Daniel McCook looks out at the world with a soft and thoughtful gaze, more like a professor or a philosopher than a soldier. But it was as soldier that he achieved high honors for himself, his family and his country, and it was as soldier that he met death in a manner that made him an American hero. On foot and with sword in hand he personally led his brigade on the ill-advised assault against the Rebels dug in atop Kennesaw Mountain. Although men were dying all around him, McCook managed to reach the top and was shot and mortally wounded in front of the breastworks. He died at home in Ohio and was buried alongside his father and his brothers Robert and Charles at the Spring Grove Cemetery in Cincinnati.

of the Cumberland. His regiment—dubbed "Harrison's Hoosiers"—was busy digging earthworks below the battleground when the shooting started. They dropped their shovels and watched in sadness and horror as their comrades buckled and died in repeated volleys of fire, noting they did all that brave men could do.[31]

Meanwhile, on the Union left, McPherson's 16th and 17th Corps were under horrific fire. When the order to advance was given, the men moved out into the open toward the Rebel works and were met by withering fire from muskets and cannons, thinning their ranks. Although taking high casualties, they forced the Rebels back. A correspondent present at the battle called it "a sublime exhibition of the superior heroism of the Federal soldiers over the sneaking obstinacy of the Rebels." The 1st Brigade of the 3rd Division that included Daniel McCooks' brother, Colonel Edwin S. McCook's 31st Illinois, was first to reach Rebel works. Hit hard, it fell back to a place of relative safety. Many officers were among the casualties and Edwin S. McCook was carried off the field of battle, "sun-struck."[32]

The multiple horrors of that fatal day forged a deep and lasting impression on Ambrose Bierce, a young soldier from Indiana who had survived Shiloh and Chickamauga, only to be wounded at Kennesaw Mountain. After the war Bierce went on to become a nationally-known journalist and writer who contributed mightily to the literature of the Civil War. The head wound Bierce suffered that June day, combined with other wartime experiences, left him with a lifetime of haunted memories, "visions of the dead and dying."[33] Kennesaw Mountain will forever be known for "the dead and dying."

For the Confederates the battle of Kennesaw Mountain was like spearing fish in shallow pond. After overcoming the shock of the unexpected assault, the Rebels unleashed a murderous fire into the blue wave that surged forward and upward. One Rebel soldier recalled that "they seemed to walk up and take death as coolly as if they were automatic or wooden men." The mental stress of the battle shock was so overwhelming that survivors from Dan McCook's 86th Illinois wandered about, acting like crazy men in a trance, clutching their pots and pans. Their behavior was so strange that the Rebels held their fire out of sympathy.[34] A Confederate soldier contended that the Union effort failed because the advancing troops were impeded by the bodies of their dead comrades.[35]

First Sergeant J. P. Parkhurst of the 86th Illinois was wounded in the assault, and when his comrades pulled back, he was left lying between the battle lines. In order to get help for his injuries, he surrendered to the Rebels and got treatment in an Atlanta hospital. Although Parkhurst lost his right arm, he survived, and 60 years later, he was reunited in Oregon with Cyrus A. B. Fox, another Union survivor of Kennesaw Mountain.

12. A Soldier's Death 189

The battle that Fox and Parkhurst fought in didn't last very long. By 10:30 in the morning, the ill-fated assault on Kennesaw Mountain was over; it had failed miserably and left in its wake heavy casualties. Wounded and dying troops were caught in the fires that ignited in the dry leaves and brush. Seeing this, the Confederates ceased fire and soon Rebels who were shooting at the Union enemy leaped out of their breastworks and ran to the rescue of burning men. It was a strange act of humanity in the midst of a terrible battle.[36]

At about 10:45 Thomas sent a testy message to Sherman: "McCook's brigade was severely handled.... Colonel McCook wounded ... the troops are all too exhausted to advance, but we will hold all that we have gained."[37] He sternly advised against any further attempts at the enemy's works, realizing the futility of it all. Those able to do so began to dig in, but their position was so close that the fighters turned diggers were still the targets of Rebel rifles.

But dig in they did the best they could with whatever implements they had at their disposal. After three days of holding their positions, a temporary truce was declared so that both sides could attend to burying the dead. Then, three days later, the Rebel army vacated Kennesaw Mountain "during the darkness of night, leaving McCook's brigade in possession of Kennesaw."[38] In a strange, bizarre way, the brigade had accomplished its mission.

The needs of wounded overwhelmed the medical staff and many were simply laid out in the sun, unattended, while maggots gathered on their bloody flesh. Later, those that were still alive were taken away by the medical corps, using every means available. Over rough trails to the railhead six miles away, more than 2,000 suffering men were transported and then loaded on trains headed for Chattanooga.

Dan McCook was placed on a train bound for Ohio. On July 7, he arrived in Cincinnati and was taken to a private residence for care. Later he was transported to Hillside, in Steubenville, the home of his older brother George. His brother, Dr. Latimer McCook, was sent to care for him, and along with their uncles, Dr. John McCook and Dr. George McCook, he did the best he could, cleaning and tending his wound. Dan's mother and his wife also contributed their love and care.[39]

Because of the severity of his wound, no one expected Dan McCook to return to duty. Nor was he the only valuable officer lost that day. And having been on the losing side of the battle of Kennesaw Mountain, W. T. Sherman was faced with reporting the disaster to the War Department in Washington, D.C. In a dispatch from Sherman, received on the morning of June 28, Edwin M. Stanton, America and the news media were informed that on the 27th, "an unsuccessful attack was made by our forces on the enemy's position, which resulted in the loss of between two and three thousand." Colonel Dan

McCook was on the list, a field officer, mortally wounded. Sherman was short on other details, saying only that McPherson attacked the southwest end of Kennesaw and Thomas struck the enemy lines about a mile further south. "Neither attack succeeded."[40]

When official battle reports went out, McCook and Harker were given special mention among the casualties. Thomas reported to Sherman that his young officers were wounded, saying that "had they not been wounded, we would have driven the enemy from his works."[41] In a reply to Thomas, Sherman said, "I regret beyond measure the loss of two such young and dashing officers as Harker and Dan McCook." Sherman was struggling to put the best face on the disaster, saying, "at times assaults are necessary and inevitable."[42]

Sherman reported the bloody result to Halleck, once again lamenting the loss of McCook and Harker. For the first time in the Georgia campaign, Sherman was less than optimistic. He told Halleck that he would continue to press Johnston so as to prevent him from re-enforcing Lee, but he would conduct no more frontal assaults as they "will cost us more lives than we can spare."[43]

General Davis believed that his brigades just ran out of gas—the intense heat was so exhausting that those lucky enough to make it to the breastworks lacked the energy to jump them. In his report, Davis wrote: "the troops failed to leap and carry the works to which their noble daring and impetuous valor had carried them." This was not meant to be critical or demeaning, for Davis praised the efforts of his officers and men, starting with "Col. Daniel McCook, long the admired and gallant commander of his brigade."[44] His losses were great and personal and Davis was saddened.

The *New York Times* correspondent called the attempt to take Kennesaw an "utter impossibility," a "reckless tempting of peril, and the piling up of dead men's bones."[45] And yet, despite the obvious tragedy, no one demonstrated any particular feelings of excessive sadness or regret. The *Times* tried to put the best possible spin on the mess, saying no ground had been lost and spirit of the army was unbroken despite the slaughter and great effusion of blood at the Rebel lines.

Ignoring the obvious mental scars on the survivors, the correspondent described the hardened army's attitude as "So what?" It had become the policy and practice of the army to fight mountains as well as men. To these obstacles, add extreme heat following heavy rainfall, and heavy casualties were the order of business; no one was indispensable. While the heroics of McCook and Harker were duly noted, after three years of war, heroes were expected and expendable. Everyone in the North expected the South to run out of its heroes first and then the terrible war would end.

Years later, when old enemies were on friendly terms, a Confederate soldier complimented the valiant effort of the Yankees at Kennesaw Mountain. In a letter to one of the Union survivors, Sergeant Major James A. Jennings said that although the slaughter was terrible, and the Southern position strong, had the Federals made one more charge, they might have succeeded, as the Rebels were running low on ammunition.[46]

Of course no one on the Union side, including Sherman, knew this. In a September 1864 report, Sherman candidly stated that although the assault failed, and he took full responsibility for it, the attack produced "good fruits, as it demonstrated to General Johnston that I would assault ... boldly."[47] In a letter to his wife, Sherman continued to rage like a war-ravaged warrior, saying that he regarded "the death and mangling of a couple of thousand men as a small affair, a kind of morning dash—and it may be well that we become so hardened."[48]

Years later when he wrote his memoir, Sherman was no longer boastful, flippant or hardened. He flatly admitted that his decision to assault Kennesaw cost the life of his "old law partner," Daniel McCook.[49]

It was one of Sherman's greatest mistakes and he knew it. A cerebral man who was not disconnected from his men, Sherman failed to understand that the mental preparation of his men was just as important as supplies, troop placement and logistics. Knowledge invests both strength and confidence in a fighter. In order for a soldier to don his "mental armor," a commander must explain the mission and its importance in the overall scheme of things. This Sherman did not do. It was wrong to wake men up early in the morning, place them in line and, without sufficient explanation, send them off to be slaughtered.

Because of the huge loss of life on Kennesaw Mountain, criticism of the top brass, especially Sherman, came sharp and quick. A soldier from the 12th Wisconsin, in a letter to a Wisconsin newspaper, mocked Sherman, saying that a charge ordered by "Gen. *Whisky*, or someone else," resulted in needless and heavy casualties.[50]

It was a recipe for failure according to General David S. Stanley, who was present at the meeting of generals when Sherman made the decision to make the assault. In his memoir, Stanley was highly critical of Sherman, saying the decision to attack was the result of his (Sherman's) "perverse mind." Stanley called it "murderous, cruel and wholly unjustifiable" and said Sherman "seemed to ... have a fiendish desire to kill off his men."[51] Although harsh on Sherman, Stanley had high praise for Dan McCook, saying he was "the best and the bravest of all the McCooks."[52]

Stanley was wrong to accuse Sherman of fiendish behavior, for the commanding general was not a man eager to use up his troops to prove his worth as a military man. He had no grandiose illusions about his role in the war that he didn't want. But it was thrust upon him, and he, the realist, was just a man doing his job the best way he knew how to do it. And he knew that his veterans would follow his orders though it meant many would die in the attempt.

Daniel McCook, just 28, had been more than willing to follow orders and accept the consequences. The badly-wounded warrior remained at Hillside in Steubenville, well cared for and attended by loving relatives all hoping against hope for his recovery. It was even reported that he was resting comfortably, "and will speedily recover, though a rifle ball passed through his chest, grazing his lungs."[53] But the severity of the wound combined with lung ailments he suffered in the past meant his chances of recovery were minimal. For soldier Daniel McCook, the war was over and his next mission waited on the other side.

On July 16, McCook received a message from Sherman. He had been promoted to brigadier general, the military honor he had long sought and risked his life to get. A soldier that had served in the 52nd Ohio recalled that McCook's wife, Julia, read the commission to him as he lay near death.[54]

Another source indicates that while on his death bed, he responded to Sherman, simply saying the promotion was too late: "return my compliments … 'I decline the honor.'"[55] The next day he died but the promotion did not and he was thereafter remembered as Brigadier General Daniel McCook. In addition to his loving wife, he left an infant daughter.

With the passing of Daniel McCook, the war was honored by another ideal death. He died the good death—a soldier's death—brave, unselfish and sacrificial in the line of duty. With courage and without complaint or blame, he endured the pain of the mortal wound, made it home to his family and died in their presence. In his death we see displayed, every form of elevated conduct so prevalent and important in the mid–19th century—everything noble, decent and manly. We have everything except his last words.

But we need not be concerned, for a correspondent with the army at Kennesaw Mountain expressed the determination and dedication of the entire command from commanding general to lowliest private, including Daniel McCook, when he wrote: "And yet it is nothing to suffer all this … to battle even to death, in the cause of human liberty, and for the restoration of a once happy Government to its original and benign purity."[56]

On the night of Daniel McCook's death, his older brother Colonel George W. McCook received the sad news by telegram at Fort Delaware. Throughout the war George had worked behind the lines, recruiting and training regiments and securing provisions, while his younger brothers and cousins did the fighting. His poor health disqualified him from the hot war but did not spare him from the sorrow caused by the death of three brothers and a father.

12. A Soldier's Death

Anxious that death was about to strike again, Colonel George W. McCook stood before his regiment, opened and read the telegram. He then immediately dismissed his troops and broke down in tears for the brother that he loved.[57]

Anson McCook believed his cousin's death was the result of poor judgment that could have been avoided. He wrote in his field manual, "like all those who fell in the assault on the 27th, he [Daniel] was sacrificed in an attempt that the experiment of both sides has show to be madness." He believed that if the army ordered further frontal assaults against entrenched troops, the "morale of the army will suffer."[58]

The family held a private funeral for Daniel, as was his wish. Then Alexander and George took their brother to Cincinnati where it was expected that there would be large public burial service. But his body had begun to decompose rapidly due to gangrene in his wound, so his brothers saw to it that he was buried quickly and quietly at Spring Grove Cemetery, next to his father and his brothers Robert and Charles.[59]

Words of sorrow over the death of Dan McCook came from both men and women. The wife of an officer who knew him confessed that "Colonel Dan McCook's death was one of the few army deaths which brought tears to my eyes." She wept because she was reminded of "his last act toward me ... one of kindness." It happened while the army was traveling through Tennessee. McCook unselfishly sent a courier to her with a package of his sandwiches, almost a luxury for an army on the move. The simple gesture had a profound effect on the woman for while she enjoyed the sandwiches, she knew that McCook was probably eating hardtack. "His was as kind a heart as ever was stilled by a rebel bullet."[60]

When Ellen Sherman learned of McCook's death, she wrote to her husband: "Poor Dan McCook is gone. I am very, very sorry and feel truly sad about it, particularly as I fear whilst serving his country he forgot his God.... What is time & what is earthly glory to poor Dan McCook?"[61] She had known Dan since 1859 and apparently followed his career close enough to understand his quest for military honors. However, had she really understood the McCook character, she would not have asked the question. For Dan McCook, like his father, uncle, brothers and cousins, was short on humility and long on personal pride and a concomitant desire to serve and succeed. For the McCooks reward followed service as a matter of course. But Ellen Sherman was devoutly religious and inward-looking and it wasn't in her nature to understand outward-looking, single-minded men like her husband and the McCooks.

The McCooks would always be a part of General Sherman's life. He was a man who admired other proud, aggressive men, and in the years following the Civil War, he loved nothing better than to visit with his soldiers and fellow officers and talk of old campaigns and campgrounds. But of all those dead and living, Daniel McCook occupied a special place in the showplace of Sherman's wartime memories. Twenty-one years after the battle of Kennesaw Mountain, Sherman wrote: "McCook was my law partner and *I* caused his death.... Since the creation, no intelligent man on earth has sacrificed his life, and all that was dear, for his Government with better grace than Gen'l Dan McCook."[62]

William T. Sherman was not afraid to send men out to certain death, for he understood full well the ugly nature of war. He had exposed himself to danger and had seen many a good man fall in battle. But if he ever reflected on or was haunted by the ghosts of the Civil War, he must have looked, from time to time, into the intense, dreamy eyes of his friend Daniel McCook, Jr.

In 1885, Blanche McCook, daughter of Daniel and Julia, contacted Sherman seeking his aid in obtaining a postmaster position at East Portland, Oregon, for herself or for her stepfather. Sherman did not hesitate. Although he hated both politics and asking for political favors, he contacted the postmaster-general because, "when the children of my old war associates appeal to me, my heart goes out and I cease to be a reasonable being." Although Blanche lost her father when she was a baby, she could count on her late father's old friend.

Sherman never forgot the valor and sacrifice of his friend. On December 28, 1886, in a letter to a friend, he recalled the assault on Kennesaw and the death of Dan McCook. As if admitting responsibility over and over again was his penance, Sherman wrote, "I ordered the assault and thereby occasioned his death. You can readily understand how deeply I feel about, for no adequate return can ever be made, by any nation or people for such services." Dan McCook and countless thousands of others fought and died to preserve the Union. With this in mind, Sherman closed his letter saying, "The government of the United States exists alone because of such sacrifices as Dan McCook made of his young life."[63]

The historian of the 52nd Ohio, Company "E," Sergeant Nixon B. Stewart, remembered "Colonel Dan" as courteous, modest and brave. "With the frankness and simplicity of a boy, he united the dash of Marion and the wisdom of a veteran." Stewart praised his colonel, noting that McCook "led us [at Kennesaw] like the tenth wave of the sea, right into the storm of splintery fire and shotted [sic] shell."[64]

When the fighting started in 1861, an enthusiastic, proud and determined Dan McCook left Kansas and law practice behind and, seemingly light-hearted, marched off to serve the Union, boasting that he would earn a colonel's epaulets or a soldier's grave. After that his duties took him to Wilson's Creek, Shiloh, Perryville, Stones River, Chickamauga and Chattanooga, and finally up to the "Dead Angle" at Kennesaw Mountain, and from there to his soldier's grave. He died a general and entered the realm of heroic soldiers forever known as the "Fighting McCooks."

Tribute: Remembering Bob and Dan

> "...the records show astonishing devotion on the part of American youth. But there is no family whose military distinction reached that of the McCooks."—*Omaha Daily Bee*, September 19, 1909

With his date with death by assassination drawing near, Abraham Lincoln acknowledged the dedication and sacrifice of the McCook family in the Civil War. In a response to a letter from Mary Jane McCook-Baldwin, he wrote: "Will [you] please see and hear Mrs. Baldwin, the bearer who is of the McCook family, so many of whom have gallantly fallen in this war?"[1]

Four of Mary's family members fell in the Civil War, or as Lincoln might have said, they were sacrificed on the altar of freedom. And by the time the South surrendered, all four were resting in Spring Grove Cemetery in Cincinnati, in graves that circled a grand marble monument. Charles, Robert, Daniel Jr., and Daniel Sr., all died of battle wounds. Having paid the ultimate price in war, they were not able to savor victory or experience the happy result of their efforts. They were unable to enjoy the peace.

Their brother, Dr. Latimer L. McCook, was able to experience peace for a short time before he passed away in 1869, having finally succumbed to the stress of two wounds received while he worked as a surgeon. Even though it was over, the Civil War had claimed another victim.

The tragic and violent death of Edwin S. McCook came in 1873 in Dakota Territory, where he had gone to serve as secretary of the territory, having been appointed to that position by President Grant. While in attendance at a public meeting, he was shot and killed by a political rival. Because he was a public official at the time, he too died in the line of duty, like the soldier he once was, and stories of his death raced across the country. The adventuresome McCooks had a penchant for attracting attention in or out of the army, but it is their participation in the Civil War that vaulted the family into historic prominence. Therefore after Edwin was gunned down in Yankton, Dakota Territory, a frontier town on the Missouri River, an Ohio newspaper struck the appropriate chord saying that he "was the youngest member of the family which has become so distinguished by the military deeds of its sons as to be termed that of 'the fighting McCooks.'"[2]

While seven McCook men were dead, George, Alexander and John—along with their cousins—were still alive and marching on, in step with all other Civil War veterans, toward that day when each would join the roll of the honored dead. Since it was widely believed that God loved the righteous and the brave, people shared a belief that a special place in paradise waited for a patriotic soldier who loved his country and never shirked his duty.

Until that final roll call, the relationships formed in the regiments on the field of battle would compel ex-soldiers to write to old colleagues and recall memories of hardships, combat, incidents of valor and thoughts of dead comrades. Bravery and sacrifice in the face of great danger created bonds of the most unbreakable material. The unity forged while in the army meant old comrades sought out the company of their mess mates and tent mates. As the passing years saw their ranks steadily diminish, old soldiers looked forward to attending ceremonies, reunions and rituals honoring their regiments. Remembering that war called ordinary men to greatness, they garnished the graves of their comrades with flowers and flags on Decoration Day.

Gradually, people came around to the idea that gathering and talking about the war was not only good for the ex-soldiers, but it was the decent thing to do, because the suffering and sacrifice was worth remembering.[3]

The regiment, which during the war was the fundamental unit of both armies, took on a new aura of respect. The men who upheld the honor of the regiments during the war kept both reputation and honor alive in ceremonies and celebrations. Magazine articles and histories were written and published by the hundreds, especially during the last quarter of the 19th century. Monuments were built and unveiled for fallen heroes such as the imminently popular Robert L. McCook, whom family and colleagues still insisted had been murdered by Frank Gurley, as opposed to being an ordinary battlefield casualty.

Wishing to permanently enshrine their "martyred Colonel," members of the 9th Ohio Infantry regiment—with music and speeches—dedicated a stately monument, approximately 16 feet tall, to Robert L. McCook at Washington Park in Cincinnati on August 23, 1877. Created by Leopold Fettweiss and resting on a pedestal of Quincy granite, the monument is topped by a three-foot-high bust of the fallen general with his name inscribed at the base. The cost was upward to $6000 and the impressive dedication ceremony was led by the mayor of Cincinnati, who graciously accepted the monument on

Tribute

The bust of Robert L. McCook atop the majestic monument erected to honor the fallen Civil War soldier looks more like a Roman god than an officer in the U.S. Army. But all the better for he, and his brother Daniel, were remembered for heroics, for larger than life accomplishments on the field of battle. The sixteen-foot-tall monument established in 1877 in Washington Park, Cincinnati, Ohio, was created by the sculptor Leopold Feitwess at a cost of approximately $6000. Surviving members of the 9th Ohio Infantry Regiment dedicated the statue with music and speeches celebrating their beloved leader's short but illustrious military career. It was one monument for one McCook, but it was one that Bob would be more than willing to share with every member of the family known as the "Fighting McCooks" (photograph by Matt Dole, author's collection).

behalf of the city. Family members in attendance included Robert's mother Martha McCook, his brothers Alexander and John, his sister Mary Baldwin, sister-in-law, Loraine, Edwin's widow, and nephew George McCook, Jr.

A massive crowd stood silently while the late General Robert L. McCook was eulogized, his short life summed up for those present, with emphasis on his Civil War exploits. He was recalled as a kind, wise and strong leader, whose dedication toward his men and "their confidence in his abilities and love for him as a man formed an attachment of peculiar force." Those gathered for the solemn occasion were reminded that McCook accepted his promotion to brigadier general with the "provision that his old regiment should be a part of his brigade." McCook and his "bully Dutchmen" were inseparable until he was brought down by "foul murder that robbed the army of a hero."[4] Truly, many in the North refused to let go of the belief that Bob McCook's death was something other than simply a casualty of war.

Not long after the dedication of the Robert L. McCook statue, George W. McCook passed away, and his service to Ohio and America was remembered. George, the older brother, the politician and die-hard Democrat, the lawyer and the acknowledged leader of the McCook clan, died on December 28, 1877, in New York City while visiting his cousin, Anson G. McCook.[5] The large, gentle man, who loved his family and the classics, was eulogized in the press for his military service in the Mexican War, his public service in Ohio, making speeches to encourage enlistment, and for organizing several infantry regiments in his home state during the Civil War. He was kept out of combat against the Rebels due to poor health, but George was still considered one of the "Fighting McCooks" for having fought and faced death in the Mexican War.

After the Civil War ended, George W. McCook stayed active in Ohio politics as a Democrat, even though other McCooks had switched to the Republican Party. In 1871, he was the Democratic candidate for governor in Ohio. Republican newspapers in Ohio slammed him, mocking his Civil War record, while ignoring his accomplishments in the Mexican War. Among the harshest critics, *The Highland Weekly News* sneeringly suggested that "he belongs to the family of *fighting* McCooks, but he is known as not the fighting McCook."[6] The mean-spirited criticism and health problems took a heavy toll and George terminated his candidacy, apparently having neither the will nor the desire to fight on.

Death in battle created many Civil War heroes, the memories of whom were enshrined for all time on the honor roll of the honored dead. Among them none stood out more dramatically than George's younger brother Daniel McCook, Jr. All the McCooks were brave and dedicated, but as it is certain that some stars shine brighter than others, it was Dan—whose start in life was that of a weak and sickly boy—who grew into the ideal 19th century man, having lived and died with honor. It was Dan who donned the mantle of the supreme hero of the family, a shining example of the citizen soldier.

Because of Dan's exalted status, and the bloody drama that played itself out on the slopes of Kennesaw Mountain in Georgia, the 52nd Ohio, his regiment, formed bonds of steel. As the years lengthened following the end of the Civil War, survivors from regiments from the victorious North gathered to celebrate the memories, accomplishments and hardships of the campaigns that stretched across four years of hardship and fighting. While every regiment was deserving of praise, none carried the torch of greatness higher and prouder than the 52nd Ohio Voluntary Infantry regiment.

On September 19, 1877, the 52nd Ohio held its third annual celebration at Barnesville, Ohio. While every member was given his due, the memory of one man, Dan McCook, was recalled with special reverence. The first speaker—one of many—extolled the brave deeds of the regiment and confessed "the great honor" of "taking the hand of the mother of the celebrated family of McCooks" and that of her daughter Mary Baldwin. Tears of joy and sorrow flowed freely when Martha McCook stepped forward to receive three cheers "for the grand old mother of the 'fighting McCooks'"

As sure as time heals all wounds, it also elevates the stature of those soldiers whose demise grateful men and women meet to remember and celebrate. The passage of time also, on occasion, colors the truth with subtle shades of fiction. Thus Colonel Daniel McCook was eulogized in a speech that not only remembered the battle of Kennesaw Mountain—where he received his death wound while bravely leading his men—but asserted that "with his dying breath ordered his regiment to the assault by which the works of the enemy were carried." While this doesn't square with what actually happened that sweltering June day of 1864, when the Union forces were repulsed, it was what the audience was willing to hear, along with cheers for the flag. On this august occasion, it was time once again to honor the "Fighting McCooks."

W. H. Reynolds of Steubenville rang the bell of pride and patriotism in a stirring address commemorating the bravery of all the soldiers, especially those who had met a soldier's death, for these special men had "died in a cause as holy as ever brightened history's page." Even more to endear them to history, they fought "against a cause as unholy and unjust as ever stained the darkest page of time; against the blackest, foulest wrong of any age—slavery."

And then, speaking directly to Martha McCook and reaching greater heights of eloquence and passion, Reynolds recalled the "hushed morning in June in that little valley before the rugged heights of Kenesaw [sic]" where the columns of Dan's brigade were readied for the deadly assault. Eager to obey the command fight for the battle objective, "we hear them plead to be given the front rank so as to be near your dear boy; again we hear his kindly words 'Not today boys, I know the 52nd will come.'" Finally, after marching with great determination against shot and shell, "with your son right in its very front," and men falling like autumn leaves, "your boy" is hit. Carried from the field, his "dying eyes rest for the last time on his loved regiment, and forgetting all else, he exclaims, 'Those boys will take their works.'"

Judge R.H. Cochran of Wheeling continued with more soaring rhetoric in a symphonic speech glorifying the deeds of the 52nd Ohio at Kennesaw Mountain where Dan McCook "won his star" and "imperishable fame." Speaking about heroes in a time of heroic deeds, Cochran said the words that were surely in the hearts and minds of those Civil War veterans in attendance: "How it must animate your souls with manly pride" to claim membership in the 52nd Ohio. Then he went on to say, "As you reflect, there rises before me form of gallant Dan McCook," a man worthy of all the outpouring of praise and admiration that gushed from the podium that day. Cochran proclaimed that none other than a Confederate once called McCook one of the "noblest and bravest and generous spirits that I ever knew. I know not where he sleeps but I should like to lay a flower upon his grave." What greater testimony to heroism than that of a former enemy?

J. T. Holmes, ex-colonel of the 52nd, spoke and further praised Dan McCook while making an impassioned plea for the unity of the country. He closed by reciting "We have Drank from the Same Canteen" and "Drake's American Flag." Then Martha McCook came forward and said that she wanted to give every member of the regiment a photograph of her late son, Dan McCook. Dan's sister Mary announced that the Society of the 52 O.V.I. should be made perpetual by giving membership to the oldest son of each member. The ceremony was over and all the participants left feeling awestruck and uplifted, as if the heroic Daniel McCook returned from the dead to smile upon them.[7]

And the memories of soldiers continued to smile on Daniel McCook. In 1903, it was announced in *The National Tribune* that members of the "Colonel Daniel McCook Brigade Association," purchased 60 acres of land on Kennesaw Mountain, known as the "Dead Angle" on Cheatham's hill. The plan—spearheaded by Colonel Allen L. Fahnestock—was to construct a monument and tablets to commemorate the deadly assault that took place on June 27, 1864, when Colonel Daniel McCook and more than 400 others from his brigade were killed or wounded.[8] The 25-foot high monument was erected on June 27, 1914.

The shibboleth "Fighting McCooks" was first used during the early stages of the war. After the war it really caught on and was repeated in the press, at

Civil War reunions, by daydreaming schoolboys, and, importantly, in history books. It was romanced into a larger-than-life tale about men of Scots-Irish descent, who, when called upon to fight, did so with a fierce dedication and for a high, moral purpose. Not long after the war ended, the state of Ohio commissioned an artist to paint a large picture of Daniel McCook, Sr., and his warrior sons. They had become America's heroes, symbolic of all that was loyal, gallant and courageous.

It wasn't so much that the McCooks were braver or better than other soldiers of high repute; rather, the sheer number of them that served in the war gave the expression "Fighting McCooks" a special glow. They were the "Fighting McCooks" because so many of them fought and did so with distinction and courage in a cause they believed in so fervently. They were heroes in an age of heroes. But they were also ordinary men for whom being a soldier was a duty, an honor not to be shirked. They stood up for the Union in a time of mortal crisis and it was right and proper for the Union to stand up for them.

Martha McCook was steadfast in her love for her boys. As the mother of war heroes, she was determined that they be appropriately honored. In a letter to President Andrew Johnson, dated February 1, 1869, she requested, as "a simple act of justice," that Robert and Daniel be awarded rank of brevet major general, that Charles be given the rank of brevet first lieutenant and John be given the rank of brevet colonel. Martha gently reminded the president that granting the request would be "a great comfort to me" and would cost the government nothing.

She entrusted the letter to her daughter Mary Baldwin, who delivered it to the White House. President Johnson nominated Robert, Dan and John, as their mother requested, but did not nominate Charles for the brevet rank. The three requests were sent to the congressional committee on military affairs where they died.[9] Martha McCook was forced to endure yet another disappointment as she moved toward her own date with death. And yet she was not entirely ignored, for she had been granted an annual federal pension of $300, a sum that was increased to $550 in 1866 by the House of Representatives.[10]

Martha "Mother McCook" died in 1879. At her grand funeral the mother of the "Fighting McCooks" was praised and mourned in a manner that acknowledged the grief and suffering she experienced at the loss of so many family members, including her husband. The tragic news delivered to her door, time and time again, was the equivalent of battle wounds. She was a veteran of the Civil War in her own right, worthy of all praise and commendation.

The same could be said for the other wives and widows of the soldier

McCooks, for whom the four-year war was an exercise in anxiety and fear. When the war ended they could count their blessings or, if need be, apply for a pension. For example, Dan's widow, Julia, who remarried, was in 1895 collecting a $30 per month pension as a result of congressional legislation.[11]

Alexander McDowell McCook came through the war without a scratch and went on to see the beginning 20th century, dying on June 12, 1903, after retiring from the army as a major general. His military career started in 1852 when as a second lieutenant he left West Point for the Far West where McCook encountered "Buffaloes" in immense herds, "as far as the eye could reach."[12] While he loved the frontier and all its natural grandeur, it was the Civil War and all its brutality that defined his military career. He had earned the highest rank of any McCook, but because of his role as a corps commander at Stones River and Chickamauga, his military record was deemed tainted and historians differ as to his leadership skills. Alexander McDowell McCook's dedication to the restoration of Union and his personal bravery, however, has never been challenged and he stands shoulder to shoulder with the select group of soldiers known as the "Fighting McCooks."

It was his popularity throughout America in the later stages of his military career that kept the light of fame beaming down on the McCooks. Since Alex was a career military man, in uniform, serving in the West, long after his brothers and cousins returned to civilian life, he, in effect, carried the soldier's torch for his family. In California, where he was widely known and highly respected, *The Herald*, a Los Angeles newspaper, praised McCook, stating that "this gallant and fiery soldier has had time to make himself popular everywhere."[13]

On September 17, 1911, John J. McCook, the youngest son of Daniel Sr. and Martha, died—the last of the "Fighting McCooks." On the occasion of his funeral, the war record of proud family was reprised in a eulogy delivered by a boyhood friend, John McTammany. He praised the McCooks, calling them "neither quarrelsome nor breeders of strife," even though they were bold and fierce fighters. On the contrary, they were a "genial, friendly and lovable body of men." While there was nothing about this Ohio family to "distinguish it from the dead level of a dozen other families residing in Carrollton" when the war broke out, they all tapped innate talent and found leadership skills. The same, he said, was true of the Grant, Sheridan and Sherman families, all from Ohio. For they, like the McCooks, rose from obscurity to deal with the emergency thrust upon the nation by the war, setting aside all personal ambition and family considerations.

McTammany's eulogy reached a new crescendo that seemed to transcend those that were given at earlier McCook funerals. Harkening back to the prewar days in Kansas when Dan McCook and W. T. Sherman were law partners,

McTammany proclaimed that the history of the "Fighting McCooks" began when the lawyers-turned-soldiers wrote on a piece of paper attached to their office door "This office is closed." Moving to the battle at Kennesaw Mountain, and as if trying to recreate the drama of what "was probably the most sanguinary struggle … in the whole history of the war," he spoke first of Sherman and his great dilemma. The general was face to face with an emergency and then and there decided that only one man was qualified to lead the attack, namely "his friend and law partner, Dan McCook." Although Dan was the only member of his family in the fight that terrible day, McTammany told the hushed audience that "God and the McCooks alone realized what it meant."

It meant, of course, that Dan McCook understood he and his men faced almost certain death. And yet Colonel McCook "felt he had been honored by his friend [Sherman] in thus being chosen to lead in such a rash and desperate struggle." He described the Rebel army as a "foe who had never been defeated," lurking on a "grim Kenesaw [sic]," a place of evil where McCook beheld a "spectre of death, with wide spread arms ready to receive him."

Taking even greater liberties with the truth, he said the assault up the slope of the mountain, "to victory and death," resulted in the "Stars and Stripes" replacing the "Stars and Bars." "Kenesaw [sic] was taken" and soon-to-become General Daniel McCook, Jr., the chosen one, died a hero.

Then, mid-stream into his eulogy, McTammany reversed course and went back to talking about the deceased, John J. McCook. The speaker reminded those in attendance that it be "impossible to write about John J. McCook without speaking of other McCooks" because the family was "one and inseparable." Their deeds of honor were somehow interconnected, so that talking about one McCook meant including the entire clan.

The latest recruit to the rolls of the honored dead, John J. McCook, proudly bore the scars of war. He was seriously wounded in May of 1864, at Shady Grove, Virginia, while serving in General Grant's Army of the Potomac. As a result he was discharged from the army. For gallantry and meritorious service, he was mustered out as a lieutenant colonel.[14] Although a "boy soldier," not more than 20 years old when the war ended, he had "'showed at every step of his military career the splendid dash of an enthusiast and the iron courage of a veteran.'"[15] High praise, but then he was a McCook.

After the war he completed undergraduate work at Kenyon College and earned a law degree from Harvard University in 1869. Thereafter he practiced law in New York City, developing a lucrative legal business. John J. McCook was a devout Presbyterian, very athletic, his favorite sport being baseball. He was once a catcher on a Steubenville, Ohio, baseball team. To round out a career marked by achievement and honors, John J. McCook was offered a cabinet post by President William McKinley—an offer he decided not to accept.

While he did not attain the high military stature of his brothers Daniel or Robert, John could claim a steady record of good service throughout the war. He fought well enough and long enough to be a "Fighting McCook," and his death almost 50 years after the war started triggered another outpouring of appreciation for America's largest and best known family of fighting men.[16]

When the sod was placed over the grave of Robert L. McCook at Spring Grove Cemetery in Cincinnati, a journalist penned a melancholy but heartfelt comment, saying that it would be unnecessary to erect a "marble monument to perpetuate his memory and virtues to posterity."[17] While it was most certainly true that the grand funeral for the fallen war hero created powerful and lasting memories of the man and his sacrifice, Robert and his warrior brothers lie buried beside the curved arches of a magnificent marble monument that will stand for all time to come in recognition of their bravery and dedication. And beyond the silence and solitude of the cemetery, the lively appellation "Fighting McCooks" became "almost as familiar as his own name to every American boy."[18]

In his book entitled *Heroes of the Civil War*, Harrison Hunt selected from the ranks of the Union army 31 men and four women to be honored as heroes. Among them are many familiar names, including generals Grant, Sherman, Thomas and Sheridan whose performances in the Civil War translated into victories that regularly attract historians. He also selected General George B. McClellan who was a skilled organizer and drill-master but otherwise a failure as a leader. McClellan never led a bayonet charge, nor did he step forward, risking his life, to rally his men in the face of great danger. In short, he did nothing heroic. He was, however, popular with the soldiers and cast a more than favorable image to the general public. But appearances have always been important and the self-styled "Napoleon," thoroughly military, looked and talked like a man with heroic qualities.

The same elevated status was bestowed on Brigadier General Robert Anderson, whose sole moment of glory came for him and his besieged men when they were pounded by Confederate cannon fire at Fort Sumter in Charleston harbor. Because he resisted, Anderson is forever known as the "hero of Fort Sumter." It was pure magic: the war had just begun, Anderson was in the spotlight, the North was angry and timing was everything. He was sidelined by illness and never fought in a major battle, but he conducted himself with great honor when the dignity of the United States was at stake and under attack by the Rebels.

Another man designated as a hero by Hunt was Colonel Ephraim E. Ellsworth, one of the earliest casualties of the war. He did not participate in a battle; he was killed on May 24, 1861, when he attempted to remove a Confederate flag from a hotel in Alexandria, Virginia. The incident was given prompt and vivid attention in the Northern press, inciting feelings of outrage toward the man who killed him. The story was well-received by the hawkish public, and the dashing, promising young officer and friend of Abraham Lincoln became a martyr and a hero.

Conspicuously absent from the list of names of the worthy men and women are members of the McCook clan. How and why were the names of Daniel and Robert McCook not on this honor roll, one may ask? After all, both men were of high rank and had wartime experiences that were the stuff of legends, and both died of wounds from enemy guns. They were looked upon as heroes by an adoring post-war public that more than appreciated the dedication and sacrifice of these two young men. Certainly they had— as the saying went—"covered themselves with glory," and most certainly, they possessed a nobility of character that was equal to of those honored by Hunt.

But while they were glorified in death, Dan and Robert, along with their kin, lacked the star quality needed to reach the highest pantheon of historic greatness. They each had their glorious moment, but it was not a magic moment like the ones that translated into the catch phrases such as the "Rock of Chickamauga" or "unconditional surrender Grant." Nor did they have the *persona*, the luck, the flash of genius or the way with words that enabled the heroic W. T. Sherman to describe war and its impact on society. He proclaimed that "war is hell" and biographers took note. The public remembered and was uplifted and made wiser.

The sheer number of McCooks who served the Union during the Civil War was something that the press and the public found both noble and unusual. In the decades that followed the war's end, newspaper articles appeared from time to time revealing the heroics of the McCook men who had earned their reputation as brave and fierce fighters. For example, in 1909, the *Omaha Daily Bee* reprised the McCook saga, declaring that while all the sons of the North contributed to victory, "there is no family whose military distinction reached that of the McCooks." Their record of service "is unparalleled in American history."[19] Among their admirers from across the American panorama was Theodore Roosevelt, a "bully" man who could appreciate military courage and accomplishment.[20]

The McCooks were truly worthy of the accolades that were cast in their direction. But while they had led lives of honor, courage and daring, their heroic deeds did not ride on the cheering express train of lasting public fascination. They were loud and visible but failed to maintain that steady drumbeat of popularity needed to march into eternity larger than life, and thus be remembered as heroes for all time to come. Lacking the magic, they gradually sank in the deep waters of history, there to rest, like most soldiers, as mere mortals.

The painting of Daniel McCook, Sr., and his sons suffered a similar fate. For some reason the state of Ohio rejected it after having ordered it. The artist sold the painting, and years later, in 1904, it was discovered in a Washington, D.C., "junk shop" by none other than John J. McCook, youngest of Daniel's sons. John bought it and hired an artist to repaint it. He then presented it the state of Ohio and it was hung in the rotunda of the state capital building at Columbus.[21] But it didn't stay there. It was moved to a museum at Ohio State University until in 1917, when, by order of the governor, it was "restored to the statehouse."[22]

Unfortunately, a painting, however artistically rendered, does not ensure lasting fame for those in paint. Like colors on a canvas, memories fade, people forget and historians form their own opinions. As a result, the McCooks lost their luster long ago. They have generally been given second-tier status by Civil War historians. Dan McCook was accorded star treatment in a book about the 52nd Ohio, but aside from a recent biography by Charles and Barbara Whalen, and a biography of General Alexander M. McCook by this writer, no one has undertaken to write in detail about the illustrious Ohio family. And aside from Anson's unpublished manuscript and Dan's article in *Harper's Weekly,* none of the McCooks wrote about the Civil War and their participation in that seminal event. Still there are some lasting and visible tributes to the McCooks. Among them, McCook County, South Dakota, is named after Edwin S. McCook and the town of McCook, Nebraska, is named in memory of Alexander M. McCook.

Although the McCooks were denied the crown of everlasting fame, their reputation as patriots, leaders and soldiers remains intact. The record forged on the many battlefields of the Civil War is clear and established for all time to come—it cannot be diminished or disparaged by fading memory or by judgmental historians. While they wanted and thought they deserved recognition, the McCooks served and fought because they were patriots doing their duty, protecting the Union and the Constitution, not for the personal desire to become heroes. They willingly stepped into the role of soldiers when soldiers were needed.

The McCooks fought for a united and strong America that many of them would never live to see—Union forever and secession nevermore. They left behind a country free from the shameful burden of slavery—an America, still young, proud, healing itself and ready to take its place among the great nations of the world. Along with countless thousands of others of all ranks who toiled in the trenches, died of disease, or were cut down on the battlefields, the McCooks were proud to serve in the Civil War and the country that Americans call home is their legacy and their gift to us.

Chapter Notes

Introduction

1. *The Intermountain Catholic* (Salt Lake City, UT), February 1, 1902.
2. Dunkelman, Mark H., *Patrick Henry Jones: Irish American, Civil War General, and Gilded Age Politician*, Baton Rouge: Louisiana State University, 2015, p. 6.
3. *St. Paul Pioneer*, December 15, 1864.
4. Davis, Kenneth C., *A Nation Rising: Untold Tales of Flawed Founders, Fallen Heroes, and Forgotten Fighters from America's Hidden History*, New York: Smithsonian Books, 2010, p. 186.
5. The Cleveland Civil War Roundtable, "The Irish in the Civil War," by Dennis Keating, 2008.
6. Goldfield, David, *America Aflame: How the Civil War Created a Nation*, New York: Bloomsbury Press, 2011, p. 88.
7. Davis, Kenneth C., p. 185.
8. Craugwell, Thomas J., *The Greatest Brigade: How the Irish Brigade Cleared the Way to Victory in the American Civil War*, Beverly, MA: Fair Winds Press, 2011, p. 21.
9. McCarthy, Karen F., *The Other Irish: The Scots-Irish Rascals That Made America*, New York: Sterling, 2011, p. ix.
10. Dolan, Jay P., *The Irish Americans, A History*, New York: Bloomsbury Press, 2008, pp. 41–42.
11. *Evening Bulletin* (Honolulu, HI), April 23, 1898.
12. Dolan, Jay P., p. 31.
13. Whalen, Charles and Barbara, *The Fighting McCooks: America's Famous Fighting Family*, Bethesda, MD: Westmoreland Press, 2006, p. 17.
14. *Ibid.*, pp. 19–20.
15. *The Mahoning Dispatch* (Canfield, OH), December 24, 1909.
16. *Fergus County Argus* (Lewistown, MT), June 24, 1903.
17. Whalen, Charles and Barbara, p. 23.
18. *Carroll Free Press* (Carrollton, OH), December 24, 1841.
19. Whalen, Charles and Barbara, p. 26.
20. *The Cambria Freeman* (Ebensburg, PA), September 24, 1875.
21. *New York Daily Tribune*, February 21, 1846.
22. *New York Daily Tribune*, February 25, 1846.
23. *The Cambria Freeman* (Ebensburg, PA), September 24, 1875; *Vermont Phoenix* (Brattleboro, VT), May 14, 1846.
24. *The Ottawa Free Trader* (Ottawa, IL), September 23, 1861.
25. Johannsen, Robert W., *Stephen A. Douglas*, New York: Oxford University Press, 1973, p. 619.
26. Anderson, Frank Maloy, *The Mystery of a Public Man: A Historical Detective Story*, Minneapolis: University of Minnesota Press, 1948, pp. 197–198.
27. *The Washington Herald* (Washington, D.C.), April 5, 1908.
28. The Cleveland Civil War Roundtable, "The Irish in the Civil War," by Dennis Keating, 2008.
29. Craugwell, Thomas J., p. 63.

30. *Holmes County Republican* (Millersburg, Holmes County, OH), May 30, 1861.
31. Muelhberger, James P., *The 116: The True Story of Abraham Lincoln's Lost Guard*, Chicago: Ankerwycke, 2015, pp. 19–20, 141.
32. Whalen, Charles and Barbara, p. 199.
33. Carroll County Historical Society, Carrollton, OH, *McCook Family Album*.
34. Lewis, Lloyd, *The Assassination of Lincoln: History & Myth*, New York: MJF Books, 1994, originally published 1929, p. 51.
35. Thomas, Benjamin P., and Hyman, Harold M., *Stanton, The Life and Times of Lincoln's Secretary of War*, New York: Alfred A. Knopf, 1962, pp. 38, 40–42, 44–45.
36. Widmer, Ted, ed., *The New York Times Disunion: 106 Articles from the New York Times Opinionator*, New York: Black Dog & Leventhal, 2013, p. 62.

Chapter 1

1. *New York Times*, July 21, 1861.
2. *New York Times* in the *Dubuque Daily Times*, August 27, 1859.
3. Nicolay, John G., *The Outbreak of Rebellion*, New York: Da Capo Press, 1995, reprint of 1881 edition, p. 138.
4. *Cincinnati Weekly Gazette*, May 8, 1861.
5. *Ibid.*, May 8, 1861.
6. *The Daily Times* (Cincinnati), October 14, 1861.
7. Burton, William L., *Melting Pot Soldiers: The Union's Ethnic Regiments*, New York: Fordham University Press, 1998, p. 94.
8. Lande, R. Gregory, *Madness, Malingering and Malfeasance: The Transformation of Psychiatry And the Law in the Civil War Era*, Washington, D.C.: Potomac Books, 2003, p. 111.
9. Reinhart, Joseph R., ed. and trans., *A German Hurrah! Civil War Letters of Friedrich Bertsch And Wilhelm Stangel, 9th Ohio Infantry*, Kent, OH: Kent State University Press, 2010, p. 12.
10. Burton, William L., p. 95.
11. *America's Civil War*, "The Eccentric German General," by Karen Koss, September 2003, p. 47.
12. Reinhart, Joseph R., ed., *August Willich's Gallant Dutchmen: Civil War Letters From the 32nd Indiana Infantry*, Kent, OH: Kent State University Press, 2006, p. 8.
13. Grebner, Constantin, *"We Were the Ninth": A History of the Ninth Regiment, Ohio Volunteer Infantry, April 17, 1861 to June 7, 1864*, trans. and ed. Frederic Trautmann, Kent, OH: Kent State University Press, 1987, pp. 4–5.
14. *The Spirit of Democracy* (Woodfield, Ohio), February 26, 1862.
15. Library of Congress, Manuscript Reading Room, McCook Family Papers, Article in the *Steubenville Herald*, August 24, 1877.
16. Neff, William B., *Bench and Bar of Northern Ohio*, Cleveland: The Historical Publishing Co., 1921, p. 144.
17. Howe, Henry, *A Brief Historical Sketch of the "Fighting McCooks,"* reprinted from the Proceedings of the Scotch-Irish Society of America, p. 10.
18. *Belmont Chronicle* (St. Clairsville, Ohio), August 14, 1861.
19. Grebner, Constantin, p. 30.
20. Howe, Henry, p. 9.
21. *The War of the Rebellion*, Official Records, Series III, Vol. I, p. 115.
22. Grebner, Constantin, p. 50.
23. McCook, Anson, *Memoirs*, Unpublished, Ohio Historical Society, Columbus, p. 8.
24. *Cincinnati Daily Commercial*, November 6, 1861.
25. *New York Times*, June 4, 1861.
26. *The Wheeling Intelligencer* in the *New York Times*, November 10, 1861.
27. *New York Times*, July 10, 1861.
28. Van Der Linden, Frank, *Lincoln, The Road to War*, Golden, CO: Fulcrum Publishing, 1998, p. 89.
29. Nicolay, John G., p. 15.
30. Kline, Michael J., *The Baltimore Plot: The First Conspiracy to Assassinate Abraham Lincoln*, Yardley, PA: Westholme, 2008, p. 52.
31. *New York Times*, June 19, 1861.

32. Perrot, Geoffrey, *Lincoln's War: The Untold Story of America's Greatest President as Commander in Chief*, New York: Random House, 2004, p. 255.
33. Williams, T. Harry, *Hayes of the 23rd: The Civil War Volunteer Officer*, Lincoln: University of Nebraska Press, 1965, p. 70.
34. *New York Tribune*, June 8, 1861.
35. *Blue and Gray Magazine*, "The Northwestern Virginia Campaign of 1861, McClellan's Rising Star—Lee's Dismal Debut," by Martin K. Fleming, Vol. X, August 1993, p. 16.
36. Nicolay, John G., pp. 144–145.
37. Williams, T. Harry, p. 90.
38. Moore, George Ellis, *A Banner in the Hills: West Virginia's Statehood*, New York: Appleton-Century-Crofts, 1963, pp. 101–102.
39. *The Daily Times* (Cincinnati), September 9, 1861.
40. *Civil War History*, Vol. 10, No. 64, December 1964, published quarterly by the University of Iowa, Robert R. Dykstra, ed., "The Bushwhacker's War: Insurgency and Counter-insurgency in West Virginia," ed. Richard O. Curry and F. Gerald Ham, p. 421.
41. Williams, T. Harry, pp. 66–67.
42. Reinhart, Joseph R., p. 18.
43. Grebner, Constantin, pp. 12–13.
44. *Ibid.*, p. 75.
45. Reid, Whitelaw, *Ohio in the War, Her Statesmen: Her Generals and Soldiers*, Vol. I, New York: Moore, Wilstach & Baldwin, 1868, p. 877.

Chapter 2

1. Reinhart, Joseph R., ed. and translator, *A German Hurrah! Civil War Letters of Friedrich Bertsch And Wilhelm Stangel, 9th Ohio Infantry*, Kent, OH: Kent State University Press, 2010, p. 47.
2. *New York Times*, July 10, 1861.
3. Beatty, John, *The Citizen Soldier or Memoirs of a Volunteer*, Cincinnati: Wilstach, Baldwin & Co., Publishers, 1879, p. 16.
4. *Blue and Gray Magazine*, Vol. IX, August 1993, "The Northwestern Virginia Campaign of 1861, McClellan's Rising Star—Lee's Dismal Debut," by Martin K. Fleming, p. 48.
5. OR, Series I, Vol. II, p. 201.
6. *National Tribune* (Washington, D.C.), February 22, 1883.
7. Moore, David G., *William S. Rosecrans and the Union Victory: A Civil War Biography*, Jefferson, NC: McFarland, 2014, pp. 12–13.
8. Grebner, Constantin, *"We Were the Ninth": A History of the Ninth Regiment, Ohio Voluntary Infantry, April 17, 1861 to June 7, 1864*, trans. and ed. Frederick Trautmann, Kent, OH: Kent State University Press, 1987, p. 64.
9. *The Daily Times* (Cincinnati), July 19, 1861.
10. Lamers, William M., *The Edge of Glory: A Biography of General William S. Rosecrans, USA*, Baton Rouge: Louisiana State University Press, 1999, p. 34.
11. McPherson, James M., *Ordeal by Fire: The Civil War and Reconstruction*, New York: McGraw-Hill Higher Education, 2001, pp. 173–174.
12. *New York Times*, July 20, 1861.
13. Grebner, Constantin, p. 64.
14. Library of Congress, Manuscript Reading Room, McCook Family Papers, letter Daniel McCook, Sr., to George McCook, August 2, 1861.
15. Reinhart, Joseph R., p. 107.
16. Lamers, William M., p. 45.
17. Williams, T. Harry, *Hayes of the 23rd: The Civil War Volunteer Officer*, Lincoln: University of Nebraska Press, 1965, p. 83.
18. Lamers, William M., p. 48.
19. *Ibid.*, p. 49.
20. OR, Series I, Vol. V, p. 142.
21. *Ibid.*, Series I, Vol. V, p. 129.
22. Grebner, Constantin, pp. 72–73.
23. Moore, George Ellis, *A Banner in the Hills, West Virginia's Statehood*, New York: Appleton-Century Crofts, A Division of Meredith Publishing Co., 1963, pp. 115–116.

24. Lamers, William M., p. 53.
25. *Cincinnati Daily Commercial,* November 6, 1861.
26. National Archives, Military Service File of Robert L. McCook.
27. Grebner, Constantin, p. 74.
28. *Daily Ohio Statesman* (Columbus, OH), October 17, 1861.
29. Lamers, William M., p. 55.
30. Grebner, Constantin, pp. 76-77.
31. Grimsley, Mark, *The Hard Hand of War, Union Military Policy Toward Southern Civilians, 1861-1865,* Cambridge: Cambridge University Press, 1995, pp. 3, 4, 8, 45-46.
32. *The Daily Times,* November 11, 1861.
33. Lamers, William M., pp. 56-60.
34. OR, Series I, Vol. V, p. 257.
35. *Civil War History,* Vol. 10, No. 64, December 1964, Published Quarterly by the University of Iowa, Robert R. Dykstra, ed., "The Bushwhacker's War: Insurgency and Counter-insurgency in West Virginia," edited by Richard O. Curry and F. Gerald Ham, p. 417.
36. McPherson, James M., pp. 175-176.
37. Buell, Thomas B., *The Warrior Generals, Combat Leadership in the Civil War,* New York: Three Rivers Press, 1997, p. 50.
38. McPherson, James M., p. 175.
39. Grebner, Constantin, p. 77.
40. *Ibid.,* pp. 79-81.
41. Reinhart, Joseph R., p. 181.
42. *Ibid.,* pp. 182-183.

Chapter 3

1. *The Ottawa Free Trader* (Ottawa, Il), September 3, 1887.
2. Engle, Stephen D., *Don Carlos Buell, Most Promising of All,* Chapel Hill: University of North Carolina Press, 1999, p. 120.
3. *Ibid.,* p. 87.
4. Widmer, Ted, ed., *The New York Times, Disunion, 106 Articles from the New York Times Opinionator,* New York: Black Dog & Leventhal, 2013, p. 118.
5. *Ohio Daily Statesman* (Columbus, OH), January 24, 1862.
6. Van Horne, Thomas B., USA, *History of the Army of the Cumberland,* Vol. I, Cincinnati: Robert Clarke & Co., 1875, pp. 53-54.
7. *The Blue and the Gray,* Vol. X, February 1993, "The Campaign and Battle of Mill Springs," by Roger Tate, p. 15.
8. OR, Series I, Vol. VII, p. 500.
9. *Ibid.,* Series I, Vol. VII, p. 501.
10. *Ibid.,* Series I, Vol. VII, p. 483.
11. Van Horne, Thomas B., USA, p. 53.
12. *The Highland Weekly News* (Hillsborough, OH), January 30, 1862.
13. *Cincinnati Daily Press,* January 24, 1862.
14. OR, Series I, Vol. VII, p. 93.
15. *Ibid.,* Series I, Vol. II, p. 93.
16. *Ibid.,* Series I, Vol. II, p. 80.
17. Grebner, Constantin, *"We Were the Ninth": A History of the Ninth Regiment, Ohio Volunteer Infantry April 17, 1861 to June 7, 1864,* trans. and ed. Frederic Trautmann, Kent, OH: Kent State University Press, 1987, p. 84.
18. OR, Series I, Vol. II, p. 94.
19. Buell, Thomas B., *The Warrior Generals Combat Leadership in the Civil War,* New York: Three Rivers Press, 1997, p. 157.
20. OR, Series I, Vol. VII, p. 94.
21. The Library of Congress, Manuscript Reading Room, McCook Family Papers, *Frank Leslie's Illustrated Newspaper,* August 30, 1862.
22. *Evening Star* (Washington, D.C.), January 23, 1862.
23. *The Highland Weekly News* (Hillsborough, OH), January 30, 1862.
24. Eicher, David J., *The Longest Night: A Military History of the Civil War,* New York: Simon & Schuster, 2001, p. 163.

25. *Cincinnati Daily Press*, January 24, 1862.
26. OR, Series I, Vol. VII, p. 94
27. Reinhart, Joseph R., ed. and trans., *A German Hurrah! Civil War Letters of Friedrich Bertsch and Wilhelm Stangel, 9th Ohio Infantry*, Kent, OH: Kent State University Press, 2010, p. 213.
28. *Evening Star*, January 23, 1862.
29. *The Blue and Gray*, Vol. X, February 1993, "The Campaign and Battle of Mill Springs," by Roger Tate, p. 53.
30. *The Blue and Gray*, Vol. IX, June 1992, "Camp Talk," ed. Neil Meier, p. 47.
31. Eicher, David J., p. 162.
32. Williams, Kenneth P., *Lincoln Finds a General: A Military Study of the Civil War*, Vol. III, New York: Macmillan, 1952, p. 176.
33. OR, Series I, Vol. VII, p. 83.
34. *Evening Star*, January 23, 1862.
35. OR, Series I, Vol. VII, p. 86.
36. *Ibid.*, Series I, Vol. VII, p. 77.
37. Reinhart, Joseph R., pp. 229–230.
38. *Cincinnati Daily Times*, February 26, 1862.
39. Reinhart, Joseph R., ed. and trans., *August Willich's Gallant Dutchmen, Civil War Letters from The 32nd Indiana Infantry*, Kent, OH: Kent State University Press, 2006, p. 60.
40. OR, Series I, Vol. VII, p. 581.
41. *The Spirit of Democracy* (Woodsfield, OH), February 26, 1862.
42. *The Cadiz Democratic Sentinel* (Cadiz, OH), March 5, 1862.

Chapter 4

1. LOC, McCook Family Papers, article in the *National Tribune*, date unknown.
2. Johnson, Mark W., *That Body of Brave Men: U.S. Regular Infantry and the Civil War in the West*, Cambridge: Da Capo Press, 2003, pp. 129–130.
3. Lowry, Thomas P., *Curmudgeons, Drunkards & Outright Fools: Courts-Martial of Civil War Union Colonels*, Lincoln: University of Nebraska Press, 2003, pp. 131–133.
4. Grebner, Constantin, *"We Were The Ninth": A History of the Ninth Regiment, Ohio Volunteer Infantry April 17, 1861 to June 7, 1864*, trans. and ed. Frederic Trautmann, Kent, OH: Kent State University Press, 1987, p. 135.
5. Johnson, Mark W., p. 133.
6. *Ibid.*, pp. 134–135.
7. *Ibid.*, pp. 136–137.
8. *Ibid.*, pp. 138–140.
9. *Ibid.*, p. 132.
10. Grebner, Constantin, p. 100.
11. Cleaves, Freeman, *Rock of Chickamauga: The Life of General George H. Thomas*, Norman: University of Oklahoma Press, 1948, p. 105.
12. Johnson, Mark W., p. 128.
13. *Ibid.*, p. 142.
14. *Ibid.*, pp. 143–145.
15. *Ibid.*, pp. 148–149.
16. *Ibid.*, p. 150.
17. *Ibid.*, pp. 150–151.
18. *Ibid.*, p. 153.
19. *Ibid.*, pp. 153–155.
20. Ambrose, Stephen A., *Halleck: Lincoln's Chief of Staff*, Baton Rouge: Louisiana State Press, 1990, p. 49.
21. *The Daily Ohio Statesman* (Columbus, OH), May 4, 1862.
22. Grebner, Constantin, p. 102.
23. Johnson, Mark W., p. 157.
24. Reinhart, Joseph R., ed. and trans., *A German Hurrah! Civil War Letters of Friedrich Bertsch and Wilhelm Stangel, 9th Ohio Infantry*, Kent, OH: Kent State University Press, 2010, p. 257.
25. *The Daily Times* (Cincinnati), May 7, 1862.

26. Johnson, R. W., *A Soldier's Reminiscences in Peace and War*, Philadelphia: J. B. Lippincott, 1886, p. 189.
27. Johnson, Mark W., pp. 160–162.
28. *Ibid.*, p. 182.
29. *Ibid.*, pp. 143–146.
30. LOC, McCook Family Papers, article in the *National Tribune*, date unknown.
31. Johnson, Mark W., p. 187.
32. Grebner, Constantin, p. 103.
33. *New York Times*, March 22, 1862.

Chapter 5

1. Grebner, Constantin, *"We Were The Ninth": A History of the Ninth Regiment, Ohio Volunteer Infantry April 17, 1861 to June 7, 1864*, trans. and ed. Frederic Trautmann, Kent, OH: Kent State University Press, 1987, pp. 104–105.
2. Reinhart, Joseph R., ed. and trans., *A German Hurrah! Civil War Letters of Friedrich Bertsch and Wilhelm Stangel, 9th Ohio Infantry*, Kent, OH: Kent State University Press, 2010, pp. 269–270.
3. *New York Times*, August 2, 1862.
4. Grebner, Constantin, p. 105.
5. OR, Series I, Vol. XVI, Part II, pp. 186–187.
6. *Ibid.*, Series I, Vol. XVI, Part II, p. 244.
7. *Ibid.*, Series I. Vol. XVI, Part I, pp. 840–841.
8. *Ibid.*, Series II, Vol. VI, p. 1032.
9. *The Spirit of Democracy* (Woodfield, Ohio), August 27, 1862.
10. Broadwater, Robert P., "Intrigue: Rebel Captain Frank Gurley Faced a Charge of Killing an Invalid Yankee General," Vol. 22, Issue 5, *Military History*, August 2005, p. 20.
11. *The Spirit of Democracy* (Woodfield, Ohio), August 27, 1862.
12. *Urbana Union* (Ohio), August 20, 1862.
13. *Cincinnati Commercial* in the *New York Times*, August 17, 1862.
14. O'Brien, Sean Michael, *Mountain Partisans, Guerrilla Warfare in the Southern App. alachians 1861–1865*, Westport CT: Praeger, 1999, pp. 102–103.
15. OR, Series I, Vol. XVI, Part I, p. 841.
16. McDonough, James Lee, *The War in Kentucky, From Shiloh to Perryville*, Knoxville: University of Tennessee Press, 1994, p. 96.
17. *The National Tribune* (Washington, D.C.), February 16, 1911.
18. Steenburn, Col. Donald H., *The Man Called Gurley*, Meridianville, AL: Elk River Press, 1999, p. 124.
19. OR, Series I, Vol. XVI, Part I, pp. 840–841.
20. *New York Times*, August 3, 1862.
21. Grebner, Constantin, pp. 109–110.
22. Sutherland, Daniel E., *A Savage Conflict, the Decisive Role of Guerrillas in the American Civil War*, Chapel Hill: University of North Carolina Press, 2009, p. xi.
23. *Belmont Chronicle* (St. Clairsville, Ohio), August 14, 1862.
24. McDonough, James Lee, p. 97.
25. LOC, McCook Family Papers, *Frank Leslie's Illustrated Newspaper*, August 30, 1862.
26. Beatty, John, *The Citizen Soldier or Memoirs of a Volunteer*, Cincinnati: Wilstach, Baldwin and Company, 1879, p. 169.
27. *New York Times*, August 9, 1862.
28. LOC, McCook Family Papers, article in the *National Republican*, circa 1880s.
29. Johnson, Mark W., *That Body of Brave Men: The U.S. Regular Infantry and the Civil War In the West*, Cambridge: Da Capo Press, 2003, pp. 212–213.
30. OR, Series I, Vol. XVI, Part II, p. 281.
31. Grebner, Constantin, p. 110.
32. *New York Times*, August 9, 1862.
33. Whalen, Charles and Barbara, pp. 138–140.
34. *The Nashville Daily Union*, August 13, 1862.
35. LOC, McCook Family Papers, letter Anson G. McCook to Martha L. McCook, August 8, 1862.

36. Connecticut Landmarks, Hartford, letter Anson G. McCook to Mary Sheldon, August 7, 1862.
37. LOC, McCook Family Papers, letter George W. McCook to Martha L. McCook, November 2, 1862.
38. Reinhart, Joseph R., p. 289.
39. *The Nashville Daily Union*, August 13, 1862.
40. OR, Series I, Vol. XVI, Part I, p. 839.
41. *Ibid.*, Series I, Vol. XVI, Part II, p. 290.
42. McDonough, James Lee, p. 96.
43. *The Goodhue Volunteer* (Red Wing, MN), August 20, 1862.
44. Holmes, J. T., *52nd O.V.I., Then and Now*, Columbus: The Berlin Printing Company, 1898, p. 41.
45. *The National Tribune*, February 20, 1896.
46. OR, Series I, Vol. XXX, Part III, p. 194.
47. *Ibid.*, Series I, Vol. XVI, Part I, pp. 325–333.

Chapter 6

1. OR, Series II, Vol. V, p. 868.
2. *Belmont Chronicle* (St. Clairsville, Ohio), December 11, 1862.
3. Hess, Earl J., *Pickett's Charge—The Last Attack at Gettysburg*, Chapel Hill: University of North Carolina Press, 2001, p. 367.
4. O'Brien, Sean Michael, *Mountain Partisans, Guerrilla Warfare in the Southern Appalachians 1861-1865*, Westport, CT: Praeger, 1999, pp. 101–102.
5. *Military History*, Vol. 22, Issue 5, August 2005, "Intrigue: Rebel Captain Frank Gurley Faced a Charge of Killing an Invalid Yankee General," by Robert P. Broadwater, p. 18.
6. O'Brien, Sean Michael, p. 104; OR, Series I, Vol. XXX, Part III, pp. 186 and 194.
7. Holmes, J. T., *52nd O.V.I., Then and Now*, Columbus: The Berlin Printing Company, 1898, pp. 123–134.
8. *Civil War Times Illustrated*, Vol. 17, December 1978, "Waiting to be Hanged," by John W. Rowell, p. 14.
9. OR, Series I, Vol. XXXI, Part I, p. 707.
10. *Ibid.*, Series I, Vol. XXXI, Part I, p. 776.
11. *Ibid.*, Series II, Vol. VI, p. 465.
12. *Ibid.*, Series II, Vol. VI, p. 521.
13. *Ibid.*, Series II, Vol. VI, pp. 691–693.
14. *Ibid.*, Series II, Vol. VI, p. 773.
15. *Ibid.*, Series II, Vol. VI, p. 831.
16. *Ibid.*, Series II, Vol. VIII, p. 741.
17. *Ibid.*, Series II, Vol. VI, pp. 1029–1033.
18. O'Brien, Sean Michael, p. 108.
19. OR, Series II, Vol. VI, pp. 1029–1033.
20. *Ibid.*, Series II, Vol. VI, p. 1031.
21. Library of Congress, Manuscript Reading Room, McCook Family Papers, Article in the *National Republican*, circa 1880s.
22. Rowell John W., pp. 12–17.
23. OR, Series II, Vol. VIII, p. 550.
24. *Ibid.*, Series II, Vol. VIII, p. 572.
25. *New York Times*, August 20, 1865.
26. *Cincinnati Commercial*, in the *St. Paul Pioneer*, December 15, 1865.
27. OR, Series II, Vol. VIII, p. 742.
28. *Ibid.*, Series II, Vol. VIII, p. 818.
29. *The Papers of Andrew Johnson*, Vol. 9, September 1865–January 1866, Knoxville: University of Tennessee Press, 1991, pp. 434–435.
30. *The Papers of Andrew Johnson*, pp. 572–574.
31. OR, Series II, Vol. VIII, pp. 820–821.
32. *Nashville Union and American* in *The Daily Empire* (Dayton, Ohio), April 30, 1866.
33. *The Papers of Ulysses S. Grant*, John Y. Simon, ed., Carbondale: Southern Illinois University Press, 1991, pp. 153–154.

34. Steenburn, Col. Donald H., *The Man Called Gurley*, Meridianville, AL: Elk River Press, 1999, p. 235.
35. Gurleyalabama.contactez.net, home of the Gurley Web Site, "From our Past XXI, a Curious Letter to Captain Frank Gurley."
36. *The Stark County Democrat* (Canton, Ohio), February 5, 1880.
37. *The National Tribune* (Washington, D.C.), December 29, 1910.
38. *Ibid.*, February 16, 1911.
39. *Daily Intelligence* (Wheeling, VA), October 21, 1862.
40. Betts, Edward Chambers, *Early History of Huntsville, Alabama 1804 to 1870*, Montgomery: The Brown Printing Co., 1916, rev. ed., p. 103.
41. Broadwater, Robert P., p. 21.

Chapter 7

1. Smith, Ronald D., *Thomas Ewing Jr., Frontier Lawyer and Civil War General*, Columbia: University of Missouri Press, 2008, p. 84.
2. LOC, McCook Family Papers, letter George W. McCook to Martha McCook, November 2, 1857.
3. Lewis, Lloyd, *Sherman, Fighting Prophet*, New York: Harcourt Brace & Co., 1932, p. 105; Howe, Henry, *A Brief Historical Sketch of the "Fighting McCooks,"* reprinted from the Proceedings of the Scotch-Irish Society of America, p. 13.
4. Smith, Ronald D., p. 23.
5. *New York Times*, March 12, 1865.
6. Lewis, Lloyd, p. 105.
7. Hirshon, Stanley P., *The White Tecumseh: A Biography of William T. Sherman*, New York: John Wiley & Sons, 1997, p. 59.
8. Smith, Ronald D., P85.
9. *Leavenworth Conservative* in the *Cleveland Morning Leader*, March 23, 1865.
10. *Ibid.*
11. Lewis, Lloyd, p. 106.
12. *Leavenworth Conservative* in the *Cleveland Morning Leader*, March 23, 1865.
13. Lewis, Lloyd, p. 106.
14. Sherman, William Tecumseh, *Memoirs of General W. T. Sherman*, New York: The Library of America, 1990, 161.
15. Hirshon, Stanley P., p. 62.
16. Leckie, Robert, *None Died in Vain: The Saga of the American Civil War*, New York: Harper-Collins, 1990, pp. 275–276.
17. Smith, Ronald D., pp. 106, 122.
18. Whalen, Charles and Barbara, *The Fighting McCooks: America's Famous Fighting Family*, Bethesda, MD: Westmoreland Press, 2006, p. 260.
19. LOC, McCook Family Papers, Scrapbook, Series I, *Daily Advocate*, Stanford, CT, October 13, 1911.
20. *The Iola Register* (Iola, KS), October 23, 1896.
21. Smith, Ronald D., p. 132.
22. Howe, Henry, p. 13.
23. *Ibid.*, p. 14; *Dakota Farmer's Leader* (Canton, SD), April 5, 1912.
24. OR, Series III, Vol. I, P 63.
25. Howe, Henry, p. 14; *Dakota Farmer's Leader* (Canton, SD), April 5, 1912.
26. Connecticut Landmarks, Hartford, letter Daniel McCook, Jr., to George W. McCook, March 10, 1861.
27. Piston, William Garrett and Hatcher III, Richard W., *Wilson's Creek: The Second Battle of the Civil War and the Men Who Fought It*, Chapel Hill: University of North Carolina Press, 2000, pp. 60–61.
28. *Cincinnati Weekly Gazette*, December 20, 1860.
29. Stiles, T. J., *Jesse James, the Last Rebel of the Civil War*, New York: Vintage, 2003, p. 37.
30. *Ibid.*, pp. 64–65.
31. *Battles and Leaders of the Civil War*, Vol. I, Edison, NJ: Castle, 1883, p. 262.
32. *Ibid.*, p. 264.
33. *Ibid.*, pp. 264–265.

34. Perret, Geoffrey, *Lincoln's War: The Untold Story of America's Greatest President as Commander on Chief*, New York: Random House, 2004, p. 80.
35. Robinson, Doane, *History of South Dakota*, Vol. I, Chicago: The American Historical Society, Inc., 1930, p. 552.
36. Nicolay, John G., *The Outbreak of Rebellion*, New York: Da Capo Press, reprint of 1881 edition, 1995, p. 118.
37. Miers, Earl Schenck, *The General Who Marched to Hell: Sherman and the Southern Campaign*, New York: Alfred A. Knopf, 1951, p. 9.
38. Krug, Mark M., ed., *Mrs. Hill's Journal—Civil War Reminiscences*, Chicago: R. R. Donnelley & Sons Co., 1980, p. 13.
39. Long, E. B. and Long, Barbara, *The Civil War Day by Day: An Almanac, 1861-1865*, Garden City, NY: Doubleday, 1971, pp. 72-73.
40. *Harper's Weekly*, New York, Vol. V, No. 231, June 1, 1861, p. 349.
41. Piston, William Garrett and Hatcher III, Richard W., p. 120.
42. McPherson, James M., *Abraham Lincoln and the Second American Revolution*, New York: Oxford University Press, 1990, p. 27.
43. Williams, T Harry., *Lincoln and His Generals*, New York: Alfred A. Knopf, 1952, p. 31.
44. *New York Times*, March 22, 1862.
45. Piston, William Garrett and Hatcher III, Richard W., pp. 62-63, 65.
46. Perret, Geoffrey, p. 83.
47. *Ibid*.
48. Long, E. B. and Long, Barbara, p. 107.
49. OR, Series I, Vol. III, p. 82-83.
50. *New York Tribune*, August 19, 1861.
51. OR, Series I, Vol. III, pp. 84-85.
52. Foote, Shelby, *The Civil War: A Narrative, Fort Sumter to Perryville*, New York: Vintage, Vol. I, 1986, p. 94.
53. *The Civil War Book of Lists*, comp. Editors of Combined Books, Combined Books, 1993, p. 101.
54. OR, Series I, Vol. III, p. 93.
55. Flood, Charles Bracelen, *1864: Lincoln at the Gates of History*, New York: Simon & Schuster, 2009, p. 33.
56. McPherson, James M., *Tried by War, Abraham Lincoln as Commander in Chief*, New York: Penguin, 2009, pp. 56-57.
57. *New York Times*, March 12, 1865.

Chapter 8

1. Leckie, Robert, *None Died in Vain: The Saga of the American Civil War*, New York: HarperCollins, 1990, p. 280.
2. Widmer, Ted, ed., *The New York Times Disunion: 106 Articles from the New York Times Opinionator*, New York: Black Dog and Leventhal, 2013, p. 267.
3. *Sioux Falls Daily Press* (Sioux Falls, DT), February 20, 1885.
4. Cleaves, Freeman, *Rock of Chickamauga: The Life of General George H. Thomas*, Norman: University of Oklahoma Press, 1948, p. 103.
5. Leckie, Robert, p. 288.
6. Widmer, Ted, ed., p. 269.
7. *Sioux Falls Daily Press* (Sioux Falls, DT), February 20, 1885.
8. Widmer, Ted, ed., p. 269.
9. *New York Times*, April 10, 1862.
10. Davis, William C., *Diary of a Confederate Soldier: John S. Jackman of the Orphan Brigade*, Columbia: University of South Carolina Press, 1990, p. 32.
11. *Harper's New Monthly Magazine*, Vol. XXVIII, "The Second Division at Shiloh," by Daniel McCook, New York: Harper and Brothers, 1864, pp. 829-830.
12. *The National Tribune* (Washington, D.C.), March 18, 1886.
13. Grimsley, Mark, *The Hard Hand of War: Union Military Policy Toward Southern Civilians, 1861-1865*, Cambridge: Cambridge University Press, 1995, p. 93.
14. OR, Series I, Vol. X, Part I, p. 381.
15. *Ashtabula Weekly Telegraph* (Ashtabula, OH), July 19, 1862.

16. *Cleveland Morning Leader*, July 24, 1862.
17. Smith, Ronald D., *Thomas Ewing Jr., Frontier Lawyer and Civil War General*, Columbia: University of Missouri Press, 2008, p. 167.
18. *Cincinnati Daily Times*, August 23, 1862.
19. OR, Series I, Vol. LII, Part I, pp. 280–281.
20. Holmes, J. T., *Then and Now: 52nd O. V. I.*, Vol. I, Columbus: The Berlin Printing Co., 1898, pp. 112–113.
21. Smith, Ronald D., p. 167.
22. *The National Tribune*, July 16, 1896.
23. Widmer, Ted, ed., p. 350.
24. van der Linden, Frank, *The Dark Intrigue: The True Story of a Civil War Conspiracy*, Golden, CO: Fulcrum Publishing, 2007, p. 39.
25. McDonough, James Lee, *Shiloh: In Hell before Midnight*, Knoxville: University of Tennessee Press, 1977, p. 16.
26. McDonough, James Lee, *War in Kentucky: From Shiloh to Perryville*, Knoxville: The University of Tennessee Press, 1994, p. 4.
27. *The Ottawa Free Trader* (Ottawa, IL), September 3, 1887.
28. Cleaves, Freeman, p. 114.
29. *The National Tribune*, September 17, 1903.
30. Sheridan, P. H., *Personal Memoirs of P. H. Sheridan*, Vol. I, New York: Charles Webster Co., 1888, p. 194.
31. OR, Series I, Vol. XVI, Part I, p. 1083.
32. Noe, Kenneth W., *Perryville: This Grand Havoc of Battle*, Lexington: University Press of Kentucky, 2001, p. 149.
33. OR, Series I, Vol. XVI, Part I, p. 240.
34. Ibid., Series I, Vol. XVI, Part I, pp. 240–241.
35. *Battles and Leaders of the Civil War*, Vol. III, New York: Castle Books, p. 59.
36. *The National Tribune*, May 17, 1906.
37. Warner, Ezra J., *Generals in Blue: Lives of the Union Commanders*, Baton Rouge: Louisiana State University Press, 1996, pp. 173–174.
38. *The National Tribune*, April 23, 1885.
39. Wheeler, Richard, *Voices of the Civil War*, New York: Thomas Y. Crowell Co., 1976, p. 229.
40. Stevens, Joseph E., *1863: The Rebirth of a Nation*, New York: Bantam Books, 2000, pp. 62–63.
41. *The Daily Green Mountain Freeman* (Montpelier, VT), January 6, 1863.
42. OR, Series I, Vol. XX, Part I, p. 445.
43. Lamers, William M., *The Edge of Glory, a Biography of General William S. Rosecrans, USA*, Baton Route: Louisiana State University Press, 1999, p. 241.
44. van der Linden, Frank, p. 14.
45. *Pittsburg Post*, in the *Spirit of Democracy* (Woodsfield, OH), January 14, 1863.
46. Stevens, Joseph E., p. 11.
47. *Cincinnati Enquirer* in the *Daily Nashville Patriot*, November 20, 1861.

Chapter 9

1. Ramage, James A., *Rebel Raider: The Life of General John Hunt Morgan*, Lexington: University Press of Kentucky, 1986, p. 55.
2. *New York Times*, March 24, 1862.
3. Winick, Jay, *April 1865: The Month That Saved America*, New York: Harper Perennial, 2001, p. 157.
4. *The Ottawa Free Trader* (Ottawa, IL), September 3, 1887.
5. OR, Series I, Vol. XX, Part I, p. 51.
6. McDonough, James Lee, *Stones River: Bloody Winter in Tennessee*, Knoxville: University of Tennessee Press, 1980, pp. 46–47.
7. Stevens, Joseph E., *1863: The Rebirth of a Nation*, New York: Bantam Books, 2000, p. 151.
8. Foote, Shelby, *The Civil War: A Narrative, Fredericksburg to Meridian*, Vol. II, New York: Vintage, 1986, p. 671.
9. Sutherland, Daniel E., *A Savage Conflict, the Decisive Role of Guerillas in the American Civil War*, Chapel Hill: University of North Carolina Press, 2009, p. 169.
10. *The Adair County News* (Columbia, Kentucky), August 12, 1903.

11. Jones, Wilmer L., *Behind Enemy Lines, Civil War Spies, Raiders and Guerrillas,* Dallas: Taylor Publishing Co., 2001, p. 198.
12. *Cincinnati Weekly Gazette,* July 15, 1863.
13. *Ibid.,* July 22, 1863.
14. Fitch, John, *Annals of the Army of the Cumberland,* Mechanicsburg, PA: Stackpole Books, 2003, reprint of 1864 edition, p. 660.
15. Scott, Robert Garth, ed., *Forgotten Valor: The Memoirs, Journals & Civil War Letters of Orlando B. Wilcox,* Kent, OH: Kent State University Press, 1999, p. 433.
16. *Cincinnati Weekly Gazette,* July 15, 1863.
17. Scott, Robert Garth, p. 432.
18. *Cincinnati Weekly Gazette,* September 9, 1863.
19. *The Salt Lake Herald,* July 19, 1903.
20. Steven, Joseph E., p. 300.
21. Foote, Shelby, Vol. II, p. 680.
22. Stevens, Joseph E., p. 299.
23. *Cincinnati Weekly Gazette,* July 22, 1863.
24. *The Portage County Democra* (Ravenna, OH), July 29, 1863.
25. *Cincinnati Weekly Gazette,* July 29, 1863.
26. *Bulletin,* Vol. 22, 1964, "Crime and No Punishment, the Death of Robert L. McCook," by James Barnett, p. 33.
27. Smith, Ronald D., *Thomas Ewing Jr., Frontier Lawyer and Civil War General,* Columbia: University of Missouri Press, 2008, p. 134.
28. *Cleveland Morning Leader,* October 24, 1861.
29. *Daily Ohio Statesman* (Columbus, OH), October 24, 1861.
30. Long, E. B. and Long Barbara, *The Civil War Day by Day: An Almanac 1861-1865,* Garden City, NY: Doubleday, 1971, p. 129.
31. *Cincinnati Enquirer* in the *Daily Ohio Statesman,* March 17, 1863.
32. *Daily Ohio Statesman* (Columbus, OH), October 7, 1863
33. Weber, Jennifer L., *Copperheads: The Rise and Fall of Lincoln's Opponents in the North,* Oxford: Oxford University Press, 2006, pp. 95-96.
34. *The Herald-Star* (Steubenville, OH), April 2, 1938, quoting from the *Steubenville Herald,* July 25, 1863.
35. OR, Series I, Vol. XXIII, Part I, p. 634.
36. *Cincinnati Weekly Gazette,* July 29, 1863.
37. OR, Series I, Vol. XXIII, Part I, pp. 656-657.
38. *Cincinnati Weekly Gazette,* July 29, 1863.
39. OR, Series I, Vol. XXIII, Part I, p. 636; Long, E. B. and Long, Barbara, *The Civil War, Day by Day: An Almanac, 1861-1865,* Garden City, NY: Doubleday, 1971, p. 391.
40. OR, Series I, Vol. XXIII, Part I, p. 657.
41. *Cincinnati Weekly Gazette,* July 29, 1863.
42. Whalen, Charles and Barbara, *The Fighting McCooks: America's Famous Fighting Family,* Bethesda, MD: Westmoreland Press, 2006, p. 213.
43. *Cleveland Morning Leader,* July 27, 1863.
44. *The Lancaster Gazette* (Lancaster, OH), August 6, 1863.
45. *Cincinnati Weekly Gazette,* December 2, 1863.
46. *The Polk County Press* (Wisconsin), September 10, 1864.
47. Foote, Shelby, *The Civil War: A Narrative, Red River to Appomattox,* Vol. III, New York: Vintage, 1986, p. 596.
48. www.equilt.com/morgan.html, "John Hunt Morgan," by David Skinner, 2000.
49. *Wichita Eagle,* July 29, 1888.
50. Warner, Ezra J., *Generals in Gray: Lives of the Confederate Commanders,* Baton Rouge: Louisiana State University Press, 1959, p. 221.
51. www.vic.com/tnchron/class/JHMorgan.htm, Tennessee History Classroom, Full History Series, "The Murder of John Hunt Morgan."

Chapter 10

1. OR, Series I, Vol. XXIII, Part II, pp. 18-19.
2. *The Nashville Daily Union,* May 21, 1863.

3. Moore, David G., *William S. Rosecrans and the Union Victory: A Civil War Biography*, Jefferson, NC: McFarland, 2014, p. 81.
4. *The Times Dispatch* (Richmond, VA), July 15, 1912. It took Troxell many years of hard work to clear his military record of the stain caused by the stubborn mules and by his equally hard-headed commanding officer.
5. Conner, Robert C., *General Gordon Granger: The Savior of Chickamauga and the Man Behind "Juneteenth,"* Philadelphia: Casemate, 2013, p. 85.
6. Conner, Robert C., p. 86.
7. OR, Series I, Vol. XXX, Part I, p. 877.
8. Cozzens, Peter, *This Terrible Sound: The Battle of Chickamauga*, Urbana: University of Illinois Press, 1992, p. 121.
9. OR, Series I, Vol. XXX, Part III, p. 727.
10. *Ibid.*,, Series I, Vol. XXX Part I, p. 115.
11. Cozzens, Peter, pp. 121–122.
12. Johnson, Mark W., *That Body of Brave Men: The U.S. Regular Infantry and the Civil War in the West*, Cambridge: De Capo Press, 2003, p. 386.
13. Cozzens, Peter, p. 122.
14. Stevens, Joseph E., *1863: The Rebirth of a Nation*, New York: Bantam Books, 2000, pp. 330–331.
15. Cleaves, Freeman, *Rock of Chickamauga, The Life of General George H. Thomas*, Norman: University of Oklahoma Press, 1948, p. 159.
16. Cozzens, Peter, p. 441.
17. OR, Series I, Vol. LII, p. 453.
18. Commager, Henry Steele, ed., *The Civil War Archive: A History of the Civil War in Documents*, New York: Black Dog & Leventhal, 2000, p. 645.
19. *Ibid.*, p. 643.
20. *The Benton Weekly Record* (Benton, MT), October 13, 1881.
21. Grant, Ulysses S., *Memoirs and Selected Letters*, New York: The Library of America, 4th Printing, 1990, p. 417.
22. Dunkelman, Mark H., *Patrick Henry Jones, Irish American, Civil War General and Gilded Age Politician*, Baton Rouge: Louisiana State University, 2015, p. 51.
23. Grant, Ulysses S., pp. 417–418.
24. *The National Tribune* (Washington, D.C.), September 25, 1902.
25. OR, Series I, Vol. XXXI, Part II, p. 106.
26. Sword, Wiley, *Mountains Touched with Fire*, New York: St. Martin's Press, 1995, p. 193.
27. OR, Series I, Vol. XXXI, Part II, p. 503.
28. Towne, Stephen E., ed., *A Fierce, Wild Joy: The Civil War Letters of Colonel Edward J. Wood, 48th Indiana Volunteer Infantry Regiment*, Knoxville: University of Tennessee Press, 2007, p. 140.
29. OR, Series I, Vol. XXXI, Part II, pp. 73–75.
30. *Cincinnati Weekly Gazette*, September 16, 1863.
31. Beatty, John, *The Citizen Volunteer*, Cincinnati: Willstach, Baldwin & Co., Publishers, 1879, p. 361.
32. OR, Series I, Vol. XXXI, Part III, p. 145.
33. *Ibid.*, Series I, Vol. XXXI, Part II, p. 504.
34. *Ibid.*, Series I, Vol. XXXI, Part II, p. 505.
35. McCook, Anson, *Memoir*, Unpublished, Columbus: Ohio State Historical Society, p. 156.
36. McPherson, James M., *This Mighty Scourge: Perspectives on the Civil War*, Oxford: Oxford University Press, 2009, p. 132.
37. *Cincinnati Weekly Gazette*, December 2, 1863.
38. Hirschon, Stanley P., *The White Tecumseh: A Biography of William T. Sherman*, New York: John Wiley & Sons, 1997, pp. 175–176.
39. Beatty, John, pp. 360–361.
40. National Archives, Military Record of Daniel McCook, Jr.

Chapter 11

1. *Dubuque Daily Times*, March 9, 1864.
2. OR, Series I, Vol. XXXII, Part I, pp. 460–461.
3. Ambrose, Stephen E., *Halleck: Lincoln's Chief of Staff*, Baton Rouge: Louisiana State University

Press, 1996, p. 160; Conger, Colonel Arthur L., *The Rise of Grant*, New York: Da Capo Press, 1996, reprint of 1931 edition, p. 312.
 4. OR, Series I, Vol. XXXII, Part II, pp. 275–276.
 5. *Ibid.*, Series I, Vol. XXX, Part I, p. 80.
 6. *The Plymouth Tribune* (Plymouth, IN), July 5, 1906.
 7. *The Polk County Press* (Wisconsin), May 8, 1864.
 8. Henig, Gerald S., and Niderost. Eric, *Civil War Firsts, The Legacies of America's Bloodiest Conflict*, Mechanicsburg, PA: Stackpole Books, 2001, p. 207.
 9. *Ibid.*, p. 207.
 10. Garrison, Webb, *Amazing Women of the Civil War: Fascinating True Stories of Women Who Made a Difference*, Nashville: Rutledge Hill Press, 1999, pp. 53–54.
 11. Davis, Stephen, *Atlanta Will Fall: Sherman, Joe Johnston and the Yankee Heavy Battalions*, S R Books, 2001, p. 19.
 12. *New York Tribune*, January 4, 1864.
 13. *New York Times*, July 1, 1864.
 14. Hess, Earl J., *Kennesaw Mountain: Sherman, Johnston, and the Atlanta Campaign*, Chapel Hill: University of North Carolina Press, 2013, p. 3.
 15. Hirshson, Stanley P., *The White Tecumseh: A Biography of William T. Sherman*, New York: John Wiley & Sons, 1997, p. 216.
 16. *The National Tribune* (Washington, D.C.), August 14, 1902.
 17. *New York Times*, June 26, 1864.
 18. *Ibid.*
 19. Hirshson, Stanley P., p. 218.
 20. Hart, B. H. Liddell, *Sherman: Soldier, Realist, American*, New York: Da Capo Press, 1993, reprint of 1929 edition, p. 264.
 21. Marszelek, John F., *Sherman: A Soldier's Passion for Order*, New York: The Free Press, 1993, p. 271.
 22. *The National Tribune*, August 14, 1902.
 23. Hess, Earl J., p. 51.
 24. *New York Times*, June 26, 1864.
 25. Marszelek, John F., p. 271.
 26. Davis, Stephen, p. 81.
 27. Hess, Earl J., p. 14.
 28. Hirshson, Stanley P., 223.
 29. Hess, Earl J., p. 50.
 30. Marszelek, John F., p. 272.
 31. *The National Tribune*, August 14, 1902.
 32. *New York Times*, July 8, 1864.
 33. Cleaves, Freeman, *Rock of Chickamauga: The Life of General George H. Thomas*, Norman: University of Oklahoma Press, 1948, p. 221.
 34. Sherman, William T., *Memoirs of General W. T. Sherman*, New York: The Library of America, 1990, pp. 530–531.
 35. Van Der Linden, Frank, *The Dark Intrigue, The True Story of a Civil Conspiracy*, Golden, CO: Fulcrum Publishing, 2007, p. 253.
 36. *New York Times*, June 15, 1864.
 37. Web Site, The Civil War and Northwest Wisconsin, letter Edwin D. Levings to his parents, June 26, 1864 (original letter in the archives of the University of Wisconsin, River Falls).

Chapter 12

 1. *The National Tribune* (Washington, D.C.), August 14, 1902.
 2. *Ibid.*
 3. Hess, Earl J., *Kennesaw Mountain: Sherman, Johnston and the Atlanta Campaign*, Chapel Hill: University of North Carolina Press, 2013, p. 67.
 4. *New York Times*, July 8, 1864.
 5. Hess, Earl J., p. 114.
 6. Royster, Charles, *The Destructive War*, New York: Alfred A. Knopf, 1991, p. 305.
 7. Hughes, Nathaniel Cheairs Jr., and Whitney, Gordon D., *Jefferson Davis in Blue, The Life of Sherman's Relentless Warrior*, Baton Rogue: Louisiana State University Press, 2002, p. 256.

8. Hicken, Victor, *Illinois in the Civil War*, 2d ed., Urbana, University of Illinois Press, 1991, p. 101.
9. Royster, Charles, pp. 306–307.
10. Holmes, J. T., *Then and Now*, Vol. I., Columbus: The Berlin Printing Company, 1898, p. 177.
11. Hess, Earl J., p. 117.
12. Royster, Charles, p. 310.
13. French, Samuel G., *Two Wars: An Autobiography of General. Samuel G. French*, Nashville: Confederate Veteran, 1901, reprint 1999 by Blue Acorn Press, p. 208.
14. *The National Tribune*, January 17, 1895, article by Major General O. O. Howard.
15. *Ibid.*
16. Royster, Charles, p. 309.
17. Stewart, Nixon B., *Dan McCook's Regiment: 52nd Ohio Volunteer Infantry 1862-1865*, published by the author, 1900, p. 118.
18. Baumgartner, Richard A., and Strayer, Larry M., *Kennesaw Mountain, June 1864: Bitter Standoff at the Gibraltar of Georgia*, Huntington: Blue Acorn Press, 2000, p. 151.
19. *Cincinnati Daily Times*, June 29, 2864.
20. *Cincinnati Gazette* in the *Belmont Chronicle* (St. Clairsville, OH), July 7, 1864.
21. *Sioux Falls Argus-Leader*, July 17, 1910, article by Col. Cyrus A. B. Fox.
22. Hess, Earl J., *The Union Soldier in Battle: Enduring the Ordeal of Combat*, Lawrence: University of Kansas Press, 1997, p. 70.
23. Baumgartner, Richard A., and Strayer, Larry M., p. 154.
24. *Ibid.*, pp. 155–156.
25. *Ibid.*, pp. 163–164.
26. Hess, Earl J., *Kennesaw Mountain: Sherman, Johnston and the Atlanta Campaign*, Chapel Hill: University of North Carolina Press, 2013, p. 124.
27. *Daily Ohio Statesman* (Columbus, OH), July 21, 1864.
28. Baumgartner, Richard A., and Strayer, Larry M., pp. 163–164.
29. Hess, Earl J., p. 126.
30. Connecticut Landmarks, Hartford, Field Manual of Anson G. McCook.
31. Perry, James, M., *Touched with Fire: Five Presidents and the Civil War Battles That Made Them*, New York: BBS, Public Affairs, 2003, p. 247.
32. *Cincinnati Daily Times*, July 8, 1864; Baumgartner Richard A., and Strayer, Larry M., p. 104.
33. Faust, Drew Gilpin, *This Republic of Suffering: Death and the American Civil War*, New York: Alfred A. Knopf, 2008, p. 196.
34. Lande, R. Gregory, *Madness, Malingering & Malfeasance, The Transformation of Psychiatry and Law in the Civil War*, Washington, D.C.: Potomac Books, Inc., 2003, p. 187.
35. Flood, Charles Bracelen, *1864: Lincoln at the Gates of History*, New York: Simon & Schuster, 2009, p. 171.
36. Sutherland, Daniel E., ed., *Reminiscences of a Private: William E. Bevens of the First Arkansas Infantry, C.S.A.*, Fayetteville: University of Arkansas Press, 1992, p. 175.
37. Royster, Charles, pp. 313–316.
38. *Sioux Falls Argus-Leader*, July 17, 1910, an article by Col. Cyrus A. B. Fox.
39. Whalen, Charles and Barbara, *The Fighting McCooks: America's Famous Fighting Family*, Bethesda, MD: Westmoreland Press, 2006, pp. 278–279.
40. *New York Times*, June 29, 1864.
41. OR, Series I, Vol. XXXVIII, Part IV, p. 611.
42. OR, Series I, Vol. XXXVIII, Part IV, p. 611.
43. *Ibid.*, Series I, Vol. XXXVIII, Part IV, p. 607.
44. *Ibid.*, Series I, Vol. XXXVIII, Part I, pp. 632–633.
45. *New York Times*, July 8, 1864.
46. Stewart, Nixon B., p. 122.
47. OR, Series I, Vol. XXXVIII, Part I, p. 69.
48. Marszalek, John F., *Sherman: A Soldier's Passion for Order*, New York: The Free Press, 1993, p. 273.
49. Sherman, William T., *Memoirs of General W. T. Sherman*, New York: The Library of America, 1990, p. 531.
50. Web Site, The Civil War and Northwest Wisconsin, letter of July 9, 1864, in *The Prescott Journal*, July 30, 1864.

51. Fordyce, Samuel W. IV, ed., *An American General: The Memoirs of David Sloan Stanley*, Santa Barbara: The Narrative Press, 2003, pp. 180–181.
52. *Ibid.*, p. 181.
53. *New York Times*, July 13, 1864.
54. *The National Tribune*, June 18, 1885.
55. Hirshson, Stanley P., *The White Tecumseh: A Biography of William T. Sherman*, New York: John Wiley & Sons, 1997, p. 224.
56. *Cincinnati Daily Times*, July 8, 1864.
57. Stewart, Nixon B., p. 123.
58. Connecticut Landmarks, Hartford, Field Manual of Anson G. McCook.
59. Whalen, Charles and Barbara, p. 286.
60. *The Benton Weekly Record* (Benton, MT), October 13, 1881.
61. Hirshson, Stanley P., p. 224.
62. Lewis, Lloyd, *Sherman: Fighting Prophet*, New York: Harcourt, Brace, p. 624.
63. Howe, Henry, *A Brief Historical Sketch of the "Fighting McCooks,"* reprinted from the Proceedings Of the Scotch-Irish Society of America, p. 16.
64. Stewart, Nixon B., p. 123.

Tribute

1. Basler, Roy P., ed., *The Collected Works of Abraham Lincoln*, Vol. VIII, 1864–1865, New Brunswick: Rutgers University Press, 1955, p. 300.
2. LOC, McCook Family Papers, *Ohio Patriot*, September 26, 1873.
3. Dunkelman, Mark H., *Brothers One and All: Esprit de Corps in a Civil War Regiment*, Baton Rouge: Louisiana State University Press, 2004, p. 251.
4. LOC, McCook Family Papers, *Steubenville Herald*, August 24, 1877.
5. *Ohio Patriot*, January 3, 1878.
6. *The Highland Weekly News* (Highland County, OH), June 15, 1871.
7. LOC, McCook Family Papers, "The Re-union, 52nd Ohio Regiment, Held at Barnesville, Ohio, September 19 and 20, 1877."
8. *The National Tribune* (Washington, D.C.), August 6, 1903.
9. *Papers of Andrew Johnson*, Vol. 15, September 1868–April 1869, Knoxville: University of Tennessee Press, 1999, p. 413.
10. *The Lancaster Gazette* (Lancaster, OH), April 19, 1866.
11. *Alexandria Gazette*, February 2, 1895.
12. *New York Sun* in *The Gainesville Star* (Gainesville, FL), November 24, 1903.
13. *The Herald* (Los Angeles), August 19, 1884.
14. *The Commoner* (Lincoln, NE), September 29, 1911.
15. *The Owosso Times* (Owosso, MI), March 5, 1897.
16. LOC, McCook Family Papers, *Daily Advocate*, Stanford, Connecticut, October 13, 1911.
17. *Cincinnati Enquirer* in *The Daily Ohio Statesman* (Columbus, Ohio), August 13, 1862.
18. *The Holt County Sentinel* (Oregon MO), July 3, 1903.
19. *Omaha Daily Bee*, September 19, 1909.
20. *New York Sun*, October 24, 1919.
21. *Evening Star* (Washington, D.C.), June 10, 1904.
22. *The Mahoning Dispatch* (Canfield, OH), April 20, 1917.

Bibliography

Books

Ambrose, Stephen E., *Halleck: Lincoln's Chief of Staff*, Baton Rouge, Louisiana State University Press, 1990.
Anderson, Frank Maloy, *The Mystery of a Public Man: A Historical Detective Story*, Minneapolis: University of Minnesota Press, 1948.
Battles and Leaders of the Civil War, Vol. III, New York: Castle Books.
Basler, Roy P., ed., *The Collected Works of Abraham Lincoln*, Vol. VIII, 1860–1861, New Brunswick: Rutgers University Press, 1955.
Beatty, John, *The Citizen Soldier or Memoirs of a Volunteer*, Cincinnati: Wilstach Baldwin, 1879.
Betts, Edward Chambers, *Early History of Huntsville, Alabama 1804 to 1870*, rev. ed., Montgomery: The Brown Printing Co., 1916.
Buell, Thomas B., *The Warrior Generals: Combat Leadership in the Civil War*, New York: Three Rivers Press, 1997.
Burton, William L., *Melting Pot Soldiers: The Union's Ethnic Regiments*, New York: Fordham University Press, New York, 1998.
Cleaves, Freeman, *Rock of Chickamauga: The Life of General George H. Thomas*, Norman: University of Oklahoma Press, 1948.
Commager, Henry Steele, ed., *The Civil War Archive: A History of the Civil War in Documents*, New York: Black Dog & Leventhal, 2000.
Conger, Arthur L., *The Rise of U. S. Grant*, 1931, New York: Da Capo Press, 1996.
Conner, Robert C., *General Gordon Granger: The Savior of Chickamauga and the Man Behind "Juneteenth,"* Philadelphia: Casemate, 2013.
Cozzens, Peter, *This Terrible Sound: The Battle of Chickamauga*, Urbana: University of Illinois Press, 1992.
Craugwell, Thomas J., *The Greatest Brigade: How the Irish Brigade Cleared the Way to Victory in the American Civil War*, Beverly, MA: Fair Winds Press, 2011.
Davis, Stephen, *Atlanta Will Fall: Sherman, Joe Johnston and the Yankee Heavy Battalions*, S R Books, 2001.
Davis, William C., *Diary of a Confederate Soldier: John S. Jackman of the Orphan Brigade*, Columbia: University of South Carolina Press, 1990.
Dolan, Jay P., *The Irish Americans: A History*, New York: Bloomsbury Press, 2008.
Dunkelman, Mark H., *Brothers One and All: Esprit de Corps in a Civil War Regiment*, Baton Rouge: Louisiana State University Press, 2004.
_____, *Patrick Henry Jones: Irish American, Civil War General, and Gilded Age Politician*, Baton Rouge: Louisiana State University, 2015.
Eicher, David J., *The Longest Night: A Military History of the Civil War*, New York: Simon & Schuster, 2001.
Engle, Stephen D., *Don Carlos Buell: Most Promising of All*, Chapel Hill: University of North Carolina Press, 1999.
Fanebust, Wayne, *Major General Alexander M. McCook, USA: A Civil War Biography*, Jefferson: McFarland, 2013.

Faust, Drew Gilpin., *This Republic of Suffering: Death and the American Civil War*, New York: Alfred A. Knopf, 2008.
Fitch, John. *Annals of the Army of the Cumberland*, 1864, Mechanicsburg, PA: Stackpole Books, 2003, reprint of 1864 edition.
Flood, Charles Bracelen, *1864: Lincoln at the Gates of History*, New York: Simon & Schuster, 2009.
Foote, Shelby, *The Civil War: A Narrative, Fort Sumter to Perryville*, Vol. I, II, & III, New York: Vintage, 1986.
Fordyce, Samuel W., IV ed., *An American General: The Memoirs of David Sloan Stanley*, Santa Barbara, CA: The Narrative Press, 2003.
Garrison, Webb, *Amazing Women of the Civil War: Fascinating True Stories of Women Who Made a Difference*, Nashville: Rutledge Hill Press, 1999.
Goldfield, David, *America Aflame: How the Civil War Created a Nation*, New York: Bloomsbury Press, 2011.
Grant, Ulysses S., *Memoirs and Selected Letters*, New York: The Library of America, 4th Printing, 1990.
Grebner, Constantin, *"We Were the Ninth": A History of the Ninth Regiment, Ohio Volunteer Infantry, April 17, 1861 to June 7, 1864*, translated and edited by Frederic Trautmann, Kent, OH: Kent State University Press, 1987.
Grimsley, Mark, *The Hard Hand of War: Union Military Policy Toward Southern Civilians, 1861–1865*, Cambridge: Cambridge University Press, 1995.
Hart, B. H. Liddell, *Sherman: Soldier, Realist, American*, 1929, New York: Da Capo Press, 1993.
Henig, Gerald S., and Niderost Eric, *Civil War Firsts: The Legacies of America's Bloodiest Conflict*, Mechanicsburg, PA: Stackpole Books, 2001.
Hess, Earl J., *Kennesaw Mountain: Sherman, Johnston, and the Atlanta Campaign*, Chapel Hill: University of North Carolina Press, 2013.
_____, *Pickett's Charge: The Last Attack at Gettysburg*, Chapel Hill: University of North Carolina Press, 2001.
_____, *The Union Soldier in Battle: Enduring the Ordeal of Combat*, Lawrence: University Press of Kansas, 1997.
Hirshson, Stanley P., *The White Tecumseh: A Biography of General William T. Sherman*, New York: John Wiley & Sons, 1997.
Holmes, J. T., *52nd O.V.I., Then and Now*, Columbus, OH: The Berlin Printing Company, OH, 1898.
Howe, Henry, *A Brief Historical Sketch of the Fighting McCooks*, Proceedings of the Scotch-Irish Society of America.
Hughes, Nathaniel Cheairs, Jr., and Whitney, Gordon E., *Jefferson Davis in Blue: The Life of Sherman's Relentless Warrior*, Baton Rouge: Louisiana State University Press, 2002.
Johannsen, Robert W., *Stephen A. Douglas*, New York: Oxford University Press, 1973.
Johnson, Mark W., *That Body of Brave Men: The U. S. Regular Infantry and the Civil War in the West*, Cambridge: Da Capo Press, 2003.
Johnson, R. W., *A Soldier's Reminiscences in Peace and War*, Philadelphia: J. B. Lippincott, 1886.
Jones, Wilmer L., *Behind Enemy Lines: Civil War Spies, Raiders and Guerrillas*, Dallas: Taylor, 2001.
Kline, Michael J., *The Baltimore Plot: The First Conspiracy to Assassinate Abraham Lincoln*, Yardley, PA: Westholme, 2008.
Krug, Mark M., ed., *Mrs. Hill's Journal: Civil War Reminiscences*, Chicago: R. R. Donnelley & Sons Co., 1980.
Lamers, William M., *The Edge of Glory: A Biography of General William S. Rosecrans, USA*, Baton Rouge: Louisiana State University Press, 1999.
Lande, R. Gregory, *Madness, Malingering and Malfeasance: The Transformation of Psychiatry and the Law in the Civil War Era*, Washington, D.C.: Potomac Books, 2003.
Leckie, Robert, *None Died in Vain, The Saga of the American Civil War*, HarperCollins, Publishers, 1990.
Lewis, Lloyd, *Sherman: Fighting Prophet*. New York: Harcourt Brace, 1932.
_____, *The Assassination of Lincoln: History & Myth*.1929. New York: MJF Books, 1994.
Long, E. B. and Barbara, *The Civil War Day by Day, an Almanac, 1861–1865*, Garden City, NY: Doubleday and Co., Inc., 1971.
Lowry, Thomas P., *Curmudgeons, Drunkards & Outright Fools, Courts-Martial of Civil War Union Colonels*, University of Nebraska Press, 2003.
McCarthy, Karen F., *The Other Irish, The Scots-Irish Rascals that Made America*, New York: Sterling, 2011.
McDonough, James Lee, *Shiloh—in Hell before Midnight*, Knoxville: The University of Tennessee Press, 1977.

_____, *Stones River—Bloody Winter in Tennessee,* Knoxville: The University of Tennessee Press, 1980.
_____, *The War in Kentucky, From Shiloh to Perryville,* Knoxville: The University of Tennessee Press, 1994.
McPherson, James M., *Abraham Lincoln and the Second American Revolution.* New York: Oxford University Press, 1990.
_____, *Ordeal by Fire, The Civil War and Reconstruction,* McGraw-Hill Higher Education, 2001.
_____, *This Mighty Scourge, Perspectives on the Civil War,* Oxford University Press, 2009.
_____, *Tried by War: Abraham Lincoln as Commander in Chief.* New York: Penguin Books, 2009.
Marszelek, John F., *Sherman, A Soldier's Passion for Order,* New York: The Free Press, a Division of Macmillan, Inc., 1993.
Miers, Earl Schenck, *The General Who Marched to Hell: Sherman and the Southern Campaign.* New York: Alfred A. Knopf, 1951.
Moore, David G., *William S. Rosecrans and the Union Victory, A Civil War Biography,* Jefferson, NC: McFarland, 2014,
Moore, George Ellis, *A Banner in the Hills, West Virginia's Statehood,* New York: Appleton-Century-Crofts, A Division of Meredith Publishing Co., 1963.
Muelhberger, James P., *The 116, The True Story of Abraham Lincoln's Lost Guard,* Ankerwycke, 2015.
Neff, William B., *Bench and Bar of Northern Ohio,* Cleveland: The Historical Publishing Co., 1921.
Nicolay, John G., *Outbreak of the Rebellion,* 1881, New York: Da Capo Press, 1995.
Noe, Kenneth W., *Perryville: This Grand Havoc of Battle,* Lexington: University Press of Kentucky, 2001.
O'Brien, Sean Michael, *Mountain Partisans: Guerrilla Warfare in the Southern Appalachians 1861–1865,* Westport CT: Praeger, 1999.
Perret, Geoffrey, *Lincoln's War: The Untold Story of America's Greatest President as Commander in Chief,* New York: Random House, 2004.
Piston, William Garrett, and Hatcher, Richard W., III, *Wilson's Creek: The Second Battle of the Civil War and the Men Who Fought It,* Chapel Hill: University of North Carolina Press, 2000.
Ramage, James A., *Rebel Raider: The Life of General John Hunt Morgan,* Lexington: University Press of Kentucky, 1986.
Reid, Whitelaw, *Ohio in the War: Her Statesmen, Her Generals and Soldiers,* Vol. I, Cincinnati: Moore, Wilstach & Baldwin, 1868.
Reinhart, Joseph R., ed. and trans., *A German Hurrah! Civil War Letters of Friedrich Bertsch and Wilhelm Stangel, 9th Ohio Infantry,* Kent OH: Kent State University Press, 2010.
_____, ed. and trans., *August Willich's Gallant Dutchmen: Civil War Letters from the 32nd Indiana Infantry,* Kent, OH, Kent State University Press, 2006.
Robinson, Doane, *History of South Dakota,* Vol. I, Chicago: The American Historical Society, Inc., 1930.
Royster, Charles, *The Destructive War: William Tecumseh Sherman, Stonewall Jackson, and the Americans,* New York: Vintage, 1993.
Scott, Robert Garth, ed., *Forgotten Valor: The Memoirs, Journals & Civil War Letters of Orlando B. Wilcox,* Kent, OH: Kent State University Press, 1999.
Sheridan, P. H., *Personal Memoirs of P. H. Sheridan,* Vol. I, New York: Charles Webster, 1888.
Sherman, William T., *Memoirs of General W. T. Sherman,* New York: Library of America, 1990.
Smith, Ronald D., *Thomas Ewing Jr., Frontier Lawyer and Civil War General,* Columbia: University of Missouri Press, 2008.
Steenburn, Col. Donald H., *The Man Called Gurley,* Meridianville, AL: Elk River Press, 1999.
Stevens, Joseph E., *1863: The Rebirth of a Nation* New York: Bantam Books, 2000.
Stiles, T. J., *Jesse James, the Last Rebel of the Civil War,* New York: Vintage, 2003.
Sutherland, Daniel E., *A Savage Conflict: The Decisive Role of Guerrillas in the American Civil War,* Chapel Hill: University of North Carolina Press, 2009.
_____, ed., *Reminiscences of a Private: William E Bevens of the First Arkansas Infantry, C.S.A.,* Fayetteville: University of Arkansas Press, 1992.
Sword, Wiley, *Mountains Touched with Fire,* New York: St. Martin's Press, 1995.
Thomas, Benjamin P., and Hyman, Harold M., *Stanton: The Life and Times of Lincoln's Secretary of War,* New York: Alfred A. Knopf, 1962.
Towne, Stephen E., ed., *A Fierce, Wild Joy: The Civil War Letters of Colonel Edward J. Wood, 48th Indiana Volunteer Infantry Regiment,* Knoxville: University of Tennessee Press, 2007.
van der Linden, Frank, *The Dark Intrigue: The True Story of a Civil War Conspiracy,* Golden, CO: Fulcrum Publishing, 2007.

_____, *Lincoln: The Road to War*, Golden, CO: Fulcrum Publishing, 1998.
Van Horne, Thomas B., *History of the Army of the Cumberland* Vol. I, Cincinnati: Robert Clarke, 1875.
Warner, Ezra J., *Generals in Blue: Lives of the Union Commanders*, Baton Rouge: Louisiana State University Press, 1996.
_____, *Generals in Gray: Lives of the Confederate Commanders*, Baton Rouge: Louisiana State University Press, 1959.
Weber, Jennifer, L. *Copperheads: The Rise and Fall of Lincoln's Opponents in the North*, New York: Oxford University Press, 2006.
Whalen, Charles and Barbara, *The Fighting McCooks: America's Famous Fighting Family*, Bethesda, MD: Westmoreland Press, 2006.
Wheeler, Richard, *Voices of the Civil War*, New York: Crowell, 1976.
Widmer, Ted, ed., *The New York Times Disunion: 106 Articles from the New York Times Opinionator*, New York: Black Dog & Leventhal, 2013.
Williams, Kenneth P., *Lincoln Finds a General: A Military Study of the Civil War*, Vol. III, New York: Macmillan, 1952.
Williams, T. Harry, *Hayes of the 23rd, The Civil War Volunteer Officer*, Lincoln: University of Nebraska Press, 1965.
_____, *Lincoln and His Generals*, New York: Alfred A. Knopf, 1952.
Winik, Jay, *April 1865: The Month That Saved America*, New York: HarperCollins, 2001.

Newspapers

The Adair County News (Columbia, KY)
Alexandria Gazette
Ashtabula Weekly Telegraph (Ashtabula, OH)
Belmont Chronicle (St. Clairsville, OH)
The Benton Weekly Record (Benton, MT)
The Cadiz Democratic Sentinel (Cadiz, OH)
The Cambria Freeman (Ebensburg, PA)
Carroll Free Press (Carrollton, OH)
Cleveland Morning Leader
Cincinnati Daily Commercial
Cincinnati Daily Press
Cincinnati Daily Times
Cincinnati Inquirer
Cincinnati Weekly Gazette
The Commoner (Lincoln, NE)
The Daily Argus-Leader (Sioux Falls, SD)
The Daily Green Mountain Freeman (Montpelier, VT)
Daily Intelligence (Wheeling, VA)
Daily Nashville Patriot
The Daily Ohio Statesman
The Daily Times (Cincinnati)
Dakota Farmer's Leader (Canton, SD)
Dubuque Daily Times
Evening Bulletin (Honolulu, HI)
Evening Star (Washington, D.C.)
Fergus County Argus (Lewistown, MT)
The Gainesville Star (Gainesville, FL)
The Goodhue Volunteer (Red Wing, MN)
The Herald (Los Angeles)
The Herald-Star (Steubenville, OH)
The Highland Weekly News (Hillsborough, OH)
Holmes County Republican (Millersburg, Holmes County, OH)
The Holt County Sentinel (Oregon MO)
The Intermountain Catholic (Salt Lake City, UT)
The Iola Register (Iola, KS)
The Lancaster Gazette (Lancaster, OH)

Leavenworth Conservative
The Mahoning Dispatch (Canfield, OH)
The Nashville Daily Union
Nashville Union and American
The National Tribune (Washington, D.C.)
New York Sun
New York Times
New York Tribune
Ohio Patriot
Omaha Daily Bee
The Ottawa Free Trader (Ottawa, IL)
The Owosso Times (Owosso, MI)
Pittsburgh Post
The Plymouth Tribune (Plymouth, IN)
The Polk County Press (WI)
St. Paul Pioneer
The Salt Lake Herald
Sioux Falls Daily Press (Sioux Falls, SD)
Steubenville Herald (OH)
The Spirit of Democracy (Woodfield, OH)
The Stark County Democrat (Canton, OH)
The Times Dispatch (Richmond, VA)
The Washington Herald (Washington, D.C.)
The Wheeling Intelligencer
Urbana Union (OH)
Wichita Eagle

Articles, Diaries, Encyclopedias and Magazines

America's Civil War, "The Eccentric German General," by Karen Koss, September 2003.
Blue & Gray Magazine, "The Campaign and Battle of Mill Springs," by Roger Tate, February 1993.
Blue & Gray Magazine, "The Northwestern Virginia Campaign of 1861, McClellan's Rising Star—Lee's Dismal Debut," by Martin K. Fleming, Vol. X, August 1993.
Bulletin, "Crime and No Punishment, the Death of Robert L. McCook," by James Barnett, Vol. 22, 1964.
Civil War History, Robert R. Dykstra, ed., "The Bushwhacker's War: Insurgency and Counterinsurgency in West Virginia," edited by Richard O. Curry, and F. Gerald Ham, Vol. 10, No. 64, Published Quarterly by the University of Iowa, December 1964.
Civil War Times Illustrated, "Waiting to be Hanged," by John W. Rowell, Vol. 17, December 1978.
Diary of Gideon Welles, Vol. I & II, New York: W. W. Norton, 1960.
Harper's Weekly, New York, Vol. V, No. 231, June 1, 1861.
Harper's New Monthly Magazine, "The Second Division at Shiloh," by Daniel McCook, Vol. XXVIII, December 1863 to May 1864, Harper & Brothers, 1864. *Military History*, "Intrigue: Rebel Captain Frank Gurley Faced a Charge of Killing an Invalid Yankee General," by Robert P. Broadwater, Vol.22, Issue 5, August 2005.
The Cleveland Civil War Roundtable, "The Irish in the Civil War," by Dennis Keating, 2008.
Archives, Manuscripts, Websites and Reference Books
Carroll County Historical Society, Carrollton, OH, *McCook Family Album*.
The Civil War Book of Lists, Compiled by the Editors of Combined Books, 1993.
Connecticut Landmarks, Hartford.
Gurleyalabama.contactez.net, Home of the Gurley Web Site, "From our Past XXI, a Curious Letter to Captain Frank Gurley."
Library of Congress, Manuscript Reading Room, McCook Family Papers.
McCook, Anson, *Memoirs*, Unpublished, Columbus: Ohio Historical Society.
National Archives, Military Service File of Daniel McCook, Jr.
National Archives, Military Service File of Robert L. McCook.
The Papers of Andrew Johnson, Vol.8 & 9, Knoxville: The University of Tennessee Press, 1991.
The Papers of Ulysses S. Grant, John Y. Simon, ed., Edwardsville: Southern Illinois Press, 1991.
War of the Rebellion, Official Records.

www.equilt.com/morgan.html, "John Hunt Morgan," by David Skinner, 2000.
www.vic.com/tnchron/class/JHMorgan.htm, Tennessee History Classroom, Full History Series, "The Murder of John Hunt Morgan."
Web Site, The Civil War and Northwest Wisconsin, letter Edwin D. Levings to his parents, June 26, 1864 (Original letter in the archives of the University of Wisconsin, River Falls).

Index

Numbers in **_bold italics_** indicate pages with illustrations

abolition 72, 103, 144
"acoustic shadow" 132
Alabama Historical Association 73
Aldrich, Cyrus 65
Alice Dean (steamer) 142
Anderson, Robert 206
Anderson, William T. "Bloody Bill" 115
Army of Southwest Missouri 131
Army of the Cumberland 152–153, 159, 161–162, 168, 170, 176
Army of the Mississippi 67
Army of the Ohio 41, 44, 54, 56, 65–66, 74, 132–133, 144, 170, 173
Army of the Potomac 138, 205
Army of the Tennessee 66–67, 120, 163, 170
Ashby, John 144
Atezrodt, George 94
Atlanta, GA 169, 173–174, 177, 184, 188

Baird, Absalom 159
"Battle Above the Clouds" 162
"Battle of Bontecou" 29
Battle of Buffington's Island 147–149
Battle of Bull Run 15, 18, 39, 44, 50, 117, 119, 126, 145, 149, 177
Battle of Carnifex Ferry 35–36
Battle of Chickamauga 40, 152, 155, 158–161, 195
Battle of Fredericksburg 136
Battle of Gettysburg 143–144, 154, 179, 183
Battle of Kennesaw Mountain 104, 183–191, 194–195
Battle of Mill Springs 43, 46–54, 60, 126
Battle of Perryville 125, 128–129, 131–133, 135, 161, 195
Battle of Philippi 26–28
Battle of Rich Mountain 31–34, 40
Battle of Shiloh 40, 54, 62, 68, 119–126, 133, 140–141, 175, 195

Battle of Stones River 134–136, 140–141, 161, 195
Battle of Vicksburg 143, 154, 179
Battle of Wilson's Creek 116–117, 119, 127, 133, 195
Battles and Leaders in the Civil War 132
Beach, Moses G. 9–10
Beatty, John 32, 77
Beatty, Margaret 14
Beauregard, Pierre Gustave Toutant 63, 68, 120–123, 127
Bell, John 45
Benham, Henry W. 35–36, 39–41
Bierce, Ambrose 188
Black regiments 137
"Black Republicans" 114, 143
Blair, Charles W. 117
Blair, Francis P. "Frank" 111
Blair, Francis P., Sr. 114, 118
Booth, John Wilkes 94
Boyle, Dr. 74
Boynton, Major 74
Bradley, Joseph C. 93
Bragg, Braxton 73, 80, 86, 92, 127, **_128_**, 129–131, 134–136, 140–141, 149, 154, 157–159, 165–168
Brandenberg, IN 142
Brannan, John M. 159
Breckinridge, John C. 11, 135
Brewer, A.L. 91–92
Brooke, Hunter 74, 76, 78, 88, 90–91
Brownlow, William G. "Parson" 45
Buchanan, James 10–11, 25, 103, 109
Buell, Don Carlos 41, 44–46, 51–52, 54, 62, 65, 67, 79, 107, 120–121, 123, 127, 129, 132–134
Burkhalter, James L. 181
Burnett, H. L. **_94_**
Burnside, Ambrose E. 138, 144, 146–149, 165–167

231

232   Index

Burt, Andrew 60, 80
bushwhackers 77, 84, 89, 115

Cameron, Simon 52, 103
Camp Dennison, Ohio 23, 125, 144
Camp Harrison, Ohio 21
Campbell, Andrew J. 151
Canterbury, Samuel 186
Carnegie, Andrew 154
Carrington, Henry B. 60, 64–65
Carrollton, OH 9, 22, 102
Chaplin River (Kentucky) 129–130
Chattanooga, TN 156, 158–159, 161, *162*, 163, 165–169, 189
Chattanooga Campaign 152–153, 195
Cheat Mountain (western Virginia) 34
Cheatham, Benjamin F. 181, 185
Chickamauga Creek 156–158, 164
Cincinnati Daily Commercial 44, 75, 92
Cincinnati Daily Times 39, 125, 185
Cincinnati Enquirer 145–146
Cincinnati Gazette 69
Cincinnati Weekly Gazette 149, 165
Cleburne, Patrick 11, 181
Clendinin, C.R. *94*
Cloud, Mason J. 144
Cochran, R.H. 202
Cole, Dr. Jack Hunt 151
Copperheads 136–137, 142–144, 146–147, 153
Corinth Campaign 54–69, 131
Cox, Jacob D. 29, 35, 37, 39, 170
Crittenden, George Bibb 47–49, 51
Crittenden, John J. 47
Crittenden, Thomas L. 133–134, 154–155, 158–159
Crockett, Davy 8
Crook, George 87

Daily Ohio Statesman 146–147
The Daily Times (Cincinnati) 31, 66
Davis, Jefferson 25, 89, 92, 121, 129, 135, 141, 143, 145, 153, 168–169, 177
Davis, Jefferson C. "Jef" 161, 166–167, 169, 180–181, 190
Decherd, Tennessee 73
Department of the Cumberland 88
Department of the Missouri 62
Department of the Ohio 19, 35
Department of the West 111
Dixon, Dr. Joseph E. 85–86
Doctor's Creek (Kentucky) 129–130
Dodge, Grenville M. 170
Douglas, Stephen A. 10
Douglass, Henry 63
Duck River 61–62, 69
Duke, Basil 142, 148–149, 151

East Tennessee loyalists 165–166
Eckley, E.R. 22
Edgerton, Sydney 65

Eighth Article of War 61
Ellsworth, Ephriam 206
Emancipation Proclamation 136–137
Engels, Friedrich 21
Ewing, Hugh 103–105, 108
Ewing, Thomas, Jr. 103–105, 107–108
Ewing, Thomas, Sr. 105

Fahnestock, Allen L. 164, 181, 202
Faulkner, William 8
Fettweiss, Leopold 198
"Fighting McCooks" 11, 54, 66, 149, 161, 170, 186, 195, 198, 200–206
Flint, G.E. 61
Floyd, John 11, 25, 35–38
Flynt, George E. 72
Foote, H.S. 85
Foote, Shelby 117
Forrest, Nathan Bedford 86, 89, 92, 138
Fort Donelson 53, 85, 119, 121
Fort Henry 53, 119, 121
Fort Lookout 112
Fort Pierre 112
Fort Randall 112
Fort Sumter 109, 121, 206
Foster, Robert S. *94*
Fox, Cyrus A.B. 188–189
Frank Leslie's Illustrated Newspaper 78
Franklin College 13
Frémont, John C. 10, 114–115, 117–118
French, Samuel G. 183
Frontier Guards 12, 145
Frost, Daniel M. 112
Fry, Birkett D. 86
Fry, Speed S. 50
Fuchshulter, Captain 80

Gallagher, Thomas J. 83
Garfield, James A. 83, 157, 161
Garnett, Robert S. 28, 31
"General Robert L. McCook's Funeral March" 80
German Immigrant Soldiers 19–23, 31, 35, 41, 50, 64, 82, 113–114, 200
Gibbon, John 86
Gilbert, Charles C. 127, 130–133
Gillem, Alvan C. 150
Goddard, C. 88
Goodhart, Dr. 144
Gookins, J.F. 69
Gorman, Dr. 74
Granger, Gordon 88, 152, *155*, 156, 158–159, 166
Grant, U.S. 53, 56, 62, 67–68, 76, 82, 85, 89, 91, 95–96, 119, *120*, 121–123, 125, 131, 154, 168–172, 175–176, 178, 197, 204–207; at Chattanooga 159, 163, 165–166
Grimshaw, Samuel 130
Gunnison, H.W. 97
Gurley, Frank B. 85–99, 147, 141, 198

Index

Halderman, John A. 116–117
Halleck, Henry W. 54–55, 62–63, 65–69, 118, 131, 136, 147–148, 163, 166, 170, 173, 176, 190
Hamrick, Joseph M. 75, 86
Hardee, William J. 174
Harker, Charles 180–181, 183–184, 190
Harmon, Oscar F. 166, 186
Harney, William S. 111
Harper's Weekly 69, 208
Harrison, Benjamin 187–188
Hart, David 32–33
Hawes, Richard 129
Hayes, Rutherford B. 27–28
Hazen, William 163
The Herald (Los Angeles) 204
Heroes of the Civil War 206
Herold, David 94
The Highland Weekly (Ohio) 200
Hobson, Edward Henry 145, 147–148
Holmes, J.T. 87, 202
Holt, Joseph 88, 93, **94**, 95, 108–109
Hood, John B. 180
Hooker, Joseph "Fighting Joe" 162–163, 165, 168, 170, 180
Hooton, Dr. Masena M. 187
Horseshoe Ridge 158, 160
Houston, Sam 8
Howard, Oliver O. 170, 174
Hughes, John 33
Hunt, Harrison 206–207
Hunter, David 118
Huntsville, Alabama 73, 75, 82, 86–87, 92–93, 99
Hurlbut, Stephen A. 89

Jackson, Andrew 8
Jackson, Claiborne F. 111, 115
James, Frank 115
James, Jesse 84, 115
James-Younger gang 84
Jefferson, Thomas 7
Jefferson College 9
Jennings, James A. 191
Johnson, Andrew 45, 80, 93, 95, **96**, 203
Johnson, Bushrod 158
Johnson, George W. 43
Johnson, Richard W. 159
Johnston, Albert Sidney 53, 121–122
Johnston, Joseph E. 89, 168–169, 172–173, 176, **177**, 183, 191
Judah, Henry M. 147–149, 170

Kammerling, Gustav 48
Kanawha Valley (western Virginia) 24, 39–40
Kansas Regiments: 1st Infantry 115–116, 118; 2nd Infantry 116–117
Kelley, Benjamin R. 26
Kennesaw Mountain 168, 173–177, 179
Kilburn, Lawson 87

Kirk, Lewis 91–92, 97
Knights of the Golden Circle 143–144
Knoxville, TN 165–167
Ku Klux Klan 95

Lander, Frederick W. 26
Lane, James H. 12, 145
Larson, O.A. 31
Latimer, Hugh 9
Leavenworth, KS 103–106, 108, 110, 167
Leavenworth Conservative 106
Leavenworth State Guard 108
Lecompte, Samuel D. 104
Lee, Robert E. 25, 28, 35, 37–41, 86, 92, 154, 165, 171, 177–178
Letcher, John 27
Levings, Edwin D. 179
Lincoln, Abraham 10, 15, 19–20, 24–25, 38, 43–45, 52, 82, 91, 93–94, 103, 108–111, 113–115, 119, 127, 153–154, 159, 166–167, 169 197, 207; and Emancipation Proclamation 136–137, 139; and slavery 178–179; versus Copperheads 143–146
Lincoln, Mary 70, 112
Logan, John A. 16, 170, 178, 180, 183
Longstreet, James "Pete" 158, 165–167
Lookout Mountain 161–163, 165–166, 168, 170
Lyon, Nathaniel 111–113, 116–117

Macaulay, Thomas Babington 181
Magoffin, Beriah 43
Manson, Mahlon D. 46
Marx, Karl 21
Mason, James M. 95, 97
McClain, Eliza 12
McClellan, George B. 19, 23–24, 26–28, 31–35, 39, 41, 46, 138, 206
McConigle, Jim 108
McCook, Alexander McDowell 12, 15–16, 19, 23, 35, 43–44, 61–63, 66, 68–69, 75, 79–80, 83, 87, 97, 118, 129, 140, 150, 154, 193, 198, 208; at Chickamauga 157–159; death 204; at Perryville 130, 132–133; at Shiloh 119, 123; at Stones River 134–135
McCook, Anson G. 19, 23, 81, 166, 170, 187, 193, 200, 208
McCook, Blanche 194
McCook, Catherine 8, 26
McCook, Charles Morris 12, 15, 20, 23, 81, 118, 145, 149, 187, 193, 197, 203; mortally wounded at Bull Run 16
McCook, Daniel, Jr. 11, 19, 44, 75, 81–82, 87, 102–103, **104**, 105–110, 115–119, 200–204, 206–208; assault on Kennesaw Mountain 180–**187**, 188–190, 201–202, 205; at Chickamauga 158–159, 161, 163–167, 170–171, 175; death 191–195, 197–198; and 52nd Ohio 125–127; at Perryville 130–132; promoted to brigadier general 192; at Shiloh 123–124; at Stones River 134–136, 150, 152, 155–157

Index

McCook, Daniel, Sr. 8–12, 16, 35, 49, 65, 104, 138, 145–147, 187, 197, 204, 208; death 149–150
McCook, Edward Moody "Horse Ed" 12, 83, 87, 140, 155, 170, 173
McCook, Edwin Stanton 12, 15–16, 53, 97–98, 170, 188, 197–198, 208
McCook, Dr. George 8, 12
McCook, George, Jr. (nephew of Robert) 200
McCook, Dr. George, Sr. 8, 189
McCook, George Wythe 12–*15*, 19, 22–23, 49, 81, 102–104, 109, 189, 192–193, 198; death 200
McCook, Dr. John, Sr. 8, 11, 26, 91–92, 189
McCook, John James 9
McCook, John James (named after his deceased older brother) 12, 16, 98, 134, 150, 155, 198; death 204–207
McCook, John "Little Johnny" (son of Dr. John, Sr.) 24, 26
McCook, Julia Tebbs 107–109, 189, 192, 194, 204
McCook, Dr. Latimer A. 12–13, 53, 189, 197
McCook, Lorraine 200
McCook, Martha Latimer 9–10, 23, 81, 104, 145, 150, 189, 200–202, 204; death 203
McCook, Robert Latimer 11, 19–24, 26–30, 32–39, 41–44, 46–48, 81–99, 118, 145, 147, 149, 151, 157, 187, 193, 203, 206–207; death 73–80, 86, 197; promoted to brigadier general 70, 72; statute dedicated to 198–*199*, 200; wounded in battle 49, 50–53, 54–63, 66–67, 69
McCook-Baldwin, Mary Jane 197, 200–203
"McCooks Avengers" 83
McCulloch, Benjamin 116
McDowell, Irwin 18, 35
McKinley, Lucy 28
McKinley, William 27–28, 205
McPherson, James B. 170, 176, 178, 180, 188, 190
McTammany, John 204–205
Meade, George G. 154, 183
Meagher, Thomas Francis 11
Memoirs and Selected Papers 163
Memoirs of W.T. Sherman 106, 167, 178
Mexican War 13, 15, 23, 44, 112, 114, 120–121, 128, 139, 169, 177
Mills, Anson 58–59
Minnesota Regiments: 2nd Infantry 44, 46, 48–49, 52, 57–59, 82
Minty, Robert 156
Missionary Ridge 161, 163, 165, 168, 170
Missouri Compromise 110
Mitchell, John G. 157, 184
Mitchell, Robert B. 155
Morgan, C.R. 149
Morgan, J. Pierpont 154
Morgan, John Hunt 138–144, 147–151
Morgan, Thomas 142

Morris, Thomas A. 28
Morton, Oliver P. 144
Murfreesboro, TN 134, 152

Nashville, Tennessee 53, 88, 90–91, 119, 135, 152
Nashville Banner 45
Nashville Daily Union 152
The National Tribune 69, 98, 130, 132, 202
Nashville Union and American 95
Nativist Party ("Know Nothings") 6, 21
New York City anti-draft riots 153
New York Daily Tribune 10
New York Times 18–19, 25, 54, 72, 78, 85, 92, 115, 122, 140, 168, 172–174, 178, 181, 190
New York Tribune 18, 117
New York Sun 10
Newton, John 180
Nicolay, John C. 25
North Chickamauga Creek 161, 164
"Northwest Confederacy" 153

Ohio (McCook) Regiments: 1st Infantry 15; 2nd Infantry 19, 170; 9th Infantry 18, 21, 23, 28–29, 32–38, 41, 43–44, 46, 48–50, 52, 57, 59, 64, 69–70, 72, 76, 80 82, 198; 23rd Infantry 27; 35th Infantry 67, 74; 52nd Infantry 83, 87, 118, 125–126 130, 152, 155–156, 161, 171, 181–182, 184, 192, 194, 202, 208
Ohio River 133, 141–142, 147–148
Omaha Daily Bee 197, 207

Palmer, B. Frank 172
Palmer, John M. 170, 187
Parkhurst, J.P. 188–189
Patterson, Robert 172
Patton, George 8
Pea Ridge 63, 69, 181
Pegram, John 32
Pittsburg Landing 55–57, 62, 65, 70, 119–121, 123–124
Polk, Leonidas 141, 174
Pope, John 67
Porterfield, George A. 26, 28
Powell (*aka* Payne), Lewis 94
Price, D.M. 69

Quantrill, William 115
Queen Mary "Bloody Mary" Tudor 9

Rauch, F.W. 80
Raymond, Henry J. 178–179
Ready, Mattie 139, 141
Reynolds, Joseph H. 159
Reynolds, W.H. 201
Rockefeller, John D. 154
Roman Catholic Irish 5–8, 11
Roosevelt, Theodore 207
Rosecrans, William S. 28, 32–40, 87, 133–135, 140–141, 146, 152–153, 155, 157–159, 170
Rousseau, Lovell H. 90, 130–131

Index

Scammon, Eliakim P. 35–36, 38–39
Schelich, Newton 28, 31
Schenk, Robert C. 39–40
Schoepf, Albin F. 46
Schofield, John M. 170, 173, 178, 180
Scotch-Irish 7–8, 11
Scully, John W. 48
Seay, James T. 186
Seddon, James A. 89
Selby, David D. 98
Seminole Indian War 44, 177
Shackelford, James M. 147–148
Shane, Colonel 186
Sheldon, Mary 81
Shepherd, Oliver L. 55–61, 64–65, 67–71, 79
Sheridan, Philip H. 11, 127, 130–131, 135, 159, 204, 206
Sherman, Ellen 104–105, 191, 193
Sherman, Thomas W. 66, 70
Sherman, William T. 44, 66, 103–106, 108, 113, 120, 122, 131, 163–168, 170–174, 204–207; at Kennesaw Mountain *175*, 176–178, 180, 183, 189–194
Sherman, Willie 113
Shield's Guards 108, 110
Shiloh Church 62, 119, 121
Sigel, Franz 116
Sill, Joshua W. 129
slavery 16, 18–19, 25, 40, 72–73, 105, 107–108, 110, 113–114, 137, 140, 148, 178–179, 208
Smith, Andrew J. 63
Smith, E. Kirby 129
Smith, W.F. "Baldy" 163
"Snake Hunters" 28–29
Sons of Liberty 143
Spring Grove Cemetery 81, 187, 193, 197, 206
"Spring Hill Riot" 57, 63
Stallo, J.B. 22, 49
Stangel, William 82
Stanley, David S. 191
Stanton, Dr. Darwin 13
Stanton, Edwin M. 13, *14*, 15, 19, 22, 25, 51–53, 65, 78, 88, 91, 102, 104, 108, 125, 136, 189
Stanton, Edwin (son of Edwin M.) *14*
Stanton, Lucy 13
Stanton, Mary 13
Stark County Democrat (Canton, OH) 97
Steubenville, OH 13, 14–15, 22, 167, 189, 192, 201, 205
Stevens, Thaddeus 10
Stewart, Nixon B. 194
Strew, Dr. W.W. 49
Stuart, James E.B. "Jeb" 138
Surratt, Mary 94–95

Tank, Henry 56, 60–61, 70
Tebbs, Algernon S. 107
Tennessee River 62, 73, 119, 122, 164–165
Thomas, George H. 44–48, 50, 61, 66–67, 70, 72–73, 76, 80, 82, 90–91, 93, 134–135, 152, 165–166, 168–171, 176, 178, 180, 187, 206; at Chickamauga 158–159, *160*, 161–162
Thomas, Lorenzo 65
Tibbs, Warren 144
Tigress steamboat 123
Tod, David 22, 52, 125, 144, 150
Todd, John B.S. 69–70, 112
Troxell, John J. 155
Tullahoma, TN 141
Tullahoma Campaign 154
Tuscumbia, Alabama 70, 72
Twain, Mark 8

Vallandigham, Clement 143–147
Van Derveer, Ferdinand 74–76, 78–79
Van Fleet, F.A. 58
Vincent, John 73–75
Volk, Charles H. 109

Wade, Benjamin F. 64
Walker, Dr. Mary 170
Wallace, Lewis "Lew" 63
war Democrats 11
War of 1812 49
Ward, William T. 187
Washington, DC 10, 18–19, 21–22, 50, 91, 125, 129, 145, 170–171, 189
Watkins, L.D. 83
West Point Military Academy 15, 19, 23, 45, 47, 63, 66, 86, 104, 111–112, 120, 127–128, 133, 169, 175, 177, 204
Western Virginia Campaign 18–42, 77
Whalen, Barbara 208
Whalen, Charles 208
Wheeler, Joseph 135, 173
The Wheeling Intelligencer 18
Whig Party 7, 105, 111
Whiskey Rebellion 8
Willard Hotel 145
Willich, Augustus 21, 23, 35, 61, 80, 135
Willoughby Medical College 12
Wise, Henry A. 25, 37
Wood, Charles 75
Wood, David L. 56–57, 60, 64, 69–70
Wood, Thomas J. 159
Wright, H.G. 125

Yankton, Dakota Territory 198

Zollicoffer, Felix K. 45–51

www.ingramcontent.com/pod-product-compliance
Ingram Content Group UK Ltd.
Pitfield, Milton Keynes, MK11 3LW, UK
UKHW041943140426
5217IPUK00014B/637